Radio and Television in Cuba

The Pre-Castro Era

Radio and Television in Cuba

The Pre-Castro Era

MICHAEL B. SALWEN

Iowa State University Press / Ames

Michael B. Salwen is associate professor, Journalism and Photography Program, School of Communication, University of Miami, Coral Gables, Florida.

© 1994 Iowa State University Press, Ames, Iowa 50014
All rights reserved

Authorization to photocopy items for internal or personal use, or the internal or personal use of specific clients, is granted by Iowa State University Press, provided that the base fee of $.10 per copy is paid directly to the Copyright Clearance Center, 27 Congress Street, Salem, MA 01970. For those organizations that have been granted a photocopy license by CCC, a separate system of payments has been arranged. The fee code for users of the Transactional Reporting Service is 0-8138-2180-0/94 $.10.

∞ Printed on acid-free paper in the United States of America

First edition, 1994

Library of Congress Cataloging-in-Publication Data

Salwen, Michael Brian
    Radio and television in Cuba: the pre-Castro era / Michael B. Salwen. — 1st ed.
    p. cm.
    Includes bibliographical references and index.
    ISBN 0-8138-2180-0 (alk. paper)
    1. Radio broadcasting—Cuba—History.   2. Television broadcasting—Cuba—History.   I. Title.
PN1991.3.C8S25 1994
384.54′097291—dc20   94-17023

Contents

Foreword *by John Spicer Nichols,* vii

Preface, xiii

1. When It All Began, 3
2. Goar Mestre and CMQ Radio, 19
3. First in Cuban Television, 34
4. Havana's Television Market, 48
5. Transition from Radio to Television, 62
6. TV Comes of Age, 77
7. Batista's Legacy of Censorship, 93
8. The Precarious Years, 108
9. Castro Comes to Power, 122
10. Freedom of the Press in Castro's Cuba, 138
11. The Great Debate over Communism, 152
12. The Omnipresent Microphones, 167

Notes, 171

Index, 201

Foreword

Revolutionary change in Cuba is inevitable, and as has been the case in the past, the electronic media will play an integral role in that change. When looking forward in anticipation of dramatic change, it is usually useful to also look back. Knowing the history of Cuban radio and television is a prerequisite to understanding what contribution the electronic media will make in the island's future.

Radio and Television in Cuba: The Pre-Castro Era is the most complete and, by far, the best history in any language of the broadcast media of pre-revolutionary Cuba. Michael B. Salwen has effectively pulled together the scattered writings on the subject and has greatly expanded the knowledge base with contemporary reporting. Of particular importance are Professor Salwen's extensive interviews with the pioneers of Cuban radio and television, many of whom later contributed to the development of the electronic media in other Latin American countries and the United States or played significant roles in the Byzantine world of anti-Castro politics. Collecting oral histories from the first generation of Cuban broadcasters before these valuable primary sources pass on and publishing the fruits of those interviews at a time of fundamental change in Cuba are major contributions to the field of international communications and Cuban studies.

At this writing in late 1993, change in Cuba is not only inevitable but, to a large extent, already under way. With the collapse of the Soviet Union, Cuba's patron for three decades, the island's economy is in a tailspin and the socialist government of Fidel Castro is in political isolation. In the early 1990s, the national income fell nearly 50 percent. Shortages in food and basic goods have led to significant popular dissatisfaction, alienation and increasing political tension. President Castro's uncompromising rhetoric of "Socialism or Death" notwithstanding, the country has been rapidly moving toward a mixed economy more closely integrated with the Western capitalist system. Some analysts believe that, with these reforms, Castro and Cuban communism might be able to weather this hurricane-force storm but re-emerge badly battered and forever transformed. Others argue that the reforms are too little, too late; that the process probably will turn violent; and that the fall of the Castro regime is imminent.[1]

In either case, Cuba is also on the threshold of radical change in the structure, function and ideology of its print and electronic media. What will this new Cuban media system look like? What role will it play for a transformed Cuban society? The stale, nearly lifeless Leninist model, under which the Cuban media now operate, will almost certainly be rejected. But, by the same token, Cubans are similarly suspicious of the crass U.S. commercial model that preceded it. Therefore, will some new, innovative formula for public communication emerge? Again, understanding the history of the Cuban media is important, perhaps essential, in answering these questions.

Salwen details how Cuban entrepreneurs of the 1930s, 1940s and 1950s built a technologically modern, advertising-financed, ratings-driven, entertainment-dominated broadcasting system that was largely modeled after that of the United States. With financial programming and logistical support from U.S. networks and advertisers, these Cuban businessmen became wealthy by airing game shows, soap operas and sports to a nation mired in poverty and inequality. Salwen further describes the ham-handed political control of radio and television by the Cuban government and occasionally by the U.S. government.

The Cuban Revolution was, in significant part, a nationalistic movement to free the country from the economic and political control of the United States and Cuban oligarchy. Castro, who had successfully used clandestine radio in his guerrilla campaign to overthrow the Batista dictatorship in Cuba, viewed the broadcast media as precious resources for fostering revolution.[2] As Salwen describes in Chapters 9, 10 and 11, all media were under official control within two years after Castro assumed the leadership of Cuba in 1959.

The most obvious purpose of government and party control of the media was to eliminate open opposition to the revolution. Castro saw little value in leaving the media in the hands of private owners who undoubtedly would use them to block revolutionary change. However, more important in Castro's view, central control of the media allowed the government to use them to achieve the major revolutionary goals of mass integration, education and mobilization. "If we want to overcome the gap which separates us from the developed world," he said, ". . . our resources [must be] used in a rational, organized way. There is no room for waste. We don't have the luxury of following the path of free competition to achieve economic development."[3] Castro believed that Cuban media resources, which were relatively well developed under private ownership during the pre-revolutionary period, must be used as a government tool for national development.

Of particular interest to Castro was the media's potential for fighting widespread illiteracy in Cuba. In the 1950s, at least 24 percent of all Cubans and 42 percent of those living in the grinding poverty of the countryside could neither read nor write a simple declarative sentence. "What is freedom to write and to speak for a man who doesn't know how to write, who doesn't know how to read?" Castro would ask those who question his decision to nationalize the media.[4]

Believing that Cuba could not hope to improve its social and economic conditions without the support and participation of a literate population, Castro and his cadre established universal literacy as a top priority. Achieving this goal required the mobilization of the entire Cuban society—including use of the media assets newly brought under government control. The centrally controlled Cuban media were coordinated to serve three important functions in the literacy campaign that began in April 1961.

First, the mass media helped to recruit an army of literacy teachers. Capitalizing on the revolutionary euphoria of the time, the print and broadcast media implored the Cuban youth to volunteer for a year's service teaching peasants in the countryside. Nearly 100,000 Cubans, mostly students between the ages of 10 and 19, responded to the call, were given a crash course in instructional methods and political indoctrination, and were sent to every corner of the island.[5]

Second, the media were mobilized in the direct instruction of illiterates and training of the volunteer literacy teachers. Expropriated newspapers were converted into textbook publishers, and within months, their presses printed nearly two million literacy primers, readers and teachers' manuals. Radio and television schools supplemented lessons of the teachers and reinforced their credibility among the peasants. The broadcast media were particularly useful in the campaign because they were capable of circumventing the illiteracy of the learners and the country's crude transportation system.[6]

The third major function of the Cuban mass media was legitimizing the literacy campaign and building support among those Cubans not directly participating in the campaign. Throughout 1961, Castro appeared frequently, sometimes several times per week, on national radio and television exhorting public cooperation. In addition, the broadcast media

glorified the work of the young literacy workers and their students.
The immediate result of the campaign was the virtual elimination of illiteracy in Cuba. By the end of 1961, the Cuban government claimed that only 4 percent of its people were illiterate—the lowest illiteracy rate in Latin America and one of the lowest in the world. To consolidate these early gains and to help build a truly educated society, the Cuban broadcast media (especially television) continued to shoulder major instructional responsibilities for the country. By the 1990s, Cuba arguably had the highest overall educational level in Latin America, despite an approximate 50 percent growth in population since 1961.[7] Although critics have questioned the accuracy of Cuba's educational statistics and quality of its school system, Jorge I. Dominguez, a leading U.S. scholar of Cuban affairs, concluded that "the quantitative educational achievements of the revolutionary government are truly impressive."[8]

The 1961 literacy campaign perhaps was the Cuban Revolution's finest hour, and the mass media were important, probably essential, in that success. On one hand, Cubans (particularly the older generations) generally recognize and appreciate their social gains, such as in education and health care, especially in comparison with their neighbors in Central America and the Caribbean. But, on the other hand, Cuba has paid a high price—perhaps too high—for this transformation. The down payment made in the 1960s was substantial. Political and economic independence from the United States came at the cost of even greater dependence on the now-defunct Soviet Union and its socialist trading bloc and endless hostility from Washington. The installment payments continue to strap the Cuban economy, limit civil and political rights of the Cuban people, and impede further social progress in the 1990s. Many among the well-educated Cuban population (especially the younger generations born after the social advances of the 1960s) have come to expect more from the government than the government is prepared or able to deliver. Cubans, who are heavy consumers of foreign broadcasting, are nearly unanimous in expecting more from their domestic media, which are too stilted, dogmatic and decreasingly relevant to everyday life of the educated population. In this respect, the revolutionary government, which with the help of state-owned media virtually eliminated illiteracy and significantly raised the educational level in Cuba, is a victim of its own success.

This turning point for Cuba presents many problems—some of potentially disastrous proportions—but also a few opportunities. In its desperate struggle to survive, the Castro government is moving rapidly toward a mixed economy open to private enterprise and foreign investment. As part of this process (sometimes called "Castroika"), the

Cuban leadership is rethinking monopoly control of the media. A top Cuban official recently told me that the Cuban radio and television system was seeking foreign investors. Programming from the U.S.-based Cable News Network already appears regularly on Cuban television, and in what may be a forerunner to foreign investment in the national broadcasting system, the government recently entered into joint ventures with Italian and Mexican companies to modernize Cuba's international and domestic telecommunications service. And in late 1993, Cuba's state television began broadcasting commercial advertising.

Given the history and ideology of the Cuban electronic media, these changes are nothing short of phenomenal. But where will these changes lead? Will these changes merely return Cuban radio and television to the pre-revolutionary model described so well by Salwen, or will the current or future leadership of Cuba learn from the successes and failures of the capitalist and Leninist models that were previously employed and adopt a unique model tailored to Cuban—not to U.S. or Soviet—needs? An understanding of the history of the Cuban media by those on both sides of the Straits of Florida, including a careful reading of *Radio and Television in Cuba,* is an important first step in arriving at enlightened answers to these questions.

John Spicer Nichols
School of Communications
The Pennsylvania State University

Preface

During his days as a charismatic rebel leader, Fidel Castro found clandestine radio a valuable medium for bypassing the country's censored commercial media. He used the airwaves to denounce the dictatorship of Fulgencio Batista and offer his own design for what he promised would be a democratic Cuba. The power of the broadcast media to influence Cuban as well as international public opinion must have left an impression on the young Castro. After coming to power in 1959, his government gradually confiscated the island's commercial radio and television systems and established what journalist Herbert Matthews described as "government by television."[1]

Scholarly inquiry of international mass communication—like the topics reported in the popular mass media—frequently focus on a limited set of "hot areas" of the world, what one group of researchers referred to as research that follows the "event agenda."[2] This was the case with Cuba after Castro came to power. A number of journals and books were published during the late 1950s and early and mid-1960s that examined how the former rebel leader used radio and television to advance his political goals.

The problem with scholarly inquiry that follows the "event agenda" is that such research does not permit time for sober reflection. Much of the research on Cuban broadcasting during the 1960s devoted little attention to the entrepreneurs who pioneered Cuban broadcasting. Even a quarter century after the revolution that brought Castro to power, research tells us little about Cuba's advanced broadcasting system before the Castro years.

This book attempts to shed some light on Cuban broadcasting during the pre-Castro years. The term "pre-Castro" refers to an era, rather than a person, to describe the period before all mass media in

Cuba were nationalized under state control. For that reason, the time span of this study does cover the early years when Fidel Castro was in power before Cuba became a Marxist state.

Cuban radio and television before Castro's revolution were richly endowed with domestically produced soap operas, live sporting events, lavish song-and-dance programs and raucous political commentators who denounced their political opponents on their "newspapers of the air." When Castro came to power, Cuba had 156 radio stations (including repeater stations of national networks) heard over 1,000,000 radio sets.[3] The island had 27 television stations and an estimated 400,000 television sets. Havana alone had six television stations, including Latin America's only color station. Three Havana television stations were the main links of national networks that blanketed the island. John S. Nichols, the foremost expert on Cuban broadcasting, wrote: "When he [Castro] came to power in 1959, Cuba's broadcast media were among the few useful assets in that extremely poor country. Most homes outside Havana lacked running water but not a radio receiver."[4]

In their battle for high ratings, the owners of Cuba's radio and television stations sought the best talent from around the world, including U.S. entertainers such as Liberace, Louis Armstrong, Cab Calloway and Josephine Baker. Cuban television networks paid large sums (by the standards of the time) for exclusive rights to broadcast baseball games and boxing matches. In 1954, one resourceful Cuban television network carried live broadcasts of the U.S. World Series baseball games by leasing a DC-3 aircraft equipped with two antennas to receive the signal from a Miami station and transmit it to Cuba.

I became interested in radio and television in pre-Castro Cuba after I had met many of Cuba's pre-Castro broadcasters in Miami and heard their stories. Obviously my location in Miami influenced my decision to write this book. I interviewed leading journalists and broadcasters from pre-Castro Cuba living in exile in Miami, New York, Puerto Rico, Colombia and elsewhere. I did not go to Cuba. While this may be regarded as a weakness of this book, it is not as serious as it might seem because almost all of the major broadcast owners whom I wished to interview had fled Cuba.

Since I relied heavily on interviews, the reader will see that much of this book reads like a journalistic account rather than a scholarly tome. As a former journalist, I did not shy away from the use of anecdotes.

I initially planned to confine the book to news and public affairs programming in radio and television on the assumption that such content had the greatest social impact. While such programming remained the focus, the research expanded to include entertainment programming. It would have been impossible to do otherwise. As much as journalism scholars such as myself are interested in "serious news," news and public affairs were only a small part of pre-Castro Cuban broadcasting.

Interviewing people many years after their experiences has advantages and drawbacks. The main drawback was that many people had gaps in their memories. Another potential danger was the tendency of sources to exaggerate their role in Cuban history. I tried to account for these deficiencies by asking the same questions of numerous people and by turning to secondary materials to confirm personal accounts.

The advantage of interviewing people years after their experiences is that after the passage of time they were often very candid. For example, some former Cuban entrepreneurs confided that they gave monetary gifts (bribes) to the press in hope of receiving favorable coverage and some journalists admitted to accepting bribes.

In addition to relying on interviews, this book draws together much of the scattered English- and Spanish-language materials on pre-Castro broadcasting. Popular Cuban periodicals of the day helped me understand the social and political atmosphere in pre-Castro Cuba. Among the most useful were *Diario de la Marina, El Mundo, The Times of Havana, The Havana Post, Revolucion, Carteles* and especially the weekly radio and television sections of *Bohemia* magazine. I also found U.S. publications such as *The New York Times, The Miami Herald, Newsweek* and *Time* valuable for offering the outsider's perspective. Declassified U.S. government documents available on microfilm also proved useful for corroboration. They were especially intriguing for their candor.

Chapter 1, "When It All Began," describes the beginnings of Cuban radio during the 1920s and 1930s. In many ways, Cuban radio developed along lines similar to that of radio in the United States. A few "amateurs" started broadcasting from their homes and gained renown. It was not long before private entrepreneurs started radio stations. Eventually national radio networks were formed. The chapter concludes by introducing Amado Trinidad Velasco and Goar Mestre Espinosa, who would figure prominently in the later age of popular and influential Cuban radio networks during the late 1930s and 1940s.

Chapter 2, "Goar Mestre and CMQ Radio," describes Mestre's contributions to the Cuban radio industry. Yale-educated Mestre introduced a number of efficient and innovative practices to Cuban radio. His contributions focused primarily on the business and management aspects of the medium rather than on the programming. The chapter also describes the fierce competition in radio that earned Mestre many business enemies.

Chapter 3, "First in Cuban Television," shifts the book's focus from radio to television in Cuba. It also introduces Gaspar Pumarejo, a popular radio personality who would play an important role in Cuban television. Pumarejo inaugurated Cuba's first television station in October 1950 from his personal residence. He sold his Union Radio television station to Manolo Alonso, a leading Cuban cinematographer and newsreel producer, in August 1951.

Chapter 4, "Havana's Television Market," describes the first television stations and networks in Cuba during the early 1950s. Several would-be television operators did not realize or appreciate the high operation costs of television. Some never advanced beyond the planning stage. This chapter introduces Amadeo Barletta, a wealthy businessman who used his fortune to construct the Telemundo television network to challenge CMQ's dominance in television.

Chapter 5, "Transition from Radio to Television," describes the impact of television on Cuba's radio industry. With the popularity of television during the 1950s, radio found its niche in the Cuban market as a "background" medium for people at work and play. Radio also became an important medium for Cuba's vitriolic political commentators. The chapter concludes by recounting the final radio campaign of Cuba's indomitable political broadcaster, Senator Eduardo ("Eddie") Chibas, a campaign that ended with Chibas' dramatic over-the-air suicide.

Chapter 6, "TV Comes of Age," describes the institutionalization of the Cuban television industry. After an initial period of flux during the early 1950s, the industry settled into several major stations and networks operated by a few wealthy owners. Pumarejo, who had sold his television station, prospered by contracting blocks of time from Cuban television owners and producing his own programs.

Chapter 7, "Batista's Legacy of Censorship," represents an abrupt change in tone and content from previous chapters. With Fulgencio Batista's military coup on March 10, 1952, politics brusquely thrust itself into the story of Cuban radio and television. During the years prior to Batista, Cuban radio and television thrived under the corrupt but democratic governments. Batista instituted varying degrees of media censorship to silence criticism of his government.

Chapter 8, "The Precarious Years," describes the final days of Batista's rule, when censorship was at its peak. Meanwhile, Fidel Castro and his rebels clashed with government soldiers in the countryside. Most Cuban industries, including radio and television, were understandably reluctant to expand during this time. Some television entrepreneurs, however, continued to prosper. During this period, Cuba inaugurated its first television station in the provinces that was not part of a national network. In addition, Pumarejo started a color television station in Havana.

Chapter 9, "Castro Comes to Power," describes the dilemma of the radio and television industries after Fidel Castro came to power. Castro promised a return to freedom of speech and press. The new government, however, displayed an intolerance to press criticism. Newspapers and radio stations suspected of having had accepted government subsidies during the Batista government were confiscated by the Castro government.

Chapter 10, "Freedom of the Press in Castro's Cuba," describes the period from 1959 through 1960 when the Castro government clamped down on newspapers. Independent newspaper publishers experienced severe labor problems. Many suspected that the government instigated labor unrest. The issue of whether the Castro government was "going Communist" became a major debate during this period.

Chapter 11, "The Great Debate over Communism," describes a verbal confrontation between two of Cuba's leading broadcast commentators that became a metaphor for the debate over the growing power of the Communist Party and the role of freedom of the press in Cuba. The dispute ended with commentator Luis Conte Aguero fleeing Cuba and Jose Pardo Llada pegged as a Castro mouthpiece.

Chapter 12, "The Omnipresent Microphones," elaborates major themes in the book that accounted for the development of broadcasting in pre-Castro Cuba.

I am indebted to numerous Cuban broadcasters, news directors, program directors, journalists and others who provided me with valuable information and documents. Their names are indicated in the footnotes. I also acknowledge the assistance of graduate and undergraduate students in the School of Communication at the University of Miami who interviewed people and located materials for me: Maria Dreschler, Irene Canel-Peterson, Abraham Chocron, Caridad Hernandez, Jennie Hausler, Aileen Sanchez, Marta Villaverde and Joanna Stavropoulos.

The manuscript was greatly improved by the comments of Gretchen Van Houten, the acquisitions editor, and Carla Tollefson, the managing editor, at Iowa State University Press. I am grateful to ISU Press for publishing this manuscript on this little-known topic. Not all publishers are willing to publish books dealing with broadcasting in a single nation. I understand their concern with expenditures and sales, and to reduce their costs I agreed to omit accent marks from Spanish words, the inclusion of which would have increased production costs.

I also have had the opportunity to publish my research on radio and television in pre-Castro Cuba in several scholarly journals. I want to acknowledge *Studies in Latin American Popular Culture;* the *Historical Journal of Film, Radio and Television;* and *World Communication* for publishing my research and helping me hone my ideas.

I also acknowledge the valuable comments of several of my colleagues at the University of Miami and other institutions: Drs. Leonardo Ferreira, Bruce Garrison, the late Sydney Head, Francis Matera, John Spicer Nichols, Kyu Ho Youm, Gonzalo Soruco, and Professors Alan Prince, C. C. Wakhisi and Paul Steinle.

I am also indebted to Dean Edward J. Pfister of the School of Communication at the University of Miami for granting me the time to devote to this project. Assistant Dean Robert Hosman was invaluable in helping me locate financial assistance.

I particularly want to acknowledge the comments and suggestions of my wife, Dr. Okhee Lee, an assistant professor in the University of Miami's School of Education. She read and reread my manuscripts and never complained. Well, hardly ever complained.

Radio and Television in Cuba

The Pre-Castro Era

CHAPTER 1
When It All Began

> My words are shot into space, driven by atmospheric waves over the agitated oceans and above the tall mountains, with sounds penetrating the ears of the citizens of the land, then reaching our hearts and evoking an echo of reciprocal effect. I want to express my deepest dreams for the prosperity, peace and progress of our republic ... and for the happiness of all who live in our powerful nation.[1]

With these grandiose words, Cuban President Alfredo Zayas

Alfonso (1921–1925) inaugurated Cuban radio station PXW on Oct. 10, 1922. The concert featured a noted cast of Cuban performers, including popular singers, a violinist, a soprano and a recitation of a "patriotic essay" written by Zayas while imprisoned by the Spanish during Cuba's War of Independence which, according to one Havana newspaper, "expressed lofty sentiments of liberty and nationalism."[2]

The station, owned by the state-run Cuban Telephone Company, a subsidiary of the American International Telephone and Telegraph (ITT) Corp., was operated from the Cuban Telephone Company's premises. At the time of the broadcast, there were an estimated 200 radio receivers in Cuba.[3] The inauguration of PWX stimulated the purchase of radio receivers.[4] Within a year after the inaugural broadcast, the island had an estimated 40,000 radio receivers.[5]

Even this early, it was apparent that the U.S. government and broadcasting industries would have an influence on the development of Cuban broadcasting. U.S. politics and economics had long played a major role in Cuban internal affairs. President Zayas, conscious of the fact that PWX's inaugural program would be monitored by amateur radio buffs in North America, scheduled his speech at 4 p.m. to meet the deadlines of U.S. evening newspapers.[6] A 1966 Cuban magazine retrospective on the first PWX broadcast described Zayas' radio comments as "so fawning and reverent to the U.S. that they are too embarrassing to repeat."[7] These were some of his words:

> Being so near to your coast, within the radius of your powerful commercial influence, and being sure, as we are, of your respect—and why not love?—for our republican national institutions, we desire to maintain the most cordial relations [with the United States], based upon a desire for a sincere and intelligent policy of mutual benefit. . . . With my words pronounced in the name of the people of Cuba, I send to the United States a true expression of respect and admiration to her national institutions and sincere friendship to her people and government. Three hurrahs to the glory of the United States! Three hurrahs to the absolute independence of Cuba![8]

While the PWX broadcast marked the "official" commencement of Cuban radio, as was the case in the United States a number of amateurs were on the air before the first regularly scheduled programs were available. Luis Casas Romero, Humberto Giquel and the brothers Guillermo and Manuel Salas were transmitting during irregular hours from the makeshift stations in their homes several months before the PWX broadcast.[9] Their programming consisted largely of spontaneous talk and phonograph recordings of musical offerings.[10] In addition to listening to these amateur broadcasters, many Cubans also tuned to programs broadcast from the United States that could be received in Cuba.[11]

Unlike the amateur broadcasters, PWX offered Cubans regularly scheduled programs other than talk and recordings. For instance, the station installed microphones in Malecon Park to broadcast army and navy band concerts each Wednesday.[12] Raul Falcon, the announcer at PWX who introduced the musical numbers, became the prototype for a generation of announcers.[13] According to one report, PWX "created an enthusiasm for radio among the citizens in which the majority became involved in the snobbery of radio, leading to increased construction of primitive receptors."[14] By late 1923, Havana was reported to have had 14 radio stations.[15]

A few celebrated PWX broadcasts stimulated radio sales. In April 1923, the National Commission of Tourism financed the arrival of the San Carlos Opera Company of Spain to perform in Havana's National Theater. PWX strung up microphones in the Theater to broadcast Gioacchino Rossini's "The Barber of Seville."[16] Later that year, the station carried a boxing match between Jack Dempsey and Argentine Luis Angel Firpo from New York's Polo Grounds. In a 1953 retrospective on the history of Cuban radio, *Bohemia* magazine[17] recounted the excitement of this match:

The fight between Dempsey, in the peak of his career, and Firpo, the famous "Savage Bull of the Pampa," was for days the topic of all conversations. In the wine cellar, at the barber, at the club, in theater lobbies and everywhere, nothing else was talked about. It was then that PWX announced the transmission, by remote control, of the great spectacle. Many thought that the offering would be impossible. "How are we going to hear in Cuba something that is happening in New York? It is a fairy tale," said one of the thousand disbelievers. And the night of the fight—14 of September 1923—Cubans crowded in front of receivers, not sure whether the transmission would be a success. But it was. The voice of the narrator arrived to all, clear and precise with vivid descriptions of the bloody encounter that ended with the victory of the champion [Dempsey].[18]

Cuba's Crowded Airwaves

The Cuban Telephone Company did not carry advertising on PWX. Most intellectuals and government officials believed that radio should not assault listeners with commercial messages.[19] Cuban entrepreneurs, however, very soon realized the financial potential for commercially supported stations. Most of these privately operated stations were in Havana.[20] In many cases, the stations were operated by the amateurs who were on the air before PWX.[21] Luis Casas Rodriguez started station 2LC.[22] Brothers Manuel and Guillermo Salas started 2MG.[23]

As was the case in the United States, major daily newspapers recognized the publicity associated with owning radio stations. In April 1923, the prestigious Havana daily *Diario de la Marina* started station 2-AZ, which primarily broadcast news and was a vehicle to promote the newspaper.[24] By June 1923, the Havana area had four powerful 500-watt stations.[25]

Even in Cuba's provinces, however, investors believed there was a future in radio. On Dec. 4, 1923, businessmen Rafael Valdes and Pedro Nogueras inaugurated the first "official" station in the provinces, 7-AZ in Camaguey.[26] A short time later American entrepreneur Frank H. Jones constructed two 100-watt stations in Santa Clara province. During the 1930s, he constructed two stations in Camaguey.[27] By 1930, Cuba had 61 radio stations, with more than 40 in Havana alone.[28]

Despite the impressive number of stations, most were small and operated on shoestring budgets. Revenues from local advertisers were insufficient to produce lavish productions. With almost a half-century of hindsight, one pioneer of Cuban radio recalled: "Radio transmissions consisted primarily of newscasts and unimaginative commercials that had little entertainment value. In some cases, the newscaster limited himself to reading the front pages of the newspaper."[29] Occasionally, the stations carried artists who received little or no pay, but were willing to perform for the publicity:

> Those were the times when the members of an orchestra received from the [radio] company the price of passage, come and go, to the broadcast station. Most worked for "the love of art" while a few—the consecrated, the stars—only earned a few pesos at the end of the month. To the orchestras and the musical groups the radio served as publicity for what really brought them benefits: playing at parties and dances. Between one song and another, one of the musicians would near the microphone and make known to listeners that they were available to liven up all classes of parties and could be reached at the following street, at the following number.[30]

By 1928, radio was a nascent Cuban industry. PWX changed its call letters to CMC after international treaty agreements required Cuban stations to begin their call letters with "CM."[31] Also during 1928, the Cuban Telephone Company expanded CMC into a national network, Cadena Nacional Telefonica. The four-station network was linked by telephone lines.[32]

Public interest in radio was growing at a rapid pace, as evidenced by the proliferation of popular mass media attention to the new medium. As early as April 1923, *Radio Grafico,* reputed to be the first Spanish-language radio magazine in the world, offered profiles and stories about radio personalities.[33] In the summer of 1928, the newspaper *Heraldo de Cuba* debuted a radio section that carried programming information and feature stories about radio personalities. Later, *Diario de la Marina* offered a regular radio section with the column of Alberto Giro.[34]

A number of creative and entrepreneurial radio announcers, known as "animators," became successful by contracting time from stations, producing their own programs and raising their own advertising. There were so many announcers that the National College of Broadcasting and the Announcers Union were founded by broadcaster Nicolas Jovino Garcia.[35]

By the early 1930s, a few programs developed into full-scale variety shows. The most famous was "Hora Multiple" ("Multiple Hour"), which appeared on CMW radio on May 2, 1931. It remained on the air for 10 years. The program's creator, Luis Aragon Dulzaides, combined a variety of formats in a single program.[36] The content ranged from popular singers and comedians to such high-brow offerings as readings of dramatic works by Leo Tolstoy and Nikolai Gogol.[37] "Multiple Hour" also had a serious segment called "La Bolsa del Saber" ("The Sack of Wisdom"), which featured discussions with prominent cultural and political figures who would respond to questions mailed in by listeners.[38]

On one occasion, "Multiple Hour" broadcast the Philharmonic Orchestra of Havana's rendition of Maurice Ravel's "Bolero." Since the station's studio could not accommodate an orchestra, the musicians performed on the roof.[39] According to Conchita Nogara, the program's musical director and Aragon's wife, the most innovative aspect of "Multiple Hour" was the creation of high-caliber commercial sketches with story lines and background music.[40] Prior to this, announcers simply read a few sentences about the products.

Radio-Newspapers

Radio evolved as an entertainment medium. News and public affairs were regarded as the domain of newspapers. Nevertheless, a few print journalists believed there was place in radio for a "radio-newspaper." In November 1933, journalists Jesus L. Lopez and Jose Benitez inaugurated "La Voz del Aire" ("The Voice of the Air") on longwave station CMCD. Two years later, the program relocated to new studios and appeared on shortwave. "The Voice of the Air" was the first all-news radio program, airing Monday through Saturday from 9 p.m. to 10:30 p.m. The program updated newspaper reports through a staff of correspondents.[41] A Sunday "Voice of the Air" served as a "literary supplement," featuring discussions with important political, artistic, literary or scientific figures. In its advertising, the program prided itself on its fairness and originality:

> Our thinking and philosophy is independent of political factions or parties. We are anti-Communist and anti-Fascist, and we are proud of the fact that we are heard in defense of the people on vital matters. We combat all sorts of tyranny and we maintain a fundamentally nationalist outlook. There are segments dealing with sports and literature as well as socio-political matters and economics. The news is given, interspersed with brief commercial announcements no longer than 40 words per announcement. . . . Our popularity and the respect that we have gained are based on the absence of any insults, coarseness and filthiness, although we are always known for telling the truth. . . . Our editorial staff consists of 19 reporters, and we do not make use of the news published [solely] in newspapers. The reporter who copies the printed news is immediately dismissed.[42]

Also in 1935, Salvador Diaz-Verson, a conservative reporter for the magazine *Carteles* and a contributor at a number of newspapers, was among a group of journalists who created a two-hour news program called "Radiario Nacional" over CMCY in Havana. Diaz-Verson brought together a group of seasoned journalists. The program's "sections" featured Cuban news, international news, political satire, literature, commentaries and social events.[43] As a serious journalist, Diaz-Verson preferred hard-news programming over frivolity. Nevertheless, the program's most popular segment was its social events calendar (the cronicas), which chronicled weddings, parties and other social activities.[44]

"Radiario Nacional" was distinguished by the editorials of Sergio Carbo, a hero of the 1933 revolution that toppled the dictator Gerardo Machado y Morales (1925–1933). Although Diaz-Verson was conservative and Carbo was liberal, Cuba's journalists prided themselves for allowing opposing viewpoints in their newspapers and radio-newspapers.[45]

Rapid Growth

The Cuban government and entrepreneurs looked to the United States as the archetypal broadcasting system. Broadcasting in the United States envisioned stations operated by private owners financed through advertising with little government involvement.[46] As in the United States, the Cuban government exercised radio "regulation" by setting power standards and assigning frequencies. But it imposed minimal control over program content.

The Cuban government sold its telephone links that comprised the Cuban Telephone Company's national network, Cadena Nacional Telefonica, to land contractor Ingeniero Cristobal Diaz Gonzalez. Cristobal Diaz used the lines to create the Radio Havana Cuba (RHC) network. The government, however, did not completely relinquish control over radio. It reserved a frequency for a 5,000-watt "educational" station in Havana, CMZ.[47]

What accounted for the rapid growth of Cuban radio during the 1930s? For one thing, more Cubans bought radio sets. For another, advertisers turned to radio to sell their products. Finally, wealthy local businesspeople purchased radio stations. In most cases, these businesspeople knew little or nothing about radio. Some were attracted to radio by the romanticism. Their resources, however, enabled them to hire the best talent in Cuba.

The influence of two large soap manufacturers—Crusellas and Sabates—was a crucial element for radio's growth. Crusellas was the Cuban subsidiary of Colgate-Palmolive. Sabates was the subsidiary of Procter and Gamble.[48] As in the United States, soap manufactures found radio the best medium for reaching the housewives who made their families' soap and other household goods purchases. Cuba had the highest per capita consumption of manufactured soap in Latin America and sixth highest in the world, behind such industrialized nations as Belgium, the United States, the United Kingdom, Sweden and the Netherlands, respectively.[49]

The economic support of the soap manufacturers came with a price. The companies demanded that their names be associated with the programs they sponsored and even with the networks' on-the-air identifications. This left the impression that the soap companies owned the networks. Throughout the late 1930s and much of the 1940s, Crusellas was associated with the CMQ radio network, while Sabates was identified with Cuba's other leading network, Radio Havana Cuba–Cadena Azul.[50]

With all the money they were investing in radio advertising and program sponsorship, advertisers started demanding to know what they were getting for their expenditures. As a result, a sophisticated audience measurement service, adapted from the United States, was introduced in Cuba during the early 1940s. The "chequos," as the service was known, was established and supervised by the Cuban Advertising Association. Hundreds of interviewers visited randomly selected homes by a pre-scheduled formula to conduct radio "coincidentals." The interviewers recorded which programs families were listening to at the time. Each of the surveys usually spanned a period of about two weeks and were based on more than 50,000 interviews.[51] The "chequos" was financed by stations, networks, major advertisers and advertising agencies, at a cost of up to $11,000 for each survey. The two major networks, CMQ and RHC–Cadena Azul, paid the largest single share—more than $2,000 each.[52]

Each survey required extensive preparation and was preceded by fanfare in entertainment sections of the press. The stations and networks knew when the interviewers would be in the field. To increase their ratings, many stations and networks carried their best talent and sponsored contests during this time. The situation was similar to the television "sweeps" in the United States, when television stations are aware that they are being monitored by the ratings services and air their best programs. The Cuban Advertising Association would append footnotes to their published ratings, noting the special efforts of stations to increase their ratings through contests and other publicity methods.[53]

Throughout the 1940s, RHC–Cadena Azul and CMQ dominated the ratings. The two networks' Havana stations frequently accounted for as much as 80 percent of the audience in the city's 30-plus station market.[54] During the 1930s and the first half of the 1940s, RHC–Cadena Azul held a consistent lead over CMQ in the ratings.[55]

A number of observers of Cuban radio praised the production quality of the two premier radio networks. A *New York Times* report on Cuban radio in 1946 hailed CMQ and RHC–Cadena Azul as "comparing quite favorably with those of stateside stations."[56] The *Times* was less impressed by the programming on Havana's many small stations, operated by single individuals who relied almost exclusively on musical recordings and talk.[57]

The *Times* also praised Havana station CMX, known as Mil Diez (the number 1010, for the place on the dial), a 10,000-watt station operated by the Communist Party. It was purchased by the party for $100,000 during the early 1940s.[58] The party rebroadcast Mil Diez programs over its international shortwave station, COCX.[59]

During most of the program day, CMX emphasized entertainment over politics. The Communist station prospered by melding into the Cuban media landscape, with the fourth largest audience in Havana.[60] Its offerings included music, dramatic sketches and what the *Times* described as largely objective news reports.[61] It also carried a daily quiz program in Marxist theory and application.[62]

CMQ Radio

CMQ was inaugurated on March 12, 1933, by co-owners Miguel Gabriel and Angel Cambo Ruiz. The two businessmen had known each other since 1930 when they were involved in contracting time on an informal late-night program called "La Hora de los Desvelados" ("The Sleepless Hour") broadcast over a small Havana station.[63] Cambo and Gabriel acquired the 250-watt station, then called CMCB, from Jose Fernandez Suviaur.[64] Cambo owned a haberdashery, La Casa de las Medias (The House of Stockings), which specialized in women's hosiery.[65] Cambo's experience in radio was limited to his advertising over CMCB. Gabriel worked as a salesman in a small U.S.-owned station called Radio Atwater-Kent. The two men incorporated as Cambo & Gabriel, S.A. The charismatic Gabriel became the public spokesperson for CMQ, while the wealthy Cambo furnished the money.[66]

These were the days of the ruthless Machado dictatorship, and CMQ gained journalistic respect in its "El Noticiero CMQ" ("CMQ News").[67] "CMQ News" carried editorials written by Jose Rodriguez Diaz and read by Manolo Serrano and Miguel Buendia. According to one popular Cuban magazine, Serrano's forceful editorials against the Machado government contributed to "alleviating the peoples' suffering under the oppression of . . . the hateful regime. Serrano was the first to suffer the rigors of the *porra* [the bludgeon] and Rodriguez and Buendia were also victims of the brutal aggression of the *energumenos* [violent people, slang for assholes], paid by the dictator."[68]

While CMQ might have gained respect in journalistic circles with its news and intrepid editorials, it gained popularity and financial success with a live amateur talent program called "La Corte Suprema del Arte" ("The Supreme Court of Art"), which began on Dec. 1, 1937.[69] The program, conceived by Gabriel, was hosted by Jose Antonio Alonso, the first of several announcers who would gain fame hosting the program. Acts that were poorly received by the studio audience were taken off the air. Gabriel himself rang a bell on the program signaling disapproval of unpopular acts. Well-received acts were invited to appear again in subsequent programs.[70] The success of "The Supreme Court of Art" is credited with being the springboard for CMQ's growth. In the years following the 1933 revolution that toppled Machado, Cambo and Gabriel purchased stations in the interior of the island that carried the Havana station's programs.[71]

Being a successful radio personality on "The Supreme Court of Art" did not guarantee instant wealth. CMQ faced little competition, and as a result it could set actors' salaries. In a 1953 interview, Alonso described his spartan working conditions:

> We lived at the station itself and we did everything. . . . [We] searched for the advertisements, did the work of the operators, we announced and we swept. Many times all we received was a sandwich and a coffee with milk. That was all that Miguel [Gabriel] would give us to fill our stomachs for the whole day. And there were occasions when we didn't have the sandwich and had to do with the coffee with milk.[72]

"The Supreme Court of Art" was a springboard for the careers of many Cuban singers and actors.[73] Stars were expected to be able to handle a variety of acting roles, and sometimes even non-acting jobs. The story of Manuel (Manolo) Reyes, who found fame on "The Supreme Court of Art," was typical. On Feb. 18, 1938, 13-year-old Reyes, an aspiring singer, beat the other acts on the program and was called back for future programs. He became a regular on "The Supreme Court of Art" and was placed on CMQ's payroll. He remained with CMQ in numerous acting, directing and sales positions until he left Cuba in August 1960.[74]

In 1940, Reyes performed the role of the son in a program called "La Familia Pilon" ("The Pilon Family," sponsored by Pilon Coffee). Almost all programs were produced and sponsored by companies that contracted the time from stations and networks.[75] Manolo Serrano, the editorial commentator on the evening news that preceded "The Pilon Family," played the father. The program's scripts were written by Jose Rodriguez Diaz, who wrote the editorials for "CMQ News." "The Pilon Family" criticized President Fulgencio Batista y Zaldivar (1940–1944, 1952–1958), after Batista had been elected in 1940. Each program concluded with the family seated around the dinner table discussing the tribulations of life in Batista's Cuba.

Serrano, Rodriguez, Reyes and others associated with "The Pilon Family" frequently received telephone calls from angered Batista supporters. The anonymous callers threatened to kidnap them and force them to drink castor oil, a punishment sometimes forced upon journalists who criticized the government. None of the people associated with the program, however, was ever harmed.[76] The program went off the air in 1945 after Ramon Grau San Martin defeated Batista in the 1944 presidential campaign.

While Reyes appeared on "The Pilon Family," Crusellas hired him to produce a 15-minute daily program called "La Guajira Guantanamera" ("The Poor People of Guantanamo"). The program was a precursor of what would later become known as "docudramas." "The Poor People of Guantanamo" adapted news reports to the popular "radionovela" (soap opera) format. Writers sifted through each day's newspapers looking for the most emotionally charged stories to dramatize into program scripts. The program, which kept the original names and places, dealt with such topics as a woman killed in a lovers' quarrel, the reunion of a family separated for many years and a woman who gave birth in the street.[77]

Radio Havana Cuba–Cadena Azul

The only radio organization that offered CMQ serious competition was Radio Havana Cuba (RHC)–Cadena Azul. CMQ built its empire in Havana and expanded into the island's interior with a network of "repeater" stations. CMQ's programming reflected the news, personalities and fast-paced entertainment of Havana. RHC–Cadena Azul, on the other hand, had a provincial flair. The network was created by Amado Trinidad Velasco (known as "El Guajiro de Ranchuelo," "the peasant from Ranchuelo," a city in Las Villas province).

With his brothers Ramon and Diego, Trinidad earned his fortune in the cigarette industry as part of the Trinidad y Hermanos (Trinidad and Brothers) cigarette company in Ranchuelo. Trinidad considered launching a radio station as early as 1935 after the brothers' business was crippled by a strike. He complained that management's position was

1. WHEN IT ALL BEGAN

not given fair treatment in the news media.[78] In 1937, Trinidad purchased stations CMHW and CMHI in Santa Clara and combined his stations into Cadena Azul (The Blue Chain or Blue Network).

Trinidad understood that radio listeners in Cuba's interior wanted programs attuned to country life, rather than the high-powered variety programs suited for the Havana audience. Success came on Aug. 26, 1939, with a program called "Pepe Cortes." The main character was played by Vicente Morin. As *Bohemia* magazine described the program, "Pepe Cortes" was a

> romantic bandit [and] peasant [who] robs the rich to help the poor. And most important, Pepe Cortes sings stanzas that are related to the plot. . . . Trinidad, a man of the land, knew the psychology of the peasant and put in the program all the elements necessary in order to captivate his [the peasant's] attention. . . . All are tuned in to the adventures of the hero who, always on his horse and gun at the belt, never lacks the time necessary to play his guitar and sing some stanzas. In front of their radio receivers, fascinated, the peasants follow the unlikely adventures of "Pepe Cortes." Those that don't have a radio go down to the caserio [small settlement] by foot and by horse to seat themselves in front of the apparatus and not miss the chapter that day.[79]

Back in Havana, Gabriel was taken by surprise at the success of "Pepe Cortes." The CMQ magnate sent a representative to entreat Morin to reprise his "Pepe Cortes" performance on CMQ. After offering Morin 300 pesos a month, five times his salary at Cadena Azul, Morin joined CMQ (a Cuban peso was roughly equivalent to a U.S. dollar).[80]

Enraged, Trinidad responded to Gabriel's assault by approaching Ingeniero Cristobal Diaz, the owner of the Radio Havana Cuba network (CMCY in Havana). Cristobal Diaz had access to important high-grade telephone lines. Trinidad negotiated with Cristobal Diaz to merge the two networks into RHC–Cadena Azul. The new network was inaugurated on April 1, 1940. Trinidad was the president and Cristobal Diaz was vice president.[81] As a result of the merger, RHC–Cadena Azul became, as it would note in its advertising, "The first telephone wired network of Cuba that blankets the whole island."[82] Like Gabriel at CMQ, Trinidad surrounded himself with creative people. Most notably, he appointed Luis Aragon Dulzaides the network's director of programming and publicity. Years earlier, Aragon created Cuba's first radio spectacular, "Multiple Hour."[83]

Trinidad received financial assistance from a number of advertisers to enhance RHC–Cadena Azul, including Sabates, the Procter and Gamble subsidiary in Cuba. Sabates' main competitor, Crusellas, the

Colgate-Palmolive subsidiary, had established a close relationship with the CMQ network. Jose Manuel Viana, Sabates' vice president of advertising, was blunt about why his company provided RHC–Cadena Azul financial assistance to compete against CMQ: "It was a need to survive against our competition that we helped to develop another national network against CMQ."[84]

Trinidad declared radio war against CMQ. Just as Morin was snatched from his organization, Trinidad set out to raid CMQ's talent. A number of CMQ's leading stars soon found a new home at RHC–Cadena Azul. CMQ responded by offering hefty salaries to Trinidad's leading performers. The war between the two networks raised the salaries of Cuban radio actors, who found marked improvements in their lifestyles. No longer would a celebrity like Jose Antonio Alonso of "The Supreme Court of Art" be expected to sweep up in the evening:

> Trinidad had done something that in the future all those who labored in front of a microphone would have to thank him. He had learned to appreciate and justly pay his valued talent. The artist, author, singer, musician who, until then, had not been treated well economically received fair pay at RHC–Cadena Azul. The salaries of $80, $100 and $150 that the magnates at CMQ thought magnificent were unknown at Amado's empire. There the actresses, actors, singers, writers received every 30 days checks of $500, $700, $1,000, $1,200.[85]

This was the state of radio in Cuba during the early 1940s. Two large national networks engaged in a self-destructive battle to rout the other. Meanwhile, other stations were vying for national prominence. The U.S. industry publication *Radio Annual* listed 34 longwave radio stations in Havana in 1941, the most powerful being CMQ's Havana station, broadcasting at 25,000 watts during the day and 15,000 at night (see Table 1.1). It was followed by CMCY, RHC–Cadena Azul in Havana, broadcasting at 15,000 watts.[86] Table 1.1 shows the stations in Havana, their owners and power in watts.

The Arrival of Goar Mestre

Since the mid-1930s, the brothers Goar, Abel and Luis Augusto Mestre operated a small product distribution company in Santiago de Cuba. The firm was an extension of their parents' business, Drogueria Mestre y Espinosa, founded by their grandfather in 1895. The brothers distributed pharmaceutical and surgical products.[87] On Oct. 10, 1938, Goar, the youngest brother, age 26, returned to Cuba. In 1936, he

Table 1.1. Radio stations in Havana, 1941

Call Letters	Owner	Power in watts
CMW	Adolfo Gil and Miguel Troncoso (RHC–Cadena Rojo)	2,500
CMCY	RHC–Cadena Azul, S.A.	15,000
CMZ	Ministry of Education	5,000
CMCD	—Suspended—	
CMQ	Cambo & Gabriel, S.A.	(Day) 25,000 (Night) 15,000
CMK	Fauto Montiel	250
CMBC	Domingo Fernandez (Radio Progreso)	(Day) 5,000 (Night) 1,000
CMBL	Radio Suaritos	5,000
CMCF	Oscar Gutierrez	5,000
CMBZ	Manuel and Guillermo Salas (Radio Salas)	250
CMCK	Luis Casas Romero	5,000
CMX	Francisco Lavin Gomez	10,000
CMCM	Transradio Columbia Company, S.A.	250
CMBY	Pages and Company	250
CMBQ	Amletto Battisti (Radio Continental)	(Day) 5,000 (Night) 1,000
CMCU	Jorge Garcia Serra (Radio Garcia Serra)	250
CMCW	Jose Villarino	250
CMBF	Cuban Radio and Television Company	5,000
CMCH	Radio Popular, S.A.	250
CMCX	Radio Popular, S.A.	250
CMBG	John L. Stowers (Radio Atwater-Kent)	1,000
CMBS	Arturo Artalejo (Radio Capital Artalejo)	250
CMOA	Juan Fernandez Duran	250
CMC	Radio Telefonica Commercial of Havana	250
CMBX	Vicente Espinosa	250
CMCB	Metropolitan Radio of Havana	250
CMBD	Luis Perez Garcia	250
CMCQ	Andres Martinez	250
CMCG	La Onda, S.A.	250
CMCA	Agusto Testar and Jose Manuel Gonzalez	250
CMOX	Perez and Chisolm, S.A.	250
CMBH	Alberto Alvarez Ferrera	5,000
CMCJ	Rafael Rodriguez	250
CMCR	Aurelio Hernandez	250

Source: Adapted from Jack Alicoate, ed., *The 1941 Radio Annual* (New York: The Radio Daily, 1942), 1002.

received a business degree at Yale University. During 1937 and 1938, he worked for the Argentine subsidiary of Union Carbide Corp. With Goar's business acumen, the distribution firm grew rapidly.[88]

In 1939, the brothers became the exclusive Cuban distributor of a powdered chocolate soft drink called Kresto. That account was immensely profitable. The Mestres purchased half of Kresto and its distributor, Bestov Products, S.A. They handled all their operations under Bestov Products. Their list of clients grew to include General Foods, Admiral, Norwich Pharmaceutical, Kolynos toothpaste, American Home Products and the General Motors divisions of GMC, Buick and Bedford.[89]

During this time, Bestov purchased air time from Cuba's two national networks, CMQ and RHC (before it merged with Cadena Azul to become RHC–Cadena Azul), to broadcast its clients' sponsored programs. Goar Mestre arranged with RHC owner Cristobal Diaz to purchase a half-hour each evening over RHC and shifted most of his clients' advertising to RHC. Then, in what Mestre regarded as an act of treachery, Cristobal Diaz canceled his contract with Bestov and leased the air time to another sponsor. Mestre engaged in a heated dispute with Cristobal Diaz, who "just walked all over me and threw me out of the station."[90]

The episode with Cristobal Diaz made Mestre realize how dependent he was on RHC and CMQ for his clients' advertising and programming. Sobered by his experience with Cristobal Diaz, Mestre brought his business back to CMQ and was grateful to Gabriel for having "rescued me." The incident, however, set Mestre thinking about establishing a "third network" in Cuba so that he would never again be subjected to the whims of a network owner. But for the 26-year-old Mestre, this seemed a dream.[91]

Meanwhile, the Mestre brothers had established a solid business reputation. In 1942, they created an advertising agency with businessman Augusto Godoy, the owner of the Publicidad Godoy advertising agency. The brothers brought their clients to the agency called Publicidad Mestre & Godoy. Godoy brought several major clients to the fledgling firm, including Pepsi Cola.[92]

During the summer of 1942, while on a business trip to New York, Goar Mestre met with Mexican radio tycoon Emilio Azcarraga in the Waldorf-Astoria Hotel. Azcarraga, a legend in Latin American radio, operated the most important radio network in Mexico and established program exchanges with the National Broadcasting Co. (NBC) in the United States.[93] Mestre had met with Azcarraga several times before to arrange for Mexican entertainers to travel to Cuba for his clients' programs.

Mestre queried Azcarraga about his idea for creating a new radio network in Cuba. Azcarraga discouraged Mestre. With the war raging in Europe, Azcarraga argued, it would be difficult to obtain the equipment to build a radio network. He advised Mestre to purchase an existing network. As Mestre recalled: "To Emilio Azcarraga, it was easy to think of buying a network. But to me and my brothers, it seemed completely

1. WHEN IT ALL BEGAN

out of the question. . . . I told Azcarraga that I didn't think that either network [CMQ or RHC–Cadena Azul] would be available. And he laughed and said something like, 'Oh, Mr. Mestre, everything is always up for sale. It all depends on the price.'"[94]

Azcarraga was right. In mid-1942, Goar Mestre queried CMQ co-owner Gabriel whether he would be willing to sell the network. Mestre did not approach RHC–Cadena Azul because he was still bitter over how Cristobal Diaz, now vice president of RHC–Cadena Azul, had spurned him in a business deal.

To Mestre's surprise, Gabriel did not reject the proposal. Gabriel wanted to discuss Mestre's offer with his partner, Cambo. In the meantime, Mestre tried to convince his brothers of the advantages to owning a network. Abel Mestre was skeptical. He had received a business degree from what was then Lehigh College in Pennsylvania, and had taken accounting courses. He was appalled by CMQ's business records: "We did not know exactly what we were getting into. We never saw a statement properly prepared by an accountant before we went into the business. The records were a mess. I remember that we got only two books—a ledger and a general accounts. And that's all the accounting that we saw."[95]

After debating the matter, the brothers offered Gabriel and Cambo a deal that would not require the brothers to take on partners. The brothers proposed purchasing half of CMQ for $725,000. Although the price was far more than the brothers could afford, they arranged to finance the purchase with a relatively small down payment of $50,000. They promised to pay the remaining $675,000 at the prevailing rate of interest over the years. Gabriel and Cambo agreed to the deal. The company was reorganized and reincorporated, changing its legal name from Cambo & Gabriel, S.A., to Circuito CMQ, S.A. Since the brothers accounted for three of the company's five directors—the three brothers along with Gabriel and Cambo—the Mestre brothers maintained effective voting control of CMQ.[96]

Gabriel, who knew Goar Mestre through numerous business dealings, agreed to accept the brothers' offer so long as Goar Mestre operated the company. Gabriel offered to teach Mestre about the radio business. According to the contract, Mestre could not devote any time to Bestov Products, the Mestre and Godoy advertising firm or any other business concern. The brothers accepted the offer, adding their own proviso that neither Gabriel nor Cambo could participate in any other radio broadcasting interests during the next five years. The deal was consummated, and on Aug. 1, 1943, the Mestre brothers became half owners of CMQ. A new era in Cuban broadcasting had begun. Under

Goar Mestre's leadership, CMQ would overtake RHC–Cadena Azul within six years and become Cuba's undisputed premier network.

CHAPTER 2
Goar Mestre and CMQ Radio

The previous chapter concluded by describing the situation in August 1943, when the three Mestre brothers (Goar, Abel and Luis Augusto) became half owners of the CMQ radio network. At this time, CMQ and RHC–Cadena Azul were in a fierce ratings war that was draining the resources of both organizations. Miguel Gabriel, the guiding force in CMQ, asked the young Goar Mestre to apply his highly vaunted business training to overcome the challenge from RHC–Cadena Azul. It did not take long for Goar Mestre to do just that.

CMQ actor and producer Manuel (Manolo) Reyes, a staple at CMQ since 1938, said that Mestre immediately instituted a policy requiring that all scripts be carefully timed so that each program ended on schedule. Mestre was annoyed by the practice of allowing sponsored programs that ran too long to continue over their allotted time, skewing the daily program schedule. Reyes recalled: "I remember that he [Mestre] told me that 'if you pay me $20 for two shirts, I'm selling you two shirts, not three. Similarly, if you buy 30 minutes, it's not 31. It's like the two shirts. You have 30 minutes, and it's off the air when your 30 minutes are over, because you have to respect the next advertiser.'"[1]

CMQ already had quality programming before Mestre joined the organization. Still, a number of programs created under Mestre's direction captured attention. On the entertainment front, Mestre instituted a series of popular daytime soap operas ("radionovelas") that touched upon risque subjects. "They are clean," Mestre told an American newsmagazine, "but there is plenty of adultery."[2] On the political front, Mestre brought the immensely popular Sen. Eduardo Rene Chibas to CMQ's microphones in 1943. Chibas's scathing radio denunciations of his political opponents brought CMQ both controversy and high ratings. Chibas had no compunctions about naming his enemies and accusing them of graft and corruption. Chibas' popularity increased when Cuban officials responded to his charges by launching libel suits and challenging him to duels. In 1946, a *New York Times* correspondent described Chibas' program this way:

> In a half hour of verbal fireworks, Senator Chibas gives his own very personal and emotional analysis of the week's news, domestic and international.... To some, Chibas is a hero, a militant voice for democracy; to others, a clown, a demagogue or worse.... He is a reporter, crusader, gossip and muckraker. His invective sizzles and he likes to name names. In short, "Eddie" puts on a good show.[3]

Mestre believed that his contribution to CMQ was in the organization's administration and business practices, not programming.[4] Mestre was disturbed by the lax and sometimes dishonest practices of Cuban radio owners. In his earlier dealings with Cuba's radio owners, when he was a product distributor and advertising agent, Mestre found that many owners informally set advertising rates during negotiations. The concept of published advertising rates was unknown. After some investigation, Mestre learned that advertising spots at CMQ ranged from $8 to $65 for a month of one-minute daily spots. Although prices for spots would be expected to vary based upon the desirability of certain time spots, there appeared to be no logic to CMQ's price discrepancies. Mestre then instituted a policy of non-negotiable advertising rates.[5]

At that time in Cuba, even after a station or network had signed a contract with an advertiser to deliver a promised number of spots, that did not always guarantee that the spots would be aired. It was common for radio owners to renege on the contracted number of advertising spots. In some cases, this would be the result of dishonesty; more often, however, it was due to mismanagement. As Mestre recalled: "I was troubled by the fact that in those days in Cuba you would buy, let's say, 50 spots, and you would try to monitor that, and you would discover that sometimes they would give you 50 spots, but more often than not they would give you 30 or 35. You would go visit the station owner, fight with him for a while and then he would give you more than the 50 you contracted. It was all very messy."[6]

Rotative Advertising

The advertising situation at CMQ was more serious than just the ad hoc rate-pricing policy or the failure to deliver the contracted number of spots. The sheer quantity of advertising was a problem. Almost 45 minutes of each daytime hour consisted of advertising. "You did not have to know a great deal about advertising to know that this situation was ridiculous," Mestre said.[7]

To learn more about network operations, Mestre traveled to NBC's Rockefeller Center in New York. CMQ had established a network affiliation with NBC's Cadena Panamerican (The Pan American Network) when Gabriel and Angel Cambo were in charge of CMQ. CBS's La Cadena de las Americas (The Network of the Americas) established a relationship with RHC–Cadena Azul.[8] The unique international network-affiliation relationship, strongly supported by the U.S. government during World War II as means to win the hearts and minds of Latin Americans to the American position in international arena, meant that the Cuban affiliates carried some U.S. programming during certain hours.[9] CMQ's network relationship with NBC continued after the war.[10]

When Mestre arrived in NBC's studios, he introduced himself as the new general manager of CMQ, NBC's affiliate in Havana. By now the U.S. networks had abandoned their grandiose plans for Pan-American networks.[11] Still, they felt obliged to assist their Latin American affiliates. John F. Royal, NBC's vice president of international relations, gave Mestre free reign to move about NBC studios and observe how the network operated. Also while in New York, Mestre visited the large Brentano's bookstore on Fifth Avenue and bought what he described as "a whole bookshelf full of books on advertising" and immediately began "to swallow them up."[12]

Upon returning to Havana, Mestre reduced the duration of long blocks of "spot" advertisements on CMQ. The blocks, which ran from five to seven minutes, consisted of a series of brief advertisements. Critics claimed that the barrage of advertisements detracted from programming.[13] The blocks were reduced to two or three minutes. "In those days, everybody bought spots," Mestre complained. "Hundreds of spots! Not one minute, but 10-second spots, 15-seconds, 20-seconds, 30-seconds. Very few one-minute spots. Whatever you wanted, they would sell you. You would buy 20, 30, 40 or 50 spots and pay a certain amount a month. That's where they used to cheat you and so forth."[14]

In addition to reducing the duration of the blocks of spots, Mestre also introduced a system called "rotative advertising." Each advertiser's spots "rotated" 15 minutes later each day into a different block of spots. In this way, over the course of each month, each advertiser's spots appeared during every time period of the day.[15]

Mestre personally visited CMQ's advertisers to persuade them to accept rotative advertising. Mestre stressed to them that while they were being asked to accept fewer spots for their monthly expenditures, their spots would appear in relative isolation in shorter blocks. In addition, as the spots rotated over the course of the broadcast day, all advertisers would receive some prime-time spots each month. To promote the concept, CMQ created the slogan "More programs and fewer commercials, but commercials that sell more."[16]

As Mestre recalled the introduction of rotative advertising, CMQ encountered surprisingly little resistance. Most advertisers could not afford the most expensive spots, so they were delighted with the new system that guaranteed occasional prime-time spots. One very important advertiser, however, the Colgate-Palmolive subsidiary of Crusellas, initially balked at the new system.

As CMQ's most important advertiser, Crusellas expected to be awarded with the most valuable spots. Crusellas had established a close relationship with CMQ when Cambo and Gabriel operated the network. For a price—$750 a month to be precise—Crusellas had purchased a "plug" in CMQ's daily station identification, which ran every 30 minutes each day.[17] CMQ's station identification began with a reverberating gong followed by an announcement: "CMQ: Belonging to Candado laundry soap [a Crusellas product], and COCQ [CMQ's shortwave call letters], belonging to Colgate dental cream and Palmolive soap, broadcasting from the soundproof RCA Victor studios located at Monte and Prado streets in Havana, Cuba."[18] CMQ also received $250 a month from RCA for mentioning RCA in the station identification. As Mestre said of Crusellas' special relationship with CMQ: "This company was the main source of financing for Cambo and Gabriel. Whenever they needed money to buy equipment, or anything else, they would ask Crusellas to give them an advance on their advertising contracts. So it [Crusellas] was almost like a bank to Cambo and Gabriel."[19]

In his efforts to persuade Crusellas to accept the new concept of rotative advertising, Mestre dealt directly with Ramon Lopez Toca, one of Crusellas' vice presidents. Mestre explained CMQ's plan for rotative advertising and eliminating Crusellas' name from the station identification. He had already arranged to drop "RCA Victor" from the identification. Mestre pleaded with Lopez Toca for Crusellas' acceptance, but, as Mestre recalled Lopez Toca's response: "He stood firm. He kept reminding me, 'But we've signed contracts, Mr. Mestre! We've signed contracts!'"

Mestre then told Lopez Toca that, if need be, CMQ would not live up to its contracts with Crusellas. This unhappy meeting led to another meeting the next day between Mestre and Ramon Francisco Crusellas

Touzet, the president of the company. To Mestre's surprise, Crusellas supported rotative advertising. Crusellas believed that if CMQ would profit from the new advertising system, so would Crusellas, because it was the main sponsor of CMQ programming.[20]

As Mestre had hoped, rotative advertising radically reduced the quantity of advertising and increased time to programming. Enrique Betancourt, who worked in Cuban radio before the Castro revolution, cited CMQ annual reports between October 1943 and October 1944 indicating that daily advertising over CMQ decreased from 415 minutes a day in 1943 to 160 minutes in 1944. Meanwhile, time dedicated to programming increased from 710 minutes to 965 minutes.[21]

All indications suggest that CMQ, and Cuban radio in general, experienced rapid growth during the late 1940s. By 1947, the island had an estimated 300,000 to 500,000 radio receivers, and almost 200,000 in the Havana area alone.[22] The Mestre brothers' advertising company, headed by Abel, was conducting regular research to track the interests and listening habits of radio listeners. Although most research remained proprietary, CMQs research director, Raul Gutierrez Serrano, made public some of the company's research in 1947 because of "the social importance of these figures."[23]

One important finding of CMQ's research was to counter the traditional notion that radio "as a medium of communication is fundamentally feminine."[24] The representative cross section of 850 Havana listeners indicated that 86 percent of the males and 85 of the females listened to radio on a daily basis.

In addition to such descriptive findings, the company also reported data which predated an area of academic study that communication researchers would later refer to as "uses and gratifications." The uses and gratifications model seeks to determine why members of the public "use" mass media and what subsequent "gratifications" they receive from the media.[25] The company's findings dispelled the traditional view that listeners used radio solely as a source of amusement while they used newspapers as a source of culture, information and public opinion.[26] While radio far exceeded newspapers as a source of entertainment, the company's findings, reported in Table 2.1, also indicate that Cubans preferred radio over newspapers in all respects.

Gabriel and Cambo Become Disenfranchised

With Goar Mestre at the helm of CMQ, the network took a number of steps to increase its ratings. As a conscious decision, CMQ's owners

Table 2.1. The Cuban public's "uses" of radio and newspapers in 1947

Use	All Respondents	Males	Females
Amusement/Entertainment			
Radio	81.2%	75.5%	86.9%
Newspapers	10.0	14.2	6.1
Both equal	8.6	10.3	7.0
Don't know	0.2	--	--
Culture			
Radio	56.1%	46.1%	65.7%
Newspapers	25.3	32.8	18.3
Both equal	18.4	21.1	16.0
Don't know	0.2	--	--
Information			
Radio	59.0%	50.0%	67.6%
Newspapers	25.1	32.8	17.8
Both equal	15.7	17.2	14.6
Don't know	0.2	--	--
Public Opinion			
Radio	51.8%	39.2%	63.7%
Newspapers	23.6	33.3	14.6
Both equal	24.1	27.0	21.7
Don't know	0.5	0.5	--

Source: Raul Gutierrez Serrano, "The Radio in Cuba," *International Journal of Opinion and Attitude Research*, 1:66 (1947).

agreed to put Goar Mestre into the public fore so that Cubans could identify CMQ with a voice on radio.[27] During the 1944 and 1948 presidential elections, CMQ provided the candidates air time to express their views.[28] Goar Mestre gained nationwide recognition and publicity for CMQ when he appeared on radio with the candidates. The network had planned to air the views of the presidential candidates again during the 1952 election on television, since CMQ had expanded into television in 1951. But the election was suspended by Gen. Fulgencio Batista's March 10, 1952, coup.[29] RHC–Cadena Azul also used the presidential elections to increase its ratings, with highly lauded campaign coverage from the candidates' headquarters.[30]

As the Mestre brothers exercised more control over CMQ, Gabriel and Cambo increasingly found themselves excluded from of the organization's decision-making processes. For Gabriel, regarded as one of the pioneers of Cuban radio, it must have been difficult to accept Goar Mestre's rise to fame.

With fame came notoriety. Oscar Luis Lopez, a former radio producer in Cuba, argued that Goar Mestre had used unethical business tactics to force Gabriel and Cambo to sell their shares of CMQ to the Mestre brothers. He maintained that Mestre used his superior business training to squeeze Gabriel and Cambo out of CMQ's decision-making processes.[31] He also asserted that prior to the Mestre brothers' purchase of half of CMQ, Goar Mestre had brought his advertising to RHC (under Ingeniero Cristobal Diaz) and later RHC–Cadena Azul (under Amado Trinidad) to financially weaken CMQ. Once weakened, Luis Lopez argued that Mestre purchased shares of CMQ:

> When the competition [between RHC–Cadena Azul and CMQ] grew to a level of personal fervor, a name unknown in broadcasting at that point entered the game—Goar Mestre. His tactics were diabolical. He supported programming on RHC through advertising aimed to injure Miguel Gabriel. When he had him [Gabriel] cornered, he bought CMQ and turned on his former ally [Amado Trinidad of RHC–Cadena Azul], destroying RHC–Cadena Azul.[32]

Bohemia magazine also noted the sharp differences between Yale-educated Goar Mestre and Trinidad, a self-described "simple peasant" ("guajiro siempre"), when the two men sparred for dominance in Cuban radio:

> It is then that appears on the scene—1943—a young, tall, fair-haired man with the accent of a Yale professor, the North American university from which he graduated.... Now began the violent battle without truce between the two rival organizations, RHC–Cadena Azul and CMQ, and between two diametrically opposed temperaments: Trinidad and Mestre. The first emotional, incapable of managing by established canons and unable to obey logic and his own impulses. The other, methodical, serene, calculating and capable, who would dominate in the end.[33]

Goar and Abel Mestre, of course, tell a different story. Goar Mestre described Luis Lopez's description as "pure fiction."[34] Abel Mestre said that the harsh portrayal of his brother's business tactics exaggerated Goar Mestre's power: "This [Luis Lopez's quote] makes Goar look like a very powerful man. He was just a young man at that time [1943, when the Mestre brothers purchased half of CMQ] with a great deal of ambition and very little money. He was not that wealthy. You could not say that Cambo and Gabriel were forced into the deal. They wanted to deal with us. We were just small-timers then."[35]

The first year after the Mestre brothers joined CMQ, the network lost $54,000. This dismayed Gabriel and Cambo. But Abel Mestre, in charge of CMQ's accounts, said that the loss reflected "depreciation" of equipment. Not until two years after the Mestre brothers joined CMQ did the organization realize profits.[36] The work paid off. The ratings report of the Cuban Advertising Association in July 1945 showed CMQ edging slightly ahead of its rival, with a rating of 7.75, compared to 7.19 for RHC–Cadena Azul. In the May 1946 ratings report, CMQ received a rating of 7.08, compared to 5.58 for RHC–Cadena Azul.[37]

Within the Mestre brothers' advertising agency of Publicidad Mestre & Co., research director Raul Gutierrez Serrano devoted much of his energy to tracking the listening habits of Cubans. Even at a time when the independent ratings reports of the Cuban Advertising Association were indicating CMQ edging past RHC–Cadena Azul, the agency reported that RHC–Cadena Azul was rated about even or slightly ahead of CMQ in Cubans' listening preferences, with 39.6 percent of the listeners preferring RHC–Cadena Azul to 38.4 percent for CMQ. Station CMBL, Radio Progreso in Havana, came in third with 8.4 percent preference, followed by the Communist-owned station, CMX, with 5.2 percent.[38]

Goar Mestre, meanwhile, devoted much of his time to the construction of a new building for CMQ—a state-of-the-art, 10-story edifice of reinforced concrete designed especially for radio. Mestre was dissatisfied with CMQ's leased building. He approached several contractors about constructing a radio center for CMQ. No doubt part of Mestre's reason for the new building was also to upstage Trinidad, who opened a "Palace of Radio" in April 1944.[39]

While driving home from work in 1946, Goar Mestre saw a plot of land where he decided to build CMQ's Radiocentro Building. He arranged to equip the building, the first in Cuba with central air conditioning, with the most advanced broadcasting equipment outside the United States. Construction on the $3 million edifice began in 1946 and was completed in 1948.[40]

In addition to housing radio facilities, CMQ leased out offices and businesses in Radiocentro. The building featured two studios, a 1,650-seat motion picture theater leased to Warner Brothers, two restaurants, a bank, an automobile showroom, a dozen shops and seven floors of office space.[41] Some land was left vacant as the site of future television studios when, and if, CMQ expanded into television.[42] Shortly after Radiocentro was inaugurated, Mexico's Emilio Azcarraga, the most well known radio broadcaster in Latin America, flew to Havana and toured CMQ's modern complex, claiming that he wanted to duplicate Radiocentro in his own proposed Radiopolis complex in Mexico City.[43]

Before Radiocentro was built, Gabriel and Cambo frequently expressed discomfort with what they viewed as Mestre's grandiose plans for a radio building and other expenses.[44] In 1945, a bitter Gabriel, whose ideas were repeatedly voted down at CMQ's board meetings, entered Goar Mestre's office and accused Mestre of squandering CMQ's finances. Gabriel told Mestre that he had purchased shares in RHC–Cadena Azul and was becoming vice president of that organization. From now on, Gabriel said, he would be working with RHC–Cadena Azul's Trinidad while retaining his shares in CMQ. The purpose of joining RHC–Cadena Azul, Gabriel said, was to offer CMQ competition so that Mestre could not squander CMQ's money. Gabriel's involvement with RHC–Cadena Azul violated the contract that he and Cambo had signed with the Mestre brothers in 1943.[45] Goar Mestre recalled the confrontational meeting with Gabriel:

> One day he [Gabriel] came in, this was about three o'clock in the afternoon, and said, "I have bought an interest in RHC–Cadena Azul." I said, "Miguel, wait a minute, you are telling me you bought an interest in Cadena Azul. What do you mean?" "I'll tell what I mean," he said. "I'm going to protect my interest here [at CMQ] because the way you are running this company you are going to wreck it, you are going to fail, so I'm going to be your competition. And I'm going to protect my interest by being your competitor, because if I don't, I'm going to lose everything that I have here." So I said to him, "But Miguel, you can't do it, because you made me sign a contract that I couldn't devote any time to any other business other than the management of CMQ, as director general, for five years. And we in turn, the Mestres, put a clause, remember, that neither you nor Angel Cambo could have any interest in any other radio organization for five years. And if you do this, you would be violating the contract. And he looked at me and said, "I shit on that contract."[46]

Goar Mestre then called Abel Mestre and Cambo to his office. Luis Augusto Mestre was not in town. Abel and Cambo were informed of what had transpired in the office. "'Well,' I told them," Goar Mestre said. "'Miguel here says that he shits on the contract,' and Miguel sat quietly in the corner nodding his head in agreement. 'What are we going to do about it?'"[47]

After Abel and Cambo agreed that Gabriel had violated the contract, Gabriel agreed to sell his shares in CMQ to the remaining owners. But Gabriel warned his partners that with Trinidad's assistance, he would destroy CMQ.[48] Half of Gabriel's 25 percent shares went to the three

Mestre brothers and the rest to Cambo. This left the brothers with 67.5 percent of CMQ. Cambo held the remaining 32.5 percent.[49] Cambo, like Gabriel, expressed reservations about CMQ's expenditures in what seemed to him like grand projects. Unlike Gabriel, the Mestre brothers never found Cambo confrontational. Cambo was more concerned about profit than his ego or personal fame.[50]

As the new vice president of RHC–Cadena Azul, Gabriel tried to build RHC–Cadena Azul into a revitalized organization to compete against CMQ. The 44-year-old Gabriel, who was severely overweight (he was known as "el gordo," "the fat man"), worked from morning to evening at RHC–Cadena Azul. But Gabriel never had an opportunity to help Trinidad. He died of a heart attack on Dec. 10, 1945.[51] He never lived to see the completion of his plan for a 1,000-seat, air conditioned studio. Gabriel hoped to use the studio for an amateur-talent program similar to CMQ's "La Corta Suprema del Arte" ("The Supreme Court of Art"), which he had created a decade earlier. When the studio was completed, Trinidad named it after Gabriel.[52]

During the late 1940s, CMQ's four directors (the three brothers and Cambo) voted to expand into television. Although Cambo approved this decision, he expressed reluctance.[53] During this time, the U.S. television industry was experiencing rapid growth. In early 1948, there were 19 stations on the air in the United States. By fall of that year, 36 were in operation.[54] Despite the growth, many stations were losing money. NBC lost $18 million in television during its first four years of operation.[55] Cambo feared similar losses for CMQ's television venture. In January 1950, Cambo met with Goar and Luis Augusto while Abel was out of town. Cambo beseeched his partners to reconsider CMQ's decision to expand into television.[56] In what Goar Mestre recalled as a friendly meeting, Cambo expressed his concerns:

> He [Cambo] said in a very solemn tone, "You know, I have been investigating on my own this television business, and I have come to the conclusion that it is a mistake to go into television." He also said that all television stations in the [United] States were losing money, which was true. I don't think that there were any television stations in 1948–49 making money in the United States, or making much money. Maybe some of them were breaking even. But the business had not yet kicked off. "Well," he said, "I don't like it. So I've come to tell you fellows that I think we should desist from going into television."[57]

By now, CMQ was committed to expanding into television. The company had arranged to purchase $500,000 worth of television equipment. It was also constructing a television annex with three television studios. Aware of Cambo's anxiety with CMQ's plans, Goar and Luis Augusto agreed that the three brothers would purchase Cambo's shares in CMQ for $500,000, making the network wholly owned by the Mestre brothers.[58] When Abel returned from his trip, he was angry with his brothers for making the decision without his approval.[59]

According to popular press reports, Cambo was retiring from CMQ because he had succeeded in his business career and he now wanted "to rest." But it apparently was no secret that CMQ's move into television was the real reason for Cambo's decision. As a *Bohemia* report noted: "Some supposedly knowledgeable person [in CMQ] said that Cambo was pulling out because he wasn't ready to face TV, a new, hard and tricky venture."[60]

Radio Reloj and CMBF

In April 1947, Goar Mestre attended a convention of the National Association of Broadcasters in Atlantic City, New Jersey. He heard a speech by Charles R. Denny, the U.S. Federal Communications commissioner. Mestre was impressed by Denny's prediction that radio's future would be in specialized stations for music, sports, news and other topics. "This," Mestre said, "is what triggered my idea for CMBF and Radio Reloj."[61]

Despite the popularity of CMQ's entertainment programs, the Mestre brothers claimed a social commitment to news and public affairs programming. CMQ met with success in radio news programming when it became the primary owner of Havana station CMCB–Radio Reloj (Radio Clock). The station was reputed to have been the first 24-hour, all-news radio station in the world.[62] Radio Reloj began in July 1947, airing 18 hours a day. It expanded to 24 hours two months later.[63]

Radio Reloj had its beginnings in April 1947 when two businessmen named Justo Carrillo Hernandez and Manolo Menendez obtained authorization from the Ministry of Communications to broadcast over 1220 kilocycles. Carrillo and Menendez made a modest investment in radio equipment and planned to copy the format of Mexican station XEQK, which announced the time every hour. The Mexican station did not feature news.[64] Carrillo, a student leader in the 1933 revolution that toppled Machado, had been in and out of Cuban politics. Years later, he would lead the anti-Batista Montecristi organization and serve as a middleman running financial donations to Fidel Castro's July 26th Movement in Mexico.[65] "But this was a business investment, nothing more," Carrillo insisted. "It was to make money."[66]

Carrillo and Menendez arranged a meeting with Goar Mestre because they lacked experience in radio and needed financial assistance.[67] Mestre agreed to have CMQ become the primary owner of Radio Reloj in partnership with Carrillo and Menendez. Carrillo and Menendez were reimbursed the approximately $12,000 they had invested. CMQ also purchased new radio equipment, including two 1-kilowatt transmitters. One was to be used as a backup.[68]

After several meetings, the owners of Radio Reloj decided upon a fast-paced news format. Each minute would begin with a announcement of the time, coordinated with the National Observatory. This would be followed by 10 seconds of advertising spots, 35 seconds of brief news announcements read one after the other by a team of fast-talking announcers and 10 more seconds of advertising spots. The last few seconds consisted of a reverberating gong. Then, with the beginning of a new minute, the time was announced and the cycle began again. All the while, a metronome ticked to simulate the sound of a clock in the background.[69]

The owners believed that Radio Reloj's frenzied pace was appropriate for Havana, where people needed news quickly. The announcement of the time was for people to set their watches. The owners decided against expanding Radio Reloj into a network, believing that the station was unsuitable for the slower pace in Cuba's interior.[70] The station was so popular that Havana residents were reported to use the phrase "Get there Radio Clock time" to mean "Get there on time."[71] Advertisers paid $58 (U.S.) each week for 135 advertising spots each day.[72]

Until CMQ concentrated all its operations in its 10-story Radiocentro complex in 1948, Radio Reloj was located in a shed on the roof of CMQ's building on the corner of Monte and Prado streets. The shed was so hot and stuffy that the announcers worked in their underwear most of the time and women were not permitted in the studio-shack.[73] By the time Radiocentro was built, public interest in Radio Reloj was so great that CMQ operated Radio Reloj in an arcade behind glass panels so that people could watch the announcers at work.[74]

The concept of Radio Reloj was a major development in radio. The station is still on the air in Cuba today, using the same fast-paced format of news announcements. In addition, many Latin American stations copied Radio Reloj's format. Miami's Spanish-language WQBA on the AM dial, known as "La Cubanisima" (the ultimate Cuban), uses a variation of the Radio Reloj format during part of its daily broadcasts.[75] Radio Reloj was one of the reasons why Goar Mestre is remembered as "the father of Latin American [radio and television] broadcasting."[76]

2. GOAR MESTRE AND CMQ RADIO

The claim, however, that Radio Reloj originated solely from CMQ and Goar Mestre is an exaggeration. Somewhere in CMQ, during several meetings among Goar Mestre, Carrillo, Menendez and CMQ program director Gaspar Pumarejo, someone conceived the idea to package Radio Reloj in an all-news format.

Carrillo said that he and Menendez conceived Radio Reloj's news format.[77] CMQ program director Gaspar Pumarejo claimed that he conceived the news format, and as a result he should have been made a partner in Radio Reloj.[78] Goar Mestre said he did not recall who suggested the news format. He thought the idea "evolved" over several meetings.[79] Mestre also said that Pumarejo never asked him about becoming a partner in Radio Reloj. Mestre agreed, however, that Pumarejo was probably angered by not having been made a partner in the profitable enterprise. Even if Pumarejo had asked to be a partner, Mestre said he would have turned Pumarejo down. To Mestre, an employee was expected to share his ideas without expectations of special rewards.[80] Embittered, Pumarejo left CMQ and started a network in competition with CMQ and became Mestre's fiercest business foe. Mestre recalled:

> One of quarrels that I know that Pumarejo took to his grave was that he felt that it [Radio Reloj] had been his idea. To be honest with you, I am not certain. In those days I used to discuss everything with Pumarejo. In that specific instance, what contribution he made and what contribution I made, I don't know. But this is one of the reasons why he left us in such an antagonistic, unfriendly, aggressive mood. That was one of the factors. What were the other factors? I don't remember, except that I know that he wanted to be his own boss. Way down deep in his heart he must have said to himself, "I have more knowledge, more experience about radio—which is true—than this upstart, this guy [Goar], Mestre."[81]

Shortly after CMQ put Radio Reloj on the air, Pumarejo started the Union Radio radio network. The network was inaugurated on Oct. 6, 1947. Soon after, Pumarejo appeared on Union Radio and attacked Goar Mestre and CMQ for "aspiring to become a monopoly in Cuban radio."[82] The attacks so angered Goar Mestre that on several occasions he wanted to appear on CMQ and respond to Pumarejo's remarks. But his brother, Abel, held him back. Abel said that nothing would have pleased Pumarejo more than to have Goar Mestre legitimize Pumarejo's allegations by responding to them.[83]

The popularity of Radio Reloj as a source of up-to-date news is evident from the fact that during periods of political turmoil its studios were commandeered by government or rebel forces. On March 10, 1952, when Batista launched a military coup, one of his first actions was to have his soldiers silence Radio Reloj. The soldiers, however, forgot to shut off the metronome after they cleared the studio. When Havana residents awoke the next morning, they tuned to Radio Reloj and only heard the ticking. Cubans then knew that something was amiss in Cuba.[84] On March 13, 1957, the station was commandeered by insurgents who coordinated with conspirators to assassinate Batista at the Presidential Palace. The insurgents broadcast Batista's death in the coup attempt. Unknown to the rebels in Radio Reloj, Batista had survived the attempt on his life.[85]

Shortly after Radio Reloj went on the air, the Mestre brothers acquired another station called CMBF. The station, inaugurated on Feb. 10, 1948, aired classical and traditional Cuban music and called itself "the Musical Wavelength of CMQ."[86] Although CMBF was not a great financial success, Goar Mestre portrayed CMBF as a public service: "That station was not intended to be a money maker. And it was never a moneymaker. We used to lose anywhere from 50 to $100,000 a year. But we kept it because we felt obliged to provide that kind of public interest service. I used to say jokingly that we had CMBF to gain forgiveness for the many sins that we had committed at CMQ."[87]

CMBF was recognized by the United Nations Educational, Scientific and Cultural Organization (UNESCO) in 1949 when it was chosen to broadcast a pre-recorded Parisian concert on the centennial of the death of composer Frederic Chopin.[88] In 1958, CMBF was honored with Italy's highest artistic award for its support of culture.[89]

The growth of CMQ and the popularity of Radio Reloj and CMBF gave Goar Mestre a reputation for business acumen and efficiency. In January 1950, when Cambo sold his shares in CMQ to the three Mestre brothers, Union Radio's Pumarejo stepped up his sometimes very personal radio attacks against Goar Mestre:

> To keep from laying awake nights thinking that Mr. Goar Mestre and CMQ intend to take over the Cuban radio industry, I would have to forget that CMQ tried to buy RHC–Cadena Azul. It used middlemen so Mr. Trinidad would not suspect who was raiding the party. I would have to skip how he got the business [CMQ] from Cambo and Gabriel by deftly getting rid of them. This and other moves have made him a fortune. He owns CMQ and the best frequencies in Cuba, and he has lately bought control of Radio Reloj and CMBF.[90]

But not only Mestre's competitors viewed the successful entrepreneur as an ingenious and perhaps underhanded businessman. So did some American officials. During September 1958, the U.S.

2. GOAR MESTRE AND CMQ RADIO

Department of State considered nominating Goar Mestre to the Foreign Leader program of the World Press Congress, to be held at the University of Missouri from March 1–7, 1959. By now, Mestre was in charge of Cuba's largest television network, as well as its largest radio network. The Department of State sought the advice of the U.S. Embassy in Havana concerning Mestre's nomination. In a response marked "confidential," Francis J. Donohue, the Embassy's cultural affairs advisor, vigorously opposed Mestre's nomination on the grounds that Mestre was a "cold businessman who tolerates a Communist cell within his CMQ-TV network.... Despite pressure brought to bear on him [Goar Mestre], he has made no efforts to rout this [Communist] cell definitely from his network. He reportedly tolerates the Reds in his organization in order to avoid any serious labor disputes. There is no evidence that he is or has ever been a Communist or fellow traveller."[91]

Donohue added that "Mr. Mestre has not proved cooperative in using USIS [United States Information Service] materials on his TV and radio outlets."[92] As an alternative to Mestre, Donohue suggested that Jose Ignacio Rivero, the editor and publisher of the conservative Havana daily newspaper *Diario de la Marina,* be nominated for the position. Rivero was later nominated.

Upon seeing the declassified document for the first time, Goar Mestre was intrigued but not surprised to see himself described as "a cold businessman" and someone who tolerated Communists in his organization. He said that much of what Donohue wrote was "quite true."[93] Donohue's description had its roots from a meeting two years earlier at the U.S. Embassy. Thomas Crain, the Embassy's first secretary, and U.S. Ambassador Arthur Gardner had invited Mestre to the Embassy to inform him that CMQ was infiltrated by a group of "Reds." Crain and Gardner presented Mestre a list of 19 CMQ employees, most of whom Mestre knew to be Communists and who made little secret of their politics. At this time, the Communist Party was a legal organization in Cuba.[94]

Regarding several names on the Embassy's list, however, Mestre laughed, claiming they could never be Communists. Mestre told Crain and Gardner: "We know who the Communists are. We are watching them. We think it is better for our own cause to know where every Communist is instead of driving them underground. In the positions that they hold, they can do no harm."[95]

CHAPTER 3
First in Cuban Television

When the Second World War ended, Cuba was ripe for the introduction of television. As in the United States, the island experienced a postwar economic boom. Middle- and upper-class Cubans had money for luxury goods such as television sets. Many had traveled to the United States and seen television. Many more read about television in the entertainment sections of their newspapers and magazines and were familiar with all the popular entertainers and programs. In addition, advertising expenditures in Cuba reached an all-time high after the war. Advertisers were looking for new media outlets to sell their goods and services.[1] Meanwhile, U.S. television set manufacturers were finding a saturated market at home and were looking to increase their sales through exports.

The widespread introduction of television in Cuba began during the early 1950s. But, as in all countries, Cuban historians traced the roots of television as far back as possible, both as an indication of the technological advancement of the nation and as a matter of national pride.

Cuban broadcast aficionado Alberto Giro, the radio and television writer at the *Diario de la Marina* newspaper, dated the origin of Cuban television to 1928.[2] In that year, Frank H. Jones, a U.S. radio operator in Cuba who constructed radio stations in the island's interior, assembled a crude television. Jones received television signals from the General Electric Company's WGY station in Schenectady, N.Y. WGY used the shortwave band of the spectrum, which allowed its signals to be transmitted over long distances. The station's thrice-a-week broadcasts were for the benefit of a small group of engineers and television enthusiasts in the United States.[3]

While Cuban newspapers reported Jones' achievement, they never explained what sort of visuals the signals contained. Although Jones had died some years before Giro's *Diario de la Marina* story, Giro obtained Jones' laboratory notes from the experimenter's son and learned that even during the 1920s the experimenter was devising plans for transmitting and receiving color television signals.[4]

It is unlikely that General Electric's technicians were even aware that their signals were being received in Cuba. If they were, they would have been proud. General Electric's chief scientist, Dr. E. F. W. Alexanderson, was proclaiming a future of international television.[5] International television, however, was not in the medium's future. The U.S. government, like other governments, would eventually confine television to very high frequency (VHF) and ultra high frequency (UHF) waves so as not to interfere with longwave and shortwave radio transmissions.[6]

The Race for Television

During 1949 and 1950, several Cuban radio networks announced plans to bring television to Cuba. According to press reports, three large networks—CMQ, RHC–Cadena Azul and Union Radio—were in a "race" to develop television.[7]

Throughout September and October 1950, Casto Mier Zurbano, a spokesman at RHC–Cadena Azul, made numerous announcements that the company would be ready to broadcast television signals by January or February 1951. The date came and passed without RHC–Cadena Azul television.[8] If Cubans expected RHC–Cadena Azul to be among the first in television, it was probably because of the network's once powerful position in Cuban radio. Although its position had declined in recent years, it was still regarded as the only serious competition to CMQ. RHC–Cadena Azul never kept its promise to bring television to Cuba.

Many prominent Cuban businesspeople expressed an interest in entering the race for television. After investigating the costs, most dropped out. Manolo Fernandez, the owner of the Radio Progreso radio network, and Ricardo Miranda Cortez, of the Cadena Oriental de Radio network, announced plans to construct television stations in Havana. Both men discontinued their plans after exploring the matter.[9] When Radio Progreso inaugurated a new, air-conditioned broadcasting facility with state-of-the-art equipment in November 1953, television facilities were conspicuously missing from the new building.[10] Guido Garcia Inclan, the owner of station COCO, held the option to broadcast over

Channel 13 in Havana and briefly considered expanding into television before abandoning the idea.[11] The *Diario de la Marina* newspaper explored the possibility of broadcasting over Channel 7, but eventually decided against it. Manuel (Manolo) Alonso, the owner of Cuba's largest newsreel company, "Noticiero Nacional," considered creating a station that would feature newsreels. He went so far as to order television equipment from RCA before canceling the order.[12]

Television proved to be an expensive venture, even for a wealthy organization like CMQ. In planning for television, CMQ's Goar Mestre originally estimated that CMQ would spend $325,000 (U.S.) to set up operations. After exceeding that amount, Mestre revised the figure to $730,000.[13]

The Regional Race

The race for television in Cuba was part of a regional race in Latin America. Mexico, Brazil and Cuba, respectively, inaugurated television stations within a 60-day period in 1950.[14] Mexico City's Romulo O'Farrill, the publisher of one of Mexico's largest daily newspapers, launched Latin America's first television station, XH-TV, on Aug. 31, 1950.[15] TV Tupi-Difusora of Sao Paulo, Brazil, went into operation less than three weeks later, on Sept. 18. The station was started by Francisco de Assis Chateaubriand, owner of 28 daily newspapers and 16 radio stations in Brazil.[16]

Unlike Mexico and Brazil, where wealthy media entrepreneurs introduced the first television stations, Cuba's first television station, CMUR-TV, Channel 4, known as Union Radio TV, was inaugurated by Gaspar Pumarejo on Oct. 24, 1950.[17] Pumarejo, director general of the Union Radio radio network, was a relatively minor media tycoon, although a well-known radio personality. During the late 1940s, most Cubans expected that CMQ's Mestre, Cuba's counterpart to O'Farrill and Chateaubriand, would be first in Cuban television.

CMQ received the first television license in 1949 and started ordering television equipment from RCA later that year.[18] At the time, CMQ was Cuba's leading radio network. A radio survey of 58,575 Havana area residents conducted in late April 1950, six months before television came to Cuba, showed that CMQ with a rating of 8.24. It was followed by RHC–Cadena Azul, 4.65; Union Radio, 3.42; and Radio Progreso, 0.59. Among the top 25 programs, 17 were on CMQ, seven on RHC–Cadena Azul and one on Union Radio.[19]

CMQ began airing television programs on Dec. 18, 1950, more than a month after Pumarejo's Union Radio TV went on the air. CMQ was officially inaugurated on March 12, 1951.[20] Once CMQ went on the air, it quickly became Cuba's premier television station and later network. Unable to compete against the vast economic resources of CMQ, Pumarejo sold Union Radio's television and radio outlets in August 1951 to Manolo Alonso of the Noticiero Nacional newsreel company.

By early 1953, Cuba was home to nine of the 20 television stations in Latin America. Mexico had five and Brazil three. Argentina, the Dominican Republic and Venezuela each had one. It was obvious, however, that Cuba, with its relatively small population compared to Mexico and Brazil, could not maintain this lead. Mexico had 23 stations under construction in early 1953, while only three were in progress in Cuba.[21]

The Critics

Many Cuban intellectuals feared that television would develop into a crass commercial medium. Participants at a July 1952 round table conference on the future of Cuban television at the University of Havana agreed on the importance of educational television. The participants also agreed that commercial broadcasters could not and would not institute educational programming. They called upon the government to support educational programming. But they knew it was unlikely that the laissez-faire government would implement their recommendations.[22]

Critics of Cuban television also charged that U.S. broadcasters encouraged Cuban and other Latin American broadcasters to develop television to create a market for U.S. equipment. Clifford W. Slaybaugh, RCA's manager of worldwide broadcast sales during the 1940s and early 1950s, said that there was no truth to this allegation.[23] Slaybaugh, who sold radio and television equipment to all of Cuba's leading broadcasters, as well as to Emilio Azcarraga of Mexico and other Latin American broadcasters, said that Cuban broadcasters approached companies in the United States for assistance in building television. "As strange as it seems," Slaybaugh said, "RCA's head of international broadcasting, Meade Brunett, tried to dissuade Cuban and other Latin Americans from rushing into television. We tried to convince them that the costs didn't justify the results. But Mexicans, Cubans and other Latin Americans are very proud and wanted television even though their countries could not afford it. While we didn't refuse to sell [television equipment] to them, we tried to advise them that this was a terribly expensive proposition."[24]

Pumarejo Leads the Way

While CMQ and RHC–Cadena Azul were planning to expand into television during 1949 and early 1950, Union Radio's flamboyant Gaspar Pumarejo was constructing his television station in his personal residence on the corner of Mazon and San Miguel streets. To Pumarejo, getting on the air first was a way of distinguishing his station from his giant competitors. Pumarejo also wanted to get his station on the air by October to carry Cuban Winter League baseball games.[25] He might have also wanted to upstage Goar Mestre, his bitter business foe.

By the summer of 1950, when it was by now apparent that Pumarejo's station would be first with television, Union Radio kept the Cuban public eagerly awaiting its first broadcast. As early as Aug. 15, Union Radio started receiving shipments of equipment from RCA.[26] Aware that Union Radio would beat CMQ to the air, CMQ spokesman Ramiro Gomez Kemp told the press that CMQ "is not running a race."[27]

Pumarejo had close connections with the Humara and Lastra RCA distribution firm in Havana since he was a teenager. In 1921, when Pumarejo was 8 years old, his family emigrated to Cuba from Spain. As a teenager, Pumarejo worked in the Humara and Lastra firm as an errand boy, running messages across town for the organization. When he cleaned the offices at night, he listened to the radio sets and developed aspirations to become a broadcaster. This may have seemed an unattainable goal because Pumarejo had a serious speech impediment. While working at Humara and Lastra, Pumarejo attended school and earned the Cuban equivalent of a high school degree. Miguel Humara and Julian Lastra befriended the young Pumarejo and helped him in his career.[28]

By all accounts, the Cuban public eagerly read the press reports about Union Radio's television activities and announcements of when test patterns would be aired. When the Oct. 6 edition of *The Havana Post* prematurely reported what was described as Union Radio's imminent broadcast that evening, it noted, "Though the pictures won't be pretty, it is expected that much beer will be sold [at bars equipped with television] and the first-nighters will be standing 10-deep in line, with consequent traffic jams."[29]

Union Radio TV: A "Kitchen Operation"

In mid-August 1950, Pumarejo received delivery of two plane-loads of television equipment from RCA, including a transmitter, dollies, cameras and monitors.[30] It would be an exaggeration to describe Pumarejo's television station as a "kitchen operation." The station consisted of rooms in the house other than just the kitchen. The station's transmitter was installed on the roof of the house, the studio in the dining room, the controls in the pantry and the projection equipment upstairs in the servants' quarters. Most of the second floor was reserved for general business purposes, such as sales offices and bookkeeping. One of the two large living rooms was used to store props. Pumarejo was rarely at home while the equipment was assembled. He was busy in the radio station. His wife, Martha Mestre Pumarejo (no relation to the Mestre brothers at CMQ), whom he married in 1941, was forced to live with relatives while the station was being constructed.[31]

Pumarejo planned to display and sell television receivers to the public in the second living room. There were rumors in Havana that once television was on the air, there would be a rush for receiver units and a shortage of sets.[32] Anticipating this shortage, Pumarejo arranged to purchase disassembled receivers in the United States and assemble them in Havana. In this way, he hoped to take advantage of the import duty waiver on television components. The plan was abandoned after the parts distributor in Miami died.[33]

Six workers labored late into the morning hours assembling the equipment. The team consisted of Alberto Mestre, Pumarejo's cousin; Nico Mestre, Pumarejo's brother-in-law; Eric Kauppe, a technician and a neighbor of Alberto Mestre; Celimo Hernandez, an amateur radio technician; Antonio Blanco, a friend of one of the other members of the team; and Alberto Vilar, who had advertising experience. A supervisor from RCA in New York, William C. Cothron, was frequently on hand to supervise the work. Cothron had recently helped Mexican entrepreneur Romulo O'Farrill establish the first Latin American television station in Mexico.[34]

The workers ran into numerous problems. A central component of the transmitter, called an 821-tube, emitted intense heat. It had to be cooled by an elaborate system of water pipes. The tube converted studio signals into signals that could be transmitted over the air. The pipes that cooled both the transmitter and the 821-tube often leaked, threatening to damage wires and other components. On several occasions, one of the men had to run to the local pharmacy to purchase feminine hygiene pads to seal the leaks.[35] The pads had the right absorbency for plugging the leaks. On other occasions, Vilar had to make airplane trips to Miami for parts and return the same day.[36]

Cuba's first television broadcast was on Oct. 12, when Union Radio conducted a closed-circuit experiment. On the afternoon of Oct. 14,

Pumarejo, his voice only, announced that a signal would be on the air at 7 p.m. As promised, Cuban viewers saw the first images on television— various test patterns and close-up images of La Competidora Gaditana cigarette packages, bottles of Cristal beer and other products that sponsored programs on Pumarejo's radio network and later would be major sponsors on Union Radio TV. The purpose of these broadcasts was for the technicians to fine tune the transmitter. The station also carried images of technicians walking about the studios and making last-minute adjustments to equipment.[37]

Not until Oct. 20 did the station begin airing programs. These programs consisted of "singers, odd shapes, music and anything else that the station takes a fancy to transmit."[38] Artists were knocking on Pumarejo's door with various acts. By now, Pumarejo was ready to start airing programs on location outside the studio.[39]

In late October, the station carried the first of what would be regular Cuban Winter League baseball games.[40] A crew drove to the stadium in a remote-control truck. The broadcasts were beamed to Pumarejo's house by microwave, where they were rebroadcast. Cameramen were positioned at first base and home plate. The station's third camera remained in the house until newsman Alberto Gandero finished his newscast. After the newscast, the third camera was carried to the stadium by taxi and positioned near third base.[41]

It was standard practice for radio and television employees to serve in several capacities. Vilar, who doubled as the station's baseball announcer and program director, anchored the games from a platform over the bleachers. The heavy television equipment was lifted to the platform by a pulley equipped with a basket while Vilar climbed a ladder. When Vilar got thirsty, he used the pulley to lower the basket and fans would send up beer and coffee.[42]

Union Radio TV was officially inaugurated in the Presidential Palace at 12:30 p.m. on Oct. 24, 1950. To receive maximum publicity, Pumarejo set the ceremony for "Journalist Day," when the island's leading news reporters were honored by President Carlos Prio Socarras. Pumarejo had virtually gotten President Prio to publicize the station. Prio was photographed hugging Pumarejo and playing the role of a cameraman, peering into the lens of a Union Radio TV camera.[43] From then on, Union Radio TV's slogan was "Union Radio, primera en television, primera en popularidad" ("Union Radio, first in television, first in popularity").[44] Much of the programming on Union Radio TV consisted of cooking programs, exercise programs, soap operas and news. A popular program featured the celebrated comedy group of Gaby, Fofo and Milike. The popular Pumarejo himself was a regular staple on Union Radio TV.[45]

After Union Radio TV went on the air, "a rush began to buy television sets, [with] dealers buying large stocks on account and restaurants, bars and shops beginning to install sets."[46] There were persistent fears of television set shortages until 1953. Despite the high cost, ranging from $350 (U.S.) for a 16-inch set to $2,000 for a 30-inch unit, the Cuban government Imports and Exports Analysis agency estimated that Cubans imported more than 100,000 television receivers by 1952.[47] For the U.S. television manufacturers, television could not have come to Cuba at a better time. The U.S. market was glutted.[48] Demand for television sets in Cuba was so great that smugglers transported receivers into Cuba from Miami and Key West, Fla., via motor boats and cargo planes.[49]

Pardo Llada on TV

Jose Pardo Llada, Pumarejo's star radio commentator, exemplified Cuba's firebrand political radio commentator. With his pencil-thin mustache and trademark sunglasses, fashionable among Cuban males of his generation, Pardo Llada would gesticulate wildly as he delivered his impassioned radio speeches. Because he was frequently pictured in magazines and newspapers, many Cubans knew what he looked like.

Pardo Llada made the transition to television with mixed success. Something of a boy wonder, at age 27 Pardo Llada was a congressman and among the leading young figures in the Ortodoxo Party (Partido del Pueblo Cubano). He practiced what he described as "denunciatory journalism," which consisted of vitriolic attacks against his opponents.[50] The main targets of his venom were President Prio and members of Prio's government.

When Pardo Llada began his career in radio, there was little to suggest that he would become a leading political commentator. He studied theater at the University of Havana but dropped out because of his inability to roll the Spanish double "r" sound. He switched to law but failed to complete his thesis. (In Cuba, a law degree was considered a doctorate which required completion of a thesis.) While still a theater student, he landed a job on CMK radio, where he read poetry and announced a tango program.[51]

Pardo Llada gained attention during a hurricane that struck Havana in 1944 while he was a news announcer at CMK. The station's generator survived the storm while other stations were forced off the air, leaving him the main source of news during and immediately after the storm. As Pardo Llada recalled:

They informed me that CMQ, [Radio] Suaritos, Radio Salas, COCO—all of them—were off the air. Our antenna was still working. It was up to me to transmit for the first time a hurricane live and direct. I would stand on the roof and see all of Havana dark—a Dante-like spectacle of fire on the docks of the bay and the ambulances, fire trucks. I played the vibrant march of "the Captain" by [the composer, John Phillip] Sousa, written in 1896, as the background while I would describe everything. . . . I would narrate it all with great enthusiasm.[52]

Pardo Llada's experience reporting the 1944 hurricane impressed upon him the power of radio to rouse listeners through the use of colorful, descriptive rhetoric. Shortly after Pumarejo started his radio network, he arranged for Pardo Llada to deliver a commentary after Union Radio's radio newscast which Pumarejo named "La Palabra" ("The Word"). On Union Radio TV, however, Pardo Llada chose to play the probing, questioning journalist rather than the ranting politician on the podium.[53] He often served as Union Radio TV's news moderator, interviewing prominent people.

According to Union Radio's Alberto Vilar, the popular Pardo Llada, known for his rasping voice, had no future in television. Pardo Llada's allure was his vitriol, not his appearance. As Vilar recalled: "When I read what Pardo Llada was about to read on radio, I said to him, 'Pardo, this is nothing.' But when he read it, he changed everything. It was in his tone, everything. But on TV it was not the same. The face of Pardo was nothing. It was big, dark glasses."[54]

Interviewed in 1992, Pardo Llada said that even in the early days of television he realized that radio and television required different styles. He clearly preferred radio, which allowed him to fully exercise his rhetorical skills:

> Radio is stronger than television. Radio has a magic power because they [the audience] do not see you. Marshall McLuhan [the famous Canadian mass communication scholar] used to say "radio has the power of imagination." McLuhan said that if Hitler had been around during television, he would have not gotten to power. His [Hitler's] medium was radio because radio was a "hot" medium in which the imagination fills up all the gaps in the audience's mind. When I am on the air, it does not matter if the audience does not know who I am. When they hear me all furious and full of emotion, only God knows how they [the audience] imagine me. On television, to be furious is bad because it is a cool medium. So radio has, and always has had, an advantage over television.[55]

Pumarejo's Plans

A short time after the inauguration of Union Radio TV, Pumarejo created a second television studio in his house-turned-television station. This one was located outdoors in his large garden. A roof was constructed over the garden-studio to protect actors from the rain. Pumarejo's neighbors would lean out their windows and look over Pumarejo's fence to watch the program productions.[56] When it rained, the actors were shielded by the overhead roof. The cameraman and the camera were covered by a plastic sheet. But television viewers saw the rain between the camera and the actors.[57]

Pumarejo had grandiose plans for Union Radio TV's expansion that were never realized. He announced that he would construct a 10-story television center that would rival CMQ's Radiocentro complex.[58] He also predicted that Union Radio would establish Cuba's first television network by late 1951 with a system of microwave links stretching from Havana to Santa Clara.[59]

In his efforts to finance his network plans, Pumarejo approached leading businesses and asked them to purchase advertising spots months in advance. With advance payments, the advertisers were promised discount rates and the best time spots. Few advertisers were willing to spend money for a product with an uncertain future.[60] Pumarejo also tried to raise money to build his network by floating $3 million in bonds in 30,000 $100 denominations.[61] Pumarejo sold some shares to buyers who saw little if any profit on their investments. The U.S. Embassy in Havana, which closely monitored the development of Cuban television for potential U.S. investors in Cuba, was skeptical about Pumarejo's network promises. However, given Pumarejo's success in being first in television, the Embassy was not about to dismiss his claims. In a classified memo, the Embassy's secretary wrote:

> Mr. Pumarejo also stated that according to studies made by "Union Radio Television, S.A.," it was learned that these profits would be substantial. This, however, remains to be seen. The Director General, a young and energetic man, voiced his hope that the network would be completed before the end of 1951. It is felt by most sources that this is too early a date. However, not quite a year ago, Mr. Pumarejo promised the Cuban public that it would have television soon, at a time when television in Cuba seemed only a remote possibility to all. Nevertheless, "Union Radio Television, S.A." was on the air in October 1950, televising the professional baseball games as promised.[62]

Pumarejo gained some success obtaining financial assistance from Trinidad and Hermanos cigarettes, part of Amado Trinidad's business holdings.[63] In a section of the classified U.S. Embassy communication marked "restricted," the memo reported that an "informed source" told Embassy officials that Trinidad and Hermanos had provided Union Radio TV $400,000 to expand into the provinces. The Embassy noted that the company, located in Ranchuelo in Las Villas province, advertised on both Union Radio TV in Havana and the CMQ-TV network. At this time, CMQ-TV was expanding its microwave network into the provinces. Trinidad might have seen an advantage to stimulating television competition in the provinces to keep advertising rates down.

To further his network plans, Pumarejo brought to bear his own charismatic personality. Pumarejo purchased a truck for his workers and actors and a car for himself to trek into Cuba's interior and sell stock in a future Union Radio TV network. Most Havana residents had at least seen television sets in department stores. Not so with many people in the provinces. They were awed by the medium. Pumarejo's workers erected temporary television systems in schools, auditoriums, clubs, restaurants, parks and elsewhere. The "programs" were produced indoors and aired by closed circuit to sets in some nearby outdoor location such as a park. Pumarejo himself introduced the traveling acts for his closed-circuit programs. After the entertainment concluded, Pumarejo appeared again with offers to sell stock to small businesspeople, manufacturers and investors.[64]

A New Owner at Union Radio

Pumarejo found that the financial operation of television far exceeded that of radio. Unlike the wealthy Mestre brothers, his organization could not sustain years of financial losses before realizing a profit. Pumarejo was often weeks and sometimes months remiss in paying his employees.[65]

In August 1951, without giving notice to his workers, Pumarejo announced the culmination of more than six months of secret, late-night negotiations to sell Union Radio's radio and television stations to Manolo Alonso, a leading figure in Cuba's film and newsreel industry. Alonso was a commercially successful filmmaker who directed Cuba's first sound feature in 1937, "La Serpiente Roja" ("The Red Serpent").[66] Joining Alonso in the purchase was Jose Luis Pelleya, an attorney. Alonso thought he could succeed where Pumarejo failed by eliminating Union Radio TV's expensive live programs and instead relying on films and newsreels.[67]

Vilar heard rumors before the sale of Union Radio that Pumarejo would sell the radio network and television station. He confronted Pumarejo with these rumors. Vilar told Pumarejo that he was about to go on vacation, and before leaving he wanted to be certain his job would be waiting for him when he returned. Pumarejo told him that there was no truth to the rumors and to enjoy his vacation. Vilar recalled: "I drove to Varadero [beach resort]. In those days it was about three hours from Havana. And when I arrived in Varadero, someone said to me, 'Hey, if you see Manolo Alonso, stand up because he's the new owner of the station.' He sold the station from one day to another, and then he took a ship to Spain to do nothing, to take a vacation!"[68]

Pumarejo was reportedly looking long and hard for a buyer. He was deep in debt. CMQ's Goar Mestre said that he was secretly contacted by Pumarejo in 1950 with a plan for CMQ to purchase or go in partnership with CMQ. Mestre said he refused the offer and the meeting ended in a bitter argument.[69] Pumarejo once made reference to this meeting during one of his public attacks against Mestre, claiming that it was Mestre who approach him about CMQ becoming partners in Union Radio.[70]

Alonso agreed to purchase Union Radio, taking over the company's estimated $1.5 million debt.[71] Alonso reportedly raised the money through a consortium of commercial interests.[72] In what proved to become a minor scandal, President Prio's brothers, Paco and Antonio, were also reported to be involved in the purchase of Union Radio.[73]

The sale of Union Radio included the radio network and Pumarejo's personal residence with the television studio and all the equipment. A *Bohemia* magazine account of the sale asserted that in his rush to beat CMQ's Mestre brothers to the air with television, Pumarejo had not properly planned television programming and relied too much on improvised programming.[74] *Bohemia* also noted that the sale of Union Radio radio and Union Radio TV to Alonso was marked by "rumors" that President Prio was indirectly involved in the purchase. The magazine reported that Prio's alleged surreptitious purchase of Union Radio was going to make Pardo Llada "jump the fence."

Pumarejo distanced himself from any scandal and expressed full support for Alonso. Upon announcing the sale to Alonso, Pumarejo said: "I believe that Manolo Alonso, who is an intelligent, enterprising businessman, will be fully successful in the task that he now undertakes. He has a thorough knowledge of cinematography, and therefore he will contribute much to the field of television. Alonso is a great fellow, and I am pleased that my two daughters—Union Radio [radio] and Union Radio TV—are in his hands."[75]

Within days after announcing the sale, Pumarejo left for Miami with his wife and daughter. From there he went to New York and then to Spain, Italy, France and Switzerland for an eight-month vacation. While he was gone, the rumors of Prio involvement in the sale of Union Radio persisted. Pardo Llada, a prominent member of the opposition Ortodoxo Party, fueled the rumors when he publicly announced that he was quitting Union Radio because of the organization's association with Prio, a member of the Autentico Party (Partido Revolucionario Cubano).[76]

The Cuban public had long suspected that politicians manipulated Cuban mass media through bribes, subsidies, stock purchases and other means. Here was one of Cuba's most popular political commentators substantiating those charges. An angry Alonso told *Bohemia* magazine that he had made an agreement with Pardo Llada, allowing the commentator to retain his position as manager and director of "La Palabra" with full editorial discretion. Alonso also said that Pardo Llada agreed to sign a contract to continue his position with Union Radio. Then, according to Alonso, Pardo Llada went public with his resignation "in a violent and improper manner."[77] Pelleya maintained that Pardo Llada and *Bohemia* publisher Miguel Angel Quevado were close friends, who were "just out for publicity."[78] Pardo Llada, who admitted a close friendship with Quevado, said that Ortodoxo leader Eduardo Chibas told him about Prio's involvement in the purchase of Union Radio.[79]

Forty years after the scandal, Alonso, the owner of Manolo Alonso Film Productions in New York, still maintained that Prio was not secretly involved in the purchase of Union Radio: "At no time was Dr. Carlos Prio Socarras involved in this operation, nor was any other Cuban politician [involved]. Concerning Sr. Pardo Llada, I personally offered him a five-year contract in which a clause existed permitting him to attack any of the proprietors [of Union Radio]. He asked for three days in which to give me an answer, but he unexpectedly went on the air arguing a series of lies which supported his political aspirations. Then he resigned."[80]

A short time after Alonso purchased Union Radio, Ortodoxo Party leader Chibas committed his dramatic suicide while on CMQ radio. When the Union Radio TV camera truck arrived at the University of Havana, where Chibas' body was on view, angry students who associated Union Radio under Alonso management with their political enemy President Prio started rocking the truck. Only after Pardo Llada went outside and told the students that the newsmen on the truck had nothing to do with Prio did the students leave.[81]

Alonso did not have enough time to leave his mark on Union Radio. About a month after Fulgencio Batista's March 10, 1952, coup, he announced that he was leaving Union Radio to devote his energies to his motion pictures business.[82] A few years later, Alonso expanded his enterprises into Noticolor, which produced color films. It is possible that the Batista government pressured Alonso—whom it perceived as a Prio crony—to leave Union Radio.[83]

Pelleya said that to the best of his knowledge, Prio was not involved in the purchase of Union Radio. In retrospect, Pelleya believed that the artful Pumarejo had sold Alonso and him a clunker in Union Radio. "He [Pumarejo] was quite a convincing salesman," Pelleya recalled. "He had us believing that we could make big money. But his debts were enormous, and they were driving us crazy. No matter how well we did, there were always debts, debts, debts. Pumarejo could sell a refrigerator to an eskimo living in an igloo."[84]

Most of Union Radio's debts were to the firm of Humara and Lastra, the exclusive distributors of RCA products in Cuba. Pelleya said that the firm happily loaned Pumarejo all the money he needed to start television because it hoped to profit by selling television sets in Cuba. Firm owners Miguel Humara and Julian Lastra were now proposing to Alonso and Pelleya that they sell Union Radio to the wealthy Amado Barletta, owner of the exclusive General Motors franchise in Cuba and part owner of the newspaper *El Mundo*. According to Pelleya, Humara and Lastra hoped that Barletta would pay the company's debts and expand into color television, which would allow Humara and Lastra to sell more television sets.[85]

Drowning in debt, Alonso and Pelleya sold Union Radio to Barletta and his partners in April 1951.[86] Barletta, however, was not interested in radio. The nine-station radio network was acquired by Luis J. Botifoll, editor-in-chief of *El Mundo,* and Pelleya.[87] Botifoll and Pelleya never paid for the network. Instead, they agreed to assume its debt. Meanwhile, Barletta took over the contracts of the best performers at the company's radio network and brought them to his television station. Lacking a lineup of stars for popular radionovelas (radio soap operas), the chief staple of successful radio programs at this time, Botifoll and Pelleya changed the network's format to mostly news, sports and recorded music.[88]

CHAPTER 4
Havana's Television Market

*Gaspar Pumarejo received six weeks of uninterrupted fa-*vorable publicity in magazines and newspaper entertainment sections after he launched Cuba's first television station on Oct. 24, 1950. Then, on Dec. 14, CMQ-TV, Channel 6 in Havana, went on the air with a lineup of lavish programs featuring some of Cuba's best talent. CMQ very quickly overshadowed Pumarejo's station. Meanwhile, CMQ's Goar Mestre was already involved in the construction of a nationwide television network.[1]

CMQ-TV offered a schedule of opulent musical productions. "Cabaret Regalias" ("Royal Cabaret") and "Casino de la Alegria" ("Casino of Joy") were among Cuba's highest rated programs until CMQ was confiscated by the Castro government in 1960. The programs recreated the "big stage spectaculars" of Havana's night clubs. CMQ producer and director Mario Barral originated Cuba's first "telenovela" (television soap opera), "Senderos de Amor" ("Paths of Love"), starring Armando Bianchi and Adela Escrin. "Telenovelas" consisted of 150 to 200 one-hour episodes during the course of a year.[2] By the summer of 1951, CMQ already had three stations in operation of what would soon become an eight-station network.[3] The "repeater" stations carried the Havana station's programs throughout the island. Meanwhile, Union Radio TV continued its schedule of low-budget cooking shows, "round tables" and talk programs.[4]

Barletta Bows Out

After Fulgencio Batista's March 10, 1952, coup, Union Radio TV was purchased by a group led by Amadeo Barletta, co-owner of the daily newspaper *El Mundo*. Joining Barletta were Miguel Humara and Julian Lastra of the Humara and Lastra RCA distributorship; Jose Ignacio de Montaner, co-owner of the newspaper *Informacion;* and Angel Cambo, former co-owner of CMQ.[5]

The owners appointed Cambo as spokesperson of the organization, perhaps because of his reputation at CMQ with the late Miguel Gabriel and Goar Mestre.[6] Barletta, however, who shunned the public spotlight, was a powerful figure in the station. A classified memo from the U.S. Embassy in Havana stated that "it is understood that Mr. Barletta is putting up most of the money for this project."[7]

The station immediately entered into negotiations with the Philco Corp. in the United States to expand into a national network.[8] In an industry where self-promotion was critical, Cambo publicly expressed bewilderment at how CMQ was attracting so much press attention for building CMQ into a national network or "chain" while his organization's network plans were ignored: "I cannot explain how Goar Mestre is able to communicate his propaganda so easily when he describes CMQ as 'the first and only microwave chain.' We are also working in the interior of the republic . . . to carry the signal of a chain."[9]

Union Radio's network plans were dashed when, in late 1952, Barletta sold his shares in the organization to his partners. Barletta then concentrated his efforts on another television venture—Telemundo, Channel 2. The station started broadcasting in February 1953. Union Radio TV, Channel 4, in the meantime, changed its name to Television Nacional.

After getting Channel 2 on the air, Barletta immediately usurped Television Nacional's network ambitions and engaged in negotiations with the Philco Corp. to expand Telemundo into an eight-station network. The network was in full operation by early 1956.[10]

Alberto Vilar, Union Radio's program director, said Barletta's decision to buy and then sell his shares in Channel 4 when he thought he could make more profit by investing in another television venture was standard practice of the magnate who at any given time held an interest in 30 to 40 businesses in Cuba. "He would buy and sell businesses like some people change their shirts," Vilar said.[11]

With CMQ-TV and Union Radio in operation, and Telemundo (also known as Radio-Television El Mundo) preparing to go on the air in mid-1952, there was every indication that Cuba would develop a thriving television market. In addition, the daily newspaper *Diario de la Marina* and the radio network Radio Havana Cuba–Cadena Azul put in applications to the Ministry of Communications to broadcast television in Cuba.[12] Table 4.1 presents a list of television stations that, as of May

1952, were authorized by the Ministry of Communications to broadcast over assigned frequencies. The list was compiled by the U.S. Embassy in Havana for the Department of State. The U.S. government gathered and shared information about broadcasting in Cuba with U.S. businesspeople interested in selling television equipment to Cuban stations.

Table 4.1. Authorized television stations in Cuba, 1952

Location and Channel	Owner	Status
Havana		
2	Radio-Television El Mundo, S.A.	Under construction
4	Union Radio Television, S.A.	In operation
6	Circuito CMQ, S.A.	In operation
7	Diario de la Marina	Reserved
11	RHC–Cadena Azul	Reserved
Matanzas		
9	Circuito CMQ, S.A.	In operation
13	RHC–Cadena Azul	Reserved
Santa Clara		
3	Radio Television El Mundo, S.A.	Under construction
5	Circuito CMQ, S.A.	In operation
8	RHC–Cadena Azul	Reserved
Ciego de Avila–Camaguey		
10	RHC–Cadena Azul	Reserved
Camaguey		
6	Circuito CMQ, S.A.	In operation
7	Union Radio	Reserved
12	RHC–Cadena Azul	Reserved
Holguin		
4	Circuito CMQ, S.A.	Reserved
9	Union Radio	Reserved
Santiago de Cuba		
2	Circuito CMQ, S.A.	In operation
5	Cadena Oriental de Radio, S.A.	Reserved
11	Union Radio	Reserved
13	RHC–Cadena Azul	Reserved

Source: Information from the Cuban Ministry of Communications gathered and reported in a declassified memorandum from Raymond L. Harrell, attache at the U.S. Embassy in Havana, addressed to the Department of State in Washington, D.C., May 7, 1952.

tions. In presenting the list, the Embassy doubted whether the market could sustain so many stations: "It is not understood how Havana, with a population of one million persons [including outlying suburbs], can support the five television transmitters which have been authorized for that city."[13] By 1954, however, Havana was supporting five television stations. Five years later, when Fidel Castro came to power, the city had six stations. Radio, meanwhile, was experiencing a slump as television gained in popularity.

Telemundo's facilities were housed in the second and third floors of Barletta's Ambar (standing for Amadeo Barletta) Motors auto dealership, the centerpiece of Barletta's business organizations. Barletta displayed cars on the first floor. The basement was a repair and service center. The fourth and fifth floors consisted of leased offices.[14]

The presence of big advertisers in beer, tobacco, oil and particularly soap and other household products spurred the growth of Cuban television. Still, cutthroat competition caused television broadcasters to discount their advertising rates and invest in expensive productions (as much as $35,000 a program during 1954) to the point where costs sometimes exceeded revenues. As the U.S. magazine *Business Week* reported: "The [Cuban television] industry's trouble stems from the fact that it has built up operations that have outrun Cuban ability to support them."[15] The competition proved to be a blessing for Cuba's entertainers, whose powerful unions exploited the demand for their talent to secure high salaries.[16]

Advertising War

When Barletta put Telemundo on the air, two other Havana television stations (CMQ and Television Nacional) had already acquired most of Cuba's best entertainers and technicians. Desperate for talent and technical assistance, Barletta sought to hire workers from the other Havana stations. One Telemundo program that quickly gained attention was "The Spirit," a children's program based on a comic strip character of the same name.[17] A few popular programs, however, could not detract from Telemundo's weak program schedule. After nearly six months on the air, the station was still referring to its broadcasts as "experimental.[18]

Telemundo could not make a significant dent in CMQ's domination of the ratings. In 1953, Barletta initiated an advertising war against CMQ, declaring that it would charge half the advertising rate of CMQ. The Mestre brothers responded by lowering their fees. The battle continued for several months before both parties accepted an unstated truce to cease hostilities.[19]

The U.S. Embassy in Havana was disturbed by the fierce Mestre-Barletta quarrel. As the Embassy attache noted: "It is unfortunate that the three networks [CMQ, Telemundo and Television Nacional, which at the time was vying for network status] could not get together on a single common relay system which would permit operating expenses to be divided, but it is understood that the personal enmity between Mr. Barletta of *El Mundo* and Mr. Goar Mestre of CMQ prevented this."[20]

The Tough-Guy Image

Sicilian-born Amadeo Barletta acquired a Cuban media empire and other businesses valued at $40 million.[21] His General Motors franchise received most of his money and attention. Still, he apparently valued his investments in the Telemundo television network and the daily newspaper *El Mundo,* from which he received respect and political power.

Barletta needed respect. He was plagued by rumors that he was a Mussolini supporter, Trujillo supporter, Mafioso leader and, after Batista's 1952 coup, Batista crony. Sociologist C. Wright Mills, in an early defense of the Castro revolution, singled out Barletta as typical of the corrupt pre-Castro media owners who sold out to Batista:

> There was a man [Barletta] who was a friend of Mussolini. When Italian fascism was defeated he came to the Americas. In the Santo Domingo republic he was in business with [dictator Rafael] Trujillo. He left there, he came to Cuba, he set up a business here.... Then he bought a big newspaper, *El Mundo,* and also radio and TV channels. He established some 43 businesses in Cuba—from selling Cadillacs to rich Cubans to the smuggling of drugs.... Now, of course, his whole illegal world has been discovered and exposed by the revolution. The files of all these businesses are somewhere in the Office for the Recuperation of Stolen Property. But that is the kind of man who was running one of our biggest newspapers.[22]

Barletta's style and demeanor fit his authoritarian image. The press was rife with stories describing how he browbeat his employees and how his body guards made it difficult for anyone—including his program producers—to meet him.[23] CMQ's Abel Mestre, aware of Barletta's disreputable reputation, said that CMQ would have relished the opportunity to obtain damaging information about its main competitor. After Barletta purchased Channel 2, Mestre contacted sources in the United States and Cuba to gather whatever negative evidence he could about Barletta. The investigation, however, yielded no damaging material. He suspected that Barletta's Italian heritage and "tough-guy" behavior accounted for the allegations.[24] Barletta had many defenders at *El Mundo* who also argued that their boss was unjustly stereotyped because of his ancestry.[25]

Barletta's alleged association with Mussolini dated to the 1930s. At the time, Barletta was the Italian consul to the Dominican Republic. He was also the exclusive U.S. distributor for General Motors while he was also involved in a number of Dominican businesses. Because of his success, he was reputed to be closely aligned with Generalissimo Trujillo. On April 4, 1935, Barletta was arrested by Dominican police. After a 15-minute trial, he was found guilty of masterminding a conspiracy to assassinate Trujillo. The arrest mushroomed into an international incident when Mussolini threatened to dispatch a warship to Santo Domingo if Barletta was not released. While the incident remained shrouded in mystery, *The New York Times* speculated that Barletta was arrested because he owned 45 percent of the Dominican Tobacco Co., which challenged the government's tobacco monopoly.[26]

At the request of the Italian government, U.S. Secretary of State Cordell Hull interceded. Hull warned Trujillo that if the Italians attacked Santo Domingo the United States would not come to Trujillo's defense. Barletta was released six weeks later and appointed Italian consul representative in Havana.[27] In Cuba, as in the Dominican Republic, he became the exclusive distributor for General Motors automobiles and attained profitable contracts with government agencies. When his name appeared on a United States blacklist of wartime Fascist sympathizers during the summer of 1941, Barletta and other alleged Axis sympathizers were expelled from Cuba at the request of the United States.[28]

Barletta waited out the Second World War in Argentina. Afterwards, he returned to Cuba. With his name still on the blacklist, the U.S. government refused to permit General Motors to grant the millionaire magnate the right to distribute its products in Cuba. In a work of legal legerdemain, the distribution business was awarded to Barletta's son, Amadeo Jr., an American citizen who had served with distinction in the American military during the war. While the enterprise was in the son's name, the elder Barletta ran the business.[29]

In 1949, Barletta headed a group of four buyers who purchased *El Mundo*. The newspaper, which had been continuously published since 1901, was considered a liberal counterweight against the archconservative *Diario de la Marina*.[30] Barletta provided the lion's share of the money and was the single largest stockholder, with 39 percent of the company's stock.[31] Barletta nonetheless maintained a low profile in the company. The stockholder who represented *El Mundo* before the public was former *Diario de la Marina* journalist Eliseo Guzman Alvarez.[32]

Barletta and the Mestre brothers were involved in negotiations to purchase the financially troubled newspaper from owner Pedro Cue Abreu.[33] Luis J. Botifoll, editor-in-chief of *El Mundo*, stated the reason for Barletta's interest in acquiring *El Mundo* in one word: "power."[34] Goar Mestre also said that he "always wanted to own a newspaper because of the power and prestige."[35]

After acquiring *El Mundo*, Barletta shamelessly promoted Telemundo's programming in its entertainment section and reported little news about other stations.[36] The journalistic quality of the once-great daily declined after Barletta became involved in the business. There is no way to know whether *El Mundo* was making a profit under Barletta. But even if it was not a profitable enterprise, Barletta might have been willing to sustain it with the profits from his many other businesses because of the power associated with owning a prestigious newspaper. John A. Lent, a leading scholar of Caribbean mass communications, referred to *El Mundo* at this time as a "morally and financially bankrupt daily."[37]

In January 1954, Botifoll parted ways with Barletta. Botifoll, once viewed as Barletta's "right-hand man," had been involved with the millionaire in about two dozen enterprises, including a bank, sales agencies and the purchase of Channel 4.[38] Now Botifoll accused Barletta of subverting *El Mundo*'s long-standing policy of political independence. Botifoll said that he was upset with what he perceived as Barletta's warm relations with the dictator Batista. He declared that Barletta ingratiated himself with each of Cuba's presidents: "He made quite a fortune during the Grau time and during the Prio time. . . . And then, when Prio was out and Batista came to power, he became friendly with Batista and promised Batista that the paper would be at his disposal."[39]

Botifoll wrote a New Year's eve editorial calling for national unity against the Batista dictatorship.[40] Barletta, who tried to work with the Batista government, saw the editorial as a personal message by Botifoll that did not represent the collective views of *El Mundo* management.[41] Barletta, accompanied by police agents, entered the newspaper during the early morning and ordered the deletion of two paragraphs from the editorial.[42] Barletta then attempted to fire Botifoll, but Botifoll refused to leave, claiming that since he owned shares in the newspaper Barletta could not unilaterally fire him. The affair dragged on in the courts for over a year before Botifoll gave up hope of winning his case. Botifoll claimed he did not have the financial resources of Barletta to continue his case.[43]

A Second Mestre-owned Network

In 1952, Goar Mestre and his brothers launched a second Havana station, CMBF, Channel 7.[44] The station, which started broadcasting in 1953, was viewed as an "experiment" by Goar Mestre.[45] In contrast to CMQ-TV, which broadcast live, local programs, Channel 7 featured foreign-dubbed films, primarily from the United States.[46] CMQ's affiliation with NBC gave it access to popular U.S. programs.[47] Its program lineup featured popular U.S. programs such as "Topper," "Alfred Hitchcock Presents," "Hopalong Cassidy," "The Cisco Kid," "Rin Tin Tin" and "The New Adventures of Charlie Chan."

A ratings report released in June 1953 indicated that CMQ had attained a commanding ratings lead in Havana's four-station market: CMQ-TV, Channel 6, 39.71; CMUR, Television Nacional (formerly Union Radio TV), Channel 4, 14.68; CMAB, Telemundo, Channel 2, 14.53; and CMBF, Channel 7, 7.09.[48] CMQ carried 24 of the top 25 programs.[49]

In early 1957, the Mestre brothers and several partners acquired the financially troubled Television Nacional, which had difficulty surviving in the competitive Havana market against CMQ-TV and Telemundo. It was never able to complete its plans to expand into a network. Angel Cambo, its president, offered to purchase the station rather than let it be sold to CMQ, but the other owners rebuffed him.[50]

The Mestre brothers transformed their newly acquired station into the flagship station of a national network called Cadena Nacional, S.A., inaugurated April 1, 1957. On their second network, the brothers continued the "experiment" they began on CMBF-TV, Channel 7, of broadcasting mostly dubbed foreign films.[51] The Mestre brothers used the familiar CMBF call letters for Channel 4. Meanwhile, Channel 7 (formerly CMBF) used the new call letters CMBA and relied largely on old movies and free promotional materials supplied by embassies.[52]

On Jan. 6, 1958, Cadena Nacional started carrying "I Love Lucy," with Lucille Ball and her husband, Cuban entertainer Desi Arnaz. Despite the presence of a Cuban co-star, the program was not the success in Cuba that it was in the United States, perhaps because women were not as dominant in the Cuban family as Ball's character, "Lucy Ricardo."[53] While Cadena Nacional was popular, it never approached CMQ's success.[54] In June 1957, with Cadena Nacional in operation two months, the Cuban Advertising Association released its television ratings report for the Havana vicinity indicating that two CMBF programs were among the top 10 in Cuba—an import from Latin America (number nine) and the melodramatic dog program "Rin Tin Tin" (number seven). The other eight top-10 programs were on CMQ.[55]

Before Cadena Nacional went on the air, Goar Mestre closed Channel 4 for three months to reorganize the station. He kept only three employees—Alberto Vilar, the program director; Mike Gutierrez, the vice president of advertising and sales; and Angel Barranco, head of technical operations.[56] Mestre provided Vilar with an attorney and ordered him to meet with each of the station's employees—actors, musicians, writers, announcers and technicians—to buy out their contracts. Some were rehired when the station reopened as the key station of a national network.[57] In addition to foreign films, Cadena Nacional added some live programming and sports to its lineup. In late March 1957, days before the new network went on the air, Cadena Nacional acquired exclusive rights to broadcast weekly boxing matches from Havana's Sports Palace.[58]

While employed by Goar Mestre, Vilar learned why Mestre was so successful. Vilar had been with Channel 4 since its inception under Pumarejo and remained with the station under different owners even after it was confiscated by the Castro government in March 1960.[59] Under Mestre, the station's business books were properly maintained. "Before Mestre," Vilar said, "it used to be that if you needed money for something the boss would dig into his pocket. Not so with Mestre. Everything had to be recorded in the book." Vilar was even surprised to see that under Mestre's management the station set and adhered to established advertising rates. Before Mestre, advertising rates were set "on the spur of the moment."[60]

A Failed American Television Venture

In 1953, there were four television stations in Havana (Channels 2, 4, 6 and 7). In this crowded market, Television del Caribe, Channel 11, financed with $500,000 of U.S. money, debuted on Nov. 11 from a plant in a Havana suburb. The station was the brainchild of George B. Storer, president of the Storer Broadcasting Co. in Toledo, Ohio. Storer ordered Albert W. Shropshire, chief engineer of a Storer radio station in Miami, to Havana in 1950 to work with Cuban engineer Manuel Autran to put the station on the air. Not until the summer of 1952 did Shropshire and Autran feel confident enough to start ordering equipment and hiring entertainers, producers and writers.[61]

Before Television del Caribe started broadcasting, it found it difficult to obtain sufficient programming to fill its schedule. Delfin Fernandez, the Channel 11's program director, negotiated with performers at other stations to interest them in joining Channel 11.[62] While many actors publicly announced that they were in negotiation, few actually made the move to Television del Caribe. The actors might have been dealing with Television del Caribe to secure better contracts with their present employers. The station's most acclaimed program was a large-cast English-language variety show called "Welcome to Cuba." The telecast was directed to tourists and Cuba's 5,000 U.S. residents and their families employed by U.S. corporations.[63] "Welcome to Cuba" and other lavish productions were later canceled because of their high production costs and replaced with inexpensive films.[64]

Television del Caribe begged for programming from the U.S. government. A letter from Television del Caribe's film director, Victor M. Fernandez, to the U.S. Department of State in Washington, D.C., requested information regarding 16-millimeter government films suitable for a foreign market. In his letter, Fernandez reminded the State Department that the Storer Broadcasting Co. held a significant interest in Television del Caribe. He also reminded the State Department that Storer operated television stations in Detroit, San Antonio, Atlanta, Birmingham and Toledo.[65]

Once on the air, Television del Caribe's biggest problem proved not to be programming but reception. Most television receivers in Havana were adjusted to receive the lower frequency broadcasts of channels 2, 4, 6 and 7. Many Havana residents complained that they could not receive Channel 11's signal.[66] To improve the reception, residents in some parts of Havana had television repairmen adjust their receivers.[67]

Television del Caribe made a brief and unimportant appearance in the Cuban television landscape when it ceased operations on April 30, 1954.[68] After Storer got out of Television del Caribe, the station changed hands a several times. But it remained a minor player with inexpensive programming that many Havana residents had trouble receiving. Its ratings were measured in fractions of a point. Television del Caribe's facilities were purchased by Amadeo Barletta.[69] After being taken off the air for reorganization, Barletta inaugurated the new Channel 11 on Aug. 5, 1954, at his Ambar Motors Building.[70]

The U.S. Embassy in Havana, which monitored Cuban television for potential U.S. investors, hoped that the sale of Channel 11 to Barletta would consolidate television operations and increase profits so that U.S. businesspeople could sell their goods in Cuba. As the Embassy's commercial attache wrote: "Although some savings are expected from the consolidation of Channels 2 and 11 under a single management, resumption of operations on Channel 11 will confront Havana broadcasters with approximately the same economic problems previously reported but with competitive interests reduced from four to three, Channels 6 and 7 [CMQ network], Channel 4 [Television Nacional] and Channels 2 and 11 [Telemundo]."[71]

In 1955, Barletta leased Channel 11's facilities to Carlos D'Mart and Nicolas Castellano, the former mayor of Havana. On April 11, Channel 11 had its third inauguration ceremony. D'Mart and Castellano scheduled inexpensive programs, featuring "round tables." Mike Alonso, the radio and television writer for the English-language *Havana Post* and publicity agent for many Cuban actors, encouraged the success of Channel 11. Alonso, who spent years in the United States and spoke fluent English, was interested in seeing Cuban television improve relations between Cuba's Spanish-speaking and English-speaking communities. He created the station's 10-minute English-language news program and a baseball quiz program called "Play Ball." He praised "Play Ball," the English-language news program and other Channel 11 programs in his columns.[72] But nothing could help the station. When D'Mart and Castellano failed to renew their lease in August 1955, few of Havana's television critics noticed the station's demise.[73]

On Dec. 1, 1956, Barletta again put the station on the air. During the station's closure, Barletta had successfully lobbied with government officials to broadcast over Channel 10 instead of Channel 11. He hoped that this move would improve the station's reception problem. Although there might have been some improvement, the problem persisted.[74]

During late 1958, only months before Batista's flight from Cuba, Barletta leased Channel 10 to a group of U.S. and Cuban businesspeople financed with capital from the National Broadcasting Corporation (NBC) in the United States. The new Channel 10, known as Television Habanera, was operated by Reuben Moulds, who had experience filming commercials. Moulds planned to turn the station into "a haven for U.S. telefilms."[75]

A report in the U.S. entertainment publication *Variety* noted the competitive situation in Cuban television and questioned whether a U.S. businessperson could operate in this environment: "The feud between Barletta and Mestre is one of the more celebrated Hatfield-McCoys of the island. . . . Just how an American tele-operator, unversed in the mores of the stormy Cuban political and competitive situations, can make out in such an atmosphere remains to be seen."[76]

Havana residents continued to have difficulty receiving Television Habanera. The station aired dubbed U.S. movies and English-language programming for Cuba's American community, known as the "American colony." Moulds launched a highly publicized premier telecast, flying U.S. entertainer Jack Paar and Paar's entire crew to Cuba for a program aired at Havana's Tropicana night club. Moulds also arranged with NBC to air such popular programs as "Victory at Sea" and "Life of Riley."[77]

It seemed unlikely that Television Habanera would succeed where others failed. But it never had an opportunity to test its mettle in the Cuban market. It went off the air with little fanfare and no explanation shortly after Batista fled Cuba and the new revolutionary government came to power in 1959.[78] Barletta resumed programming on the station until his properties were confiscated by the Castro government in March 1960.[79]

World Series Broadcasts

Among various sports, baseball and boxing were the most popular in Cuba. During August 1953, Gaspar Pumarejo negotiated exclusive rights to televise Cuban Winter League Baseball. In addition to the plays, the games also featured sometimes scantily clad women who racked up the scorecards of runs, hits and errors. Pumarejo obtained the rights to air the games even though he did not own a station and did not yet sign a contract with any interested party to carry the games.[80] He entered into negotiations with Television Nacional and Barletta's Channel 2 to lease time to carry the games. He did not even approach his business enemy Goar Mestre about contracting time over CMQ-TV.[81]

Perhaps to improve his bargaining position, Pumarejo also negotiated with Television del Caribe, Channel 11, which was not yet on the air. He eventually arranged to broadcast the games over Channel 2.[82] Pumarejo hoped to arrange to broadcast the Winter League games in the future. His plans were thwarted, however, by his archrival Goar Mestre. In August 1956, CMQ spent $1 million for an exclusive five-year contract to carry Cuban Winter League Baseball games over radio and television.[83]

In 1953, CMQ-TV aired filmed broadcasts of the U.S. World Series using a method known as "kinescope recording." This method involved filming the games directly from special monitors. The kinescopes were filmed in Miami and flown to Havana, where they were processed and on the air in Cuba about a three hours later. Sports announcer Cuco Conde provided the Spanish voice-over of the play-by-plays. CMQ fueled the publicity about the games, broadcasting the airport arrival of the kinescopes and arranging for police motorcades to escort the van transporting the films from Rancho Boyeros Airport to the Radiocentro Building.[84]

In mid-September of 1954, CMQ-TV announced it would broadcast the World Series live to Cuba. It was widely publicized that this was the first live broadcast from one nation to another. But there obviously were unintentional cross-border "spillovers" before this broadcast. In addition, a broadcast by Pope Pius XII from Vatican City earlier that summer was carried live in several European cities.[85]

The first World Series broadcast was on Sept. 29 at 12:30 p.m. To accomplish the then unheard of feat, CMQ arranged with the U.S. Federal Communications Commission and Miami station WTVJ to relay the Miami station's signals of the games to Cuba. CMQ rented a DC-3 aircraft from Cuban Airlines, fitted with two antennae and a $14,000 10-watt RCA transmitter. The plane circled 8,500 feet over the Florida Keys. The signal was received by CMQ's Channel 9 station in Matanzas and relayed to Havana. The audio was supplied by announcers Cuco Conde, Fernandito Menendez, Jess Losada and Gabino Delgado.[86] In following years, the signal of the games was transmitted to all CMQ stations.

By all accounts, CMQ's World Series broadcasts were clear, with only brief fade-outs.[87] There was a good deal of preparation, planning and testing weeks in advance. After the games were over, CMQ rebroadcast kinescope versions of the games over its Channel 7 station in Havana.[88] While the World Series broadcast satiated most Cubans' interests in American baseball, Abel and Goar Mestre fretted throughout the broadcasts. If any of the games ran into extra innings, forcing the plane to land and refuel, the game might have had to be taken off the air just as public interest in the game was its height.[89] During the last game, a tropical storm threatened to ground the airplane.[90] Mike Alonso, in his column, described how CMQ officials got the "scare of their lives" that day:

> In the last inning of the game, the plane—flying in a 10-kilometer circle—got into a stormy zone. The plane started jumping up and down and the pilot was unable to get out of the zone—otherwise the picture signals from Miami would have been lost. The plane went through the ordeal and after a while the pilot radioed Rancho Boyeros tower asking for instructions. He was advised to "use his own judgment." Fortunately, the game ended soon after and the plane made the return trip. Since gas was running low, the pilot decided to land in Varadero, but the airport was closed, and that's when the boys really got scared. But the pilot went directly to Santa Clara, where he made a three-point landing. Less than 20 gallons of gas were left in the DC-3's tanks.[91]

The National Broadcasting Company (NBC) in the United States was so impressed by CMQ's World Series broadcast that in 1955 it worked with CMQ personnel to present the first live television broadcast from a foreign nation (Cuba) to the United States on a segment of its "Wide Wide World" program. American viewers saw scenes of Havana. The program was accomplished by beaming a signal from Havana to a C-47 aircraft flying a figure-eight pattern between Havana and Miami. The signal was transmitted to an antenna atop Miami Beach's 16-story Fontainbleu Hotel. From there, the signal was relayed to the other transmitters.[92]

CMQ-TV continued to carry the World Series broadcasts in 1955 and 1956 using the plane fitted with dual antennas. In 1957, 1958 and 1959, the games were broadcast in Cuba through the newly inaugurated "over-the-horizon" link between Florida and Cuba. International Telephone and Telegraph (IT&T) established the system in September 1957 for telephone communications between the two nations.[93]

The over-the-horizon link consisted of gigantic parabolic reflectors connected to 10-kilowatt transmitters in Guanabo, Cuba, and Florida City, Florida. The Florida station sent arch-shaped signals over the horizon to the Cuban receiving station that did not interfere with other signals. In contrast to the 50-mile distance of conventional television, the over-the-horizon system could transmit clear signals 180 miles.[94] When the signal was received in Cuba, CMQ retransmitted it through its microwave relays.

When CMQ was confiscated by the Castro government in 1960, the World Series broadcasts were replaced with Cuban baseball games.[95] Cubans did not have an opportunity see a live broadcast of the World Series again until 1990, when the Voice of America (VOA) purchased the rights to carry the games over the U.S. propaganda stations Radio Marti and TV Marti, adding Spanish-language commentary to the coverage.[96] The Cuban government's largely successful efforts at jamming TV Marti made it highly unlikely that many Cuban viewers were able to receive the program.[97]

By 1958, live television broadcasts between the United States and Cuba were no longer novelties. CMQ used the over-the-horizon system to relay boxing matches and professional baseball games from the United States over the Cadena Nacional network. In January 1958, U.S. entertainer Steve Allen and an entire cast of 60 technicians and performers flew to Havana to broadcast his regular Sunday evening variety program from the Havana Riviera Hotel to the United States. The cast included singer Steve Lawrence, Edgar Bergen and his puppet Charlie McCarthy, Mamie Van Doren, Lou Costello of the Abbot and Costello comedy team and comedians Louis Nye, Tom Poston and Don Knotts.[98]

CHAPTER 5
Transition from Radio to Television

When television came to Cuba in 1950, few Cuban media owners anticipated the impact of television on radio listening. In September 1950, several weeks before Cuba's first television station went on the air, CMQ's Goar Mestre confidently predicted that radio would weather the inevitable competition from the new medium because radio and television served different functions: "Television will never replace radio," Mestre said. "It is impossible to spend all hours of the day and night with our eyes fixed on a screen. As long as there is a housewife that needs to do the dishes and other chores, radio will maintain its audience.... Radio will decline in the evening and at night, when the workday ends and the family is together."[1]

But, like many media experts, Mestre underestimated television's effect on radio. By 1954, television had become the undisputed leading broadcast medium in Cuba. Table 5.1 shows radio listening data in Cuba from 1949–1953. The data indicate that the decline started in 1952 and continued in 1953. As Mestre had predicted, the evening hours experienced the greatest declines. Radio listening during the early and midday hours scarcely declined at all. But after 6 p.m., when husbands in Cuba's nuclear families returned home and watched television with their families, radio listening declined sharply.

By the mid-1950s, television sets had become fixtures in middle-class Cuban homes. By early 1956, Cuba was reported to have had 200,000 television receivers, the highest penetration in Latin America. By year's end, there were 275,000 television receivers on the island.[2] Most were in the Havana area.

Radio Havana Cuba (RHC)–Cadena Azul, Cuba's dominant radio

Table 5.1. Radio listening (ratings) in Cuba, 1949–1953

Hours	1949	1950	1951	1952	1953	Change 1949–1953
9–10 a.m.	9.30	9.90	12.03	11.87	10.02	+0.72
10–11	13.79	13.24	19.26	15.98	15.20	+1.41
11–Noon	23.81	21.44	26.30	22.18	22.16	-1.65
Noon–1 p.m.	33.26	28.36	32.12	29.48	24.81	-8.45
1–2	30.93	32.27	31.11	33.33	25.26	-5.67
2–3	18.51	19.50	26.16	25.31	20.40	+1.89
3–4	20.78	15.97	20.37	19.99	17.60	-3.18
4–5	14.71	12.16	19.31	18.54	15.54	+0.83
6–7	22.84	19.47	21.20	19.45	17.74	-5.10
7–8	37.50	33.83	38.06	33.24	27.14	-10.36
9–10	34.81	36.71	39.22	29.62	23.05	-11.76
Total	24.92	22.74	26.17	23.39	19.82	-5.10

Source: "Estado Comparativo de Audiencia Potencial (1) de la Radio," *Bohemia,* March 29, 1953, 44.

Note: The ratings data during 1949 were collected during January, while the data for the other years were collected during February.

network during the 1930s and much of the 1940s, did not expand into television. By the late 1940s and early 1950s, RHC–Cadena Azul declined to third and sometimes fourth in the ratings reports behind CMQ, Union Radio and Radio Progreso. Finally, on April 29, 1952, RHC–Cadena Azul owner Amado Trinidad Velasco sold the network to a group of U.S. and Cuban businessmen.[3] The last ratings report before the sale of RHC–Cadena Azul indicated CMQ with a 7.07 rating. It was followed by Radio Progreso, 2.74; RHC–Cadena Azul, 1.04; and Union Radio, 0.91.[4]

CMQ dominated Cuban television from when it went on the air in 1950 to when it was confiscated 10 years later. The Cuban Advertising Association's May 1953 television survey of the Havana area showed CMQ, Channel 6, with a 16.24 rating. It was followed by CMUR, Television Nacional, Channel 4 (formerly Union Radio TV), 7.99; CMAB, Telemundo, Channel 2, 7.24; and the Mestre brothers' second television station, CMBF-TV, Channel 7, 5.87.[5]

The caliber of radio programming deteriorated as broadcasters diverted their money and talent into television. During April 1953, *The Havana Post*'s radio-television columnist despaired over the state of

Cuban radio programs:

> Quality of radio programs today is way below that of a couple of years ago. Television is no doubt the cause. Many advertisers, however, seem to forget that Havana is not all of Cuba. Radio in Santa Clara, Camaguey and Oriente is still the cheapest way of advertising. . . . More than two million radio listeners feel very unhappy about the poor quality of programs presented.[6]

In November 1954, Manuel (Manolo) Reyes, who had been with CMQ since 1938 as a radio actor and producer, was appointed to oversee an advertising sales staff of 10 men in the Mestres' three radio enterprises—CMQ, CMBF and CMCB–Radio Reloj.[7] Reyes' position proved to be as difficult as he had expected. The big advertisers in the soap industry believed that the future of Cuban broadcasting was in television. Advertisers were gradually shifting their sponsorship from radionovelas (radio soap operas) to telenovelas (television soap operas) and other types of television programs.[8]

Looking for radio advertising revenue during these times was a constant frustration. Reyes had to be careful not to lure advertising dollars away from CMQ-TV to CMQ-radio. "Remember," Reyes said, "that television was the left pocket of the Mestres and radio was the right pocket. You could not have one pocket stealing from the other. So I had to try to drain the (advertising) budgets from magazines, papers and other radio and television stations. It was not easy."[9]

The Other Networks

In addition to Cuba's "Big Two" radio networks of CMQ and RHC–Cadena Azul, other smaller networks were established during the late 1940s and early 1950s. By the mid-1950s, after RHC–Cadena Azul went off the air, Cuba boasted five national radio networks—CMQ, Union Radio, Radio Progreso, Cadena Oriental de Radio and Circuito Nacional Cubano (CNC). The stations in these networks are listed in Tables 5.2 to 5.6.

Cadena Oriental de Radio, under the ownership of Ricardo Miranda Cortez (known as "El Chino, the Chinaman," because of the name of the network), featured a news and political commentary format. The network carried some of Cuba's most popular political commentators from Cuba's two major parties—the Autenticos (Partido Revolucionario Cubano) and Ortodoxos (Partido del Pueblo Cubano). The most popular were Ortodoxo spokesmen Jose Pardo Llada and Luis Conte Aguero. The

Table 5.2. Stations in the CMQ Radio Network (Circuito CMQ, S.A.)

Location	Call Letters	Frequency	Power in Kilowatts	
Havana	CMQ	630 KC	25	(DA)
			1	(EM)
			50	(AA)
Havana	CMCB	1330 KC	1 and 1	(EM)
Havana	CMBF	950 KC	10	(DA)
Pinar del Rio	CMAQ	920 KC	1	
Santa Clara	CMHQ	640 KC	15	(DA)
Camaguey	CMJL	920 KC	10	(DA)
Holguin	CMKJ	740 KC	10	(DA)
Santiago de Cuba	CMKU	850 KC	2	

President: Goar Mestre
President, Board of Directors: Abel Mestre
Director: Luis Augusto Mestre
Treasurer: Alberto S. Ventura
Technical Director: Raul Lopez Guiral

KEY for Tables 5.2–5.6:
D = Power authorized for day use
N = Power authorized for night use (after sunset)
DA = Directional antenna in use
EM = Emergency (substitute) transmitter
AA = Increase in power authorized

Table 5.3. Stations in the Radio Progreso Radio Network (Estaciones Radiodifusoras Radio Progreso, S.A.)

Location	Call Letters	Frequency	Power in Kilowatts	
Havana	CMBC	690 KC	50	(DA)
Pinar del Rio	CMAF	680 KC	1	
Santa Clara	CMHG	670 KC	1	(D)
Cienfuegos*		680 KC	1	
Ciego de Avila	CMJI	700 KC	1	(D)
			0.5	(N)
Camaguey	CMJE	680 KC	1	
Holguin	CMKP	670 KC	1	(DA)
Santiago de Cuba	CMDE	680 KC	1	(D)
			0.5	(N)

President: Ovidio Fernandez
Director General: Manuel Fernandez
Technical Director: Carlos Estrada

*The Cienfuegos station was under construction.

Table 5.4. Stations in the Union Radio Network (Union Radio, S.A.)

Location	Call Letters	Frequency	Power in Kilowatts	
Havana	CMCF	910 KC	10	
Pinar del Rio*				
Santa Clara	CMHD	890 KC	1	
Ciego de Avila	CMJD	1190 KC	0.25	
Camaguey	CMJB	880 KC	1	
Holguin	CMKM	560 KC	5	
Santiago de Cuba	CMDB	1170 KC	1	
Matanzas*				
Sancti Spiritus	CMHB	780 KC	1	(DA)

President and Director: Dr. Luis J. Botifoll
Vice President and Manager: Dr. Jose Luis Pelleya
Vice President: Jose Luis Maso
Technical Director: Luis Val

*Stations not in operation but authorized and under construction.

Table 5.5. Stations in the Cadena Oriental de Radio Network (Cadena Oriental de Radio, S.A.)

Location	Call Letters	Frequency	Power in Kilowatts
Havana	CMCI	1260 KC	5
Santa Clara	CMHM	1130 KC	1
Ciego de Avila	CMJY	760 KC	1
Camaguey	CMJG	1000 KC	1
Holguin	CMKD	970 KC	1
Santiago de Cuba	CMDL	800 KC	2
Matanzas	CMGL	1400 KC	0.25
Colon	CMGU	1340 KC	0.25
Victoria de las Tunas*			
Bayamo	CMDE	1260 KC	0.25
Guantanamo	CMKA	1250 KC	0.25

President: Ricardo Miranda Cortez
Manager: Guillermo Henriques
Technical Director: Agustin Mederes

Note: Cadena Oriental de Radio also relayed its programs using its own chain of 13 FM stations.
*Stations not in operation but authorized and under construction.

Table 5.6. Stations in the Circuito Nacional Cubano (Compania Operadora de Radiodifusion, S.A.)

Location	Call Letters	Frequency	Power in Kilowatts	
Havana	CMW	590 KC	2.5	
Santa Clara	CMHI	570 KC	10	(DA)
Santa Clara	CMHW	810 KC	1	(DA)
Ciego de Avila	CMJM	840 KC	0.5	
Camaguey	CMJM	960 KC	1	
Holguin	CMKV	600 KC	1	
Santiago de Cuba	CMKM	930 KC	1	
Matanzas	CMGF	930 KC	0.25	
Pinar del Rio	CMAN	840 KC	1	
Jovellanos	CMGN	960 KC	0.5	

President: Jose Luis Piedra
Vice President: Alberto Sotolongo
Vice President: Fernando Zapata
Treasurer and Technical Director: Adolfo Gil

Source: "Cuban Radio and Television Broadcasting Stations," declassified document prepared by the U.S. Embassy in Havana for the U.S. Department of State, June 22, 1955.

network also carried the commentaries of Ortodoxo commentators Mario Rivadulla, Orlando Castro, Max Lesnick and Autentico commentators Armando Garcia Sifredo and Primitivo Rodriguez.[10]

Pardo Llada described the style of the commentators on Cadena Oriental de Radio as the "journalism of denunciation" because they virulently denounced their opponents, often with shrill voices and fists pounding.[11] In addition to commenting on politics, the commentators also defended Cuban culture, the beauty of Cuban women and the virility of Cuban men.[12] Pardo Llada said that Cadena Oriental de Radio offered him an opportunity to practice his unique radio style:

> I could have never worked at CMQ or at [RHC–]Cadena Azul. With my journalism of denunciation, I would have gotten into trouble with various important people—with [presidents] [Ramon] Grau, [Carlos] Prio, [Fulgencio] Batista. I would have caused trouble for the powerful chains [the common Cuban word for "networks"]. . . . That is the type of thing that they [the powerful networks] could not afford because of the special interests they represented. I had to settle with the small stations.[13]

Ortodoxos and Autenticos alike praised Miranda Cortez for displaying no favoritism toward commentators from either of Cuba's leading political parties, although the network carried more Ortodoxo than Autentico programs.[14] As the opposition party during the Grau (1944–1948) and Prio (1948–1952) governments, the Ortodoxos naturally had more and more boisterous commentators.

Despite Cadena Oriental de Radio's preponderance of Ortodoxo commentators, commentator Garcia Sifredo, a member of the Autentico Party, described Miranda as "very fair to everyone who wanted to use his microphones. He never favored any [commentators] over the others. Nor did he show any [political] ambitions."[15] Garcia Sifredo recalled that President Grau once approached Miranda with a proposition to make the network available for "free propaganda" to the Autenticos. In return, Grau promised Miranda political support in attaining political office. Miranda refused.[16] Pardo Llada also described Miranda as fair to all the political commentators on Cadena Oriental de Radio:

> I think that deep inside he saw all of us [political commentators] with fondness because we represented rebellion. "El Chino" Miranda did not get involved in commentaries. Perhaps he made some editorials, but that was not his forte. What he wanted was for his station to be heard, and that is why we were there. That was our function. El Chino Miranda was basically an entrepreneur, not a politician.[17]

During the summer of 1956, executives at Cadena Oriental de Radio considered purchasing or leasing a recently closed Havana television station, Channel 11. They quickly abandoned the idea after the costs of operating a television station became apparent.[18]

CNC was a latecomer network, inaugurated on Aug. 1, 1954, shortly after RHC–Cadena Azul went off the air. CNC hoped to fill the vacuum left by RHC–Cadena Azul's demise by providing programming for listeners in the provinces.[19] CNC's director general, Ruben Romeu, developed a number of programs about life and heroes in the countryside.[20] Even in news, CNC aired a program called "Noticiero Guajiro" ("Country People's News") about cities in the provinces.[21]

CNC was started by cigar manufacturer Jose Luis Piedra and Alberto Sotolongo, the head of the publicity firm of Mercado, Survey y Publicidad and a former publicist and director of programming at Radio Progreso.[22] Piedra's death during the summer of 1956 curbed the network's plans for expansion. Although CNC never attained high ratings in Havana, it had a following in the island's interior.[23] During 1957, the majority of the shares in the network was thought to have been secretly purchased by friends of dictator Fulgencio Batista.[24]

Radio Progreso was inaugurated as station 2AF on Dec. 15, 1929,

5. TRANSITION FROM RADIO TO TELEVISION

by owner Domingo Fernandez and his sons, Manolo and Ovidio. When international treaty agreements required Cuban radio stations to use the call letters "CM," the station became CMBC.[25] The sons took charge of the station, expanded it into a network and established a reputation for comedy programming. Radio Progreso became known as "the Radio Wave of Happiness."[26] The network also featured the popular daily evening music variety program "Alegrias de Hatuey" ("The Joys of Hatuey," named after the beer company that sponsored the program), hosted by Israel Pimentel Molina. A teenage Celia Cruz, who would later become Cuba's most famous salsa singer, sang regularly on Pimentel's program.[27]

Radio Progreso briefly considered entering Cuban television during 1950, before television was on the air in Cuba. But Manolo Fernandez wisely withdrew his plans for television, realizing that his network could not compete against the powerful economic forces of CMQ and RHC-Cadena Azul, both of which had announced plans to expand into television.[28]

As noted in Chapter 3, Union Radio was created by former CMQ program director and radio announcer Gaspar Pumarejo. He left CMQ after a bitter dispute with Goar Mestre and inaugurated Union Radio on Oct. 6, 1947. More than just an entrepreneur, Pumarejo was a charismatic radio personality. People who knew Pumarejo described him as a quiet man in personal dealings with a serious speech impediment. But when he spoke on radio, the stutter disappeared and he became fluent and loquacious. Even Goar Mestre, who usually had little positive to say about Pumarejo, was impressed by Pumarejo's mastery behind the microphone:

> When I had conversations with Pumarejo he would stutter and I had to follow him closely. You would never imagine that this man had the ability to speak so well, so fluently, so naturally. But when you put a microphone in front of Pumarejo, it was as if some miraculous transformation occurred. He could speak without preparation. The words just came to him. It was amazing. Now, in my position at CMQ I frequently spoke over radio, and I think I was pretty good. But I could not compare to Pumarejo. I was not natural. . . . I had writers prepare my scripts for me. I practiced reading the scripts over and over before I went on the air.[29]

In 1951, Union Radio (and Union Radio TV) was acquired by cinematographer Manuel (Manolo) Alonso and attorney Jose Luis Pelleya. In 1952, after Alonso sold his shares in the network, Pelleya and newsman Luis J. Botifoll owned Union Radio until late 1957. Botifoll and Pelleya sold the station to the Confederation of Cuban Workers (Spanish initials CTC), an umbrella organization for an amalgamation of unions. The bosses at the CTC were purported to be close to Batista, and Pelleya said he suspected that Batista was behind the purchase.[30]

Although Cuban television was witnessing rapid growth during the mid- and late-1950s, Cuba remained a leader in Latin American radio. Table 5.7 presents United Nations data on radio in Latin America during the mid-1950s. Cuba had among the highest penetration (per 1,000 population) of radio in the region, second only to Uruguay and ahead of such regional giants as Mexico, Argentina and Brazil.

Radio's Swan Song

Radio and television developed as entertainment media in Cuba. Nevertheless, radio at least carried a few serious news and public affairs programs. CMQ's "Ante la Prensa" ("Meet the Press"), a Cuban version of the program with the same name in the United States, served as a forum for a panel of journalists to question leading political figures. In addition, radio was the favorite medium of Cuba's vitriolic politicians. Just

Table 5.7. Radio receivers in selected Latin American nations

Country	Receiver Units	Per 1,000 Population	Year
Argentina	2,900,000	158	1953
Bolivia	200,000	62	1956
Brazil	3,500,000	61	1954
Chile	650,000	99	1954
Costa Rica	50,000	55	1954
CUBA	**1,100,000**	**176**	**1956**
Ecuador	100,000	26	1956
El Salvador	24,000	11	1956
Guatemala	36,030	11	1954
Haiti	19,000	6	1956
Honduras	30,000	18	1956
Mexico	2,500,000	84	1955
Nicaragua	30,000	25	1954
Panama	95,000	110	1953
Paraguay	80,000	53	1953
Puerto Rico	200,000	88	1956
Uruguay	500,000	189	1956
Venezuela	230,000	39	1956

Source: Abstracted from George A. Codding Jr., *Broadcasting Without Barriers* (Paris: United Nations Educational, Scientific and Cultural Organization, 1959), 148.

5. TRANSITION FROM RADIO TO TELEVISION

as television made its appearance in Cuba, the charismatic Eduardo Rene Chibas led his most sensational political crusade over radio. It ended with Chibas' dramatic over-the-air suicide.

Shortly after the Mestre brothers became partners in CMQ during the summer of 1943, Cuba's 1944 presidential campaign began. President Batista, elected in 1940, was constitutionally prohibited from seeking a second term. His party nominated Carlos Saladrigas, regarded as Batista's hand-picked successor. Saladrigas was supported by a coalition which included the military, big business, leading intellectuals and even the Communist Party.[31] The opposition Autentico Party selected Ramon Grau San Martin, who served four months as provisional president following the overthrow of dictator Gerardo Machado in 1933. Saladrigas purchased substantial radio time from CMQ and ran a well-orchestrated campaign.

So successful was Saladrigas' radio campaign that CMQ and other radio organizations were accused of favoring Saladrigas. Mestre actively encouraged Autentico leaders to speak for Grau on CMQ to dispel this allegation. Chibas, a prominent member of the Autentico party, came forward. Chibas purchased a 30-minute program each Sunday evening to represent Grau and the Autenticos.[32] From the beginning, Chibas' program, full of invective and denunciations, was very popular. Visitors to Cuba wrote about how they could walk down Cuba's empty streets when Chibas was on the air and hear Chibas' radio harangues from every open window.[33] To Mestre's disappointment, what was at first meant to be a program to represent Grau and the Autenticos during the election remained on the air until 1951. As Goar Mestre recalled these early days after Chibas first appeared on CMQ:

> We got more than we bargained for because he went on the air and he was vicious, ruthless and demagogic from the start. He paid for the first two or three months. He was late, but he paid. But after Grau Martin was elected, he wouldn't pay his bills. At first I tried to collect from him, personally. And he would look at me and smile and say, "But Goar, you have a hell of a program with the highest rating that you could imagine. You are not going to make me pay for this time slot, are you?" And I'd say, "Of course you have to pay." And we lived through this comedy [of CMQ demanding payment and Chibas refusing] for years, but we never got paid.[34]

Grau was elected president by a substantial margin. During the early years of the Grau administration, Chibas was regarded as a loyal Grau supporter, although he never served in the cabinet. Shortly after taking office, Grau's popularity plummeted following a series of scandals. Although Cuban politicians had a reputation for dishonesty, the Grau administration took corruption, graft and nepotism to new levels. Chibas and other Autenticos also grew disillusioned with their leader.

During early 1947, Chibas broke with the Autenticos and founded the Ortodoxo Party. Politically, there was little to distinguish the Autenticos from the Ortodoxos other than the issue of honesty in government. In fact, the name Ortodoxo was meant to signify that the Ortodoxos were true or orthodox Autenticos who were not corrupted. Chibas' slogan was "verguenza contra dinero" (roughly translated as dignity or shame versus money). The symbol of the party was a broom, to signify that the Ortodoxos meant to "sweep away" the corruption of the Autenticos.[35]

Chibas' popularity rested on his unquestioned integrity, acknowledged even by his critics. William S. Stokes, a University of Wisconsin political science professor, interviewing Cuban political leaders in Havana to study Cuban politics during the 1948 presidential campaign, wrote of Chibas: "His opponents and even some of his friends argue that he is a man without profound appreciation of public issues and problems and without great administrative ability, but every person I talked to agreed that Chibas was a man of unblemished probity."[36]

Chibas railed against corruption in the Autentico Party and built a loyal national following for his new party through his radio program. His radio attacks against his opponents resulted in a number of pistol and saber duels with leading political figures. No one was killed, and both men left the field of honor with their reputations in tact. Surviving duels was more the norm than dying. The purpose was to publicly defend one's reputation. A flesh wound from a duel was worn as a badge of honor. Each duel seemed to enhance Chibas' reputation. During September 1947, Chibas was grazed by an assassin's bullet during an open-air speech. Unfazed, he bared his chest and cried, "Go ahead and shoot! The Ortodoxos need a martyr."[37]

Chibas was the Ortodoxo's presidential candidate in 1948. Despite his late entry into the race and lack of financing, he received 20 percent of the vote in a three-way election, but lost to Autentico candidate Carlos Prio Socarras.[38]

CMQ, meanwhile, had all but given up trying to collect payment for Chibas' Sunday evening program. Although Goar Mestre conceded that CMQ had profited from Chibas' program because of the publicity and high rates it charged for the advertisements before and after the program, he felt uncomfortable with Chibas' unsubstantiated accusations against his foes being aired over CMQ. Mestre was particularly incensed by Chibas' habit of running over his allotted air time.[39] When it came to dealing with Chibas, Mestre was not as quick to order his technicians to

5. TRANSITION FROM RADIO TO TELEVISION

cut Chibas' program off the air as he was to cut off other sponsors' programs that ran over their time. Mestre knew from experience that silencing Chibas in midspeech would meet with considerable public opposition.[40] On the few occasions when CMQ cut Chibas off the air, the network experienced a barrage of complaints:

> We wavered and hesitated and didn't know what to do with this guy. But we had to cut him off now and then, to let him know that we would cut him off. If we did not do that once in awhile, he would have kept on talking for another 20 minutes or a half hour, God knows. When we did that [cut Chibas off], our switchboard would light up and [callers would] call us all sorts of names, insult us, call us the most incredible things.[41]

As Chibas' became more famous, his idiosyncracies became more apparent. As historian Hugh Thomas wrote:

> [I]t was becoming evident that despite his great gifts, his strong mesmeric personality, the streak of [ir]rationality in him was growing stronger with age: he would often fast, he would invite women to lunch with him and appear at five o'clock, he would remain in the bath under running water for long periods, his telephoning of friends was frenetic, his speeches had more and more hysteria of madness as much as genius.[42]

Goar Mestre found himself constantly defending CMQ for carrying Chibas' program. On Aug. 9, 1950, the Prio government responded to Chibas' radio attacks by promulgating a "right to reply" law (Decree No. 2273). The law permitted anyone personally attacked over radio to petition the Ministry of Communications for free air time on the offending station.[43] Former President Batista, who harbored ambitions to regain the presidency, saw the law as an opportunity to portray the Prio government as an opponent to freedom of speech and the press. Batista publicly denounced the law as having "an appearance of protection of freedom of thought, when its real object is to destroy that freedom."[44]

Based on the ratings, Chibas' scathing denunciations were well received by the public. At the same time, many Cubans believed that the attacks were unjust and irresponsible. Abel Mestre recalled that CMQ's opposition to the right-to-reply law was unpopular.[45] On Aug. 18, executives from 10 Havana radio organizations signed their names to a letter backing the law. The letter was reprinted in newspapers and magazines. The signature of Amado Trinidad, president of the RHC-Cadena Azul network, CMQ's main competitor, appeared on top of the letter.[46]

Although Goar Mestre opposed the law on principle, he privately harbored negative feelings toward Chibas. It is interesting, however, that in criticizing the right-to-reply law, Goar Mestre did not defend Chibas' veracity. Instead, he took the position that, as a leading political figure, Chibas had a right to express his views.[47] Without mentioning Chibas by name, Mestre agreed that political commentators frequently abused their power: "It is true that for years we have suffered from verbal gangsterism on the radio. But the solution of the problem is to give citizens protection through streamlined libel laws, which should replace our present antiquated legislation, and not by regulations which throw the burden on the radio stations."[48]

The law received its first test on Feb. 18, 1951. After a bomb was found in the house of a prominent Ortodoxo leader, Chibas appeared on his program and accused Congressman Rolando Masferrer Rojas, a Prio supporter, of masterminding the plot. Masferrer obtained authorization from the Ministry of Communications to appear on the air during Chibas' program time to refute the charges.[49]

CMQ issued an announcement restating its opposition to the right-to-reply law, and that it was seeking to get the law declared unconstitutional in the courts. It added, however, that until the law was abrogated, the network was legally obliged to permit Masferrer to rebut Chibas' charges over CMQ's microphones.[50]

On the day of Masferrer's reply, the congressman shoved his way through a crowd of Chibas' supporters who, at Chibas' command, attempted to block the congressman's entry into CMQ's Radiocentro Building. But Masferrer eventually entered the building and spoke. Meanwhile, back at Chibas' house, a crowd of sympathizers sought to accompany Chibas to the Radiocentro Building. Riots pursued, and one person was killed by police.[51]

As the election year of 1952 approached, it was evident that Chibas was forging another attempt for the presidency. He rhetoric grew more accusatory. As Thomas wrote:

> During the early months of 1951 he appeared as a real demagogue, half preacher, half scourge, one of the most effective orators in Latin American history; by his accusations, week after week, he effectively completed the discrediting of all surviving political institutions in Cuba, describing this [the Prio Administration], the last democratic government in Cuba, as "a scandalous bacchanalia of crimes, robberies and mismanagement." . . . It was impossible not to listen to him. The vagueness of his ultimate program, his omission to mention any precise policies of economic or social control meant that many people of differing long-term views could assemble behind him.[52]

5. TRANSITION FROM RADIO TO TELEVISION

During the summer of 1951, Chibas led what would be his final radio crusade against government corruption. He lashed out against President Prio's Minister of Education, Dr. Aureliano Sanchez Arango. Chibas accused Sanchez Arango of embezzling funds for schoolchildren's breakfasts and investing the money in Guatemalan real estate. Sanchez Arango publicly challenged the Ortodoxo leader to produce evidence to support the allegations. Chibas responded that he had the proof in his briefcase:

> Next Sunday at half past nine at night before the television cameras and microphones, I shall be ready to open my portmanteau and show the nation the proof of the embezzlement in respect of the school textbooks, furniture and meals, the Guatemala district and other things even worse to prove that this government of Carlos Prio is the most corrupt in the history of Cuba.[53]

When Chibas opened the briefcase two weeks later it was generally agreed, even by Ortodoxo members, that his documents were unconvincing.[54] Chibas' opponents used the phrase "Abrir la maleta" ("Open the briefcase") to taunt him and disgrace him.[55] The Sanchez Arango affair hurt Chibas politically. A presidential poll indicated that while Chibas was still popular, his support was waning.[56]

When Chibas appeared on his Aug. 5, 1951, program, the pressure on him to present convincing evidence against Sanchez Arango was intense. Pardo Llada began the program, defending Chibas for 20 minutes before Chibas took the microphone. Chibas repeated his charges against Sanchez Arango and launched into a morality tale about how Galileo lacked evidence to prove his claim that the earth revolved around the sun.[57] Just as the program went off the air, Chibas reached under the jacket of his trademark double-breasted white suit and shot himself in the stomach with a .38 Colt Special.

CMQ technicians cut the program off the air before the gun went off. Goar Mestre was at home listening to Chibas' program. When Chibas was silenced in midsentence, Mestre assumed that it was because Chibas had run over his allotted time. "Ten minutes later," Mestre recalled, "they [CMQ employees] called me and said, 'Chibas shot himself in studio number three.' They put up all the signs and said they would cut him off. And he didn't think we would dare cut him off that night."[58]

Chibas was rushed to the hospital. After 11 days in critical condition, the 43-year-old political leader died during the early morning hours of Aug. 16. Chibas' death was followed by an outpouring of public grief and a funeral procession through Havana on Aug. 17. All regular radio transmissions were suspended and replaced with religious music and biographical information about Chibas. The churches were packed as mourners prayed for the martyred leader. Balconies were decked with black ribbons.[59]

Chibas became the model for the next generation of Cuba's radio commentators. Both Pardo Llada and Conte Aguero praised Chibas in their speeches, writings and radio commentaries.[60] Chibas' death also left a leadership vacuum in the Ortodoxo Party. Tad Szulc, *The New York Times* Cuban correspondent, recalled how Chibas' brother, Raul, and a young Fidel Castro successfully urged Pardo Llada and other Ortodoxo leaders to put Chibas' body on display at the University of Havana because his career started at the university and his popularity among the young.[61] Pardo Llada also recalled Castro's suggestion to display Chibas' body in order to fuel public anger against Prio and produce a coup d'etat. Pardo Llada argued against the idea: "I knew it could be done. It was logical that we could have succeeded with only a little bloodshed—we really don't know—but it wasn't in me to do it."[62]

To this day, many Cuban exile leaders claim that Chibas' suicide was responsible for a chain of events that led to Castro's rise to power. Castro, like other Ortodoxo leaders, would frequently pay homage to Chibas during later years. In an interview with an American journalist during 1969, Castro praised Chibas: "I trusted his [Chibas'] rebellious temperament, his personal honesty and his feeling of obligation to the masses. While he lived, I always had some hope that a revolutionary movement could come out of that movement."[63]

CHAPTER 6
TV Comes of Age

By the mid-1950s, two dynamic broadcast magnates dom-
inated Havana's television market—CMQ's Mestre brothers (Channels 4, 6 and 7) and Telemundo's Amadeo Barletta (Channels 2 and 10). The Mestres owned two national television networks (Channels 4 and 6) while Barletta owned one (Channel 2). Amado Trinidad, Cuba's other leading broadcast tycoon, never started a television station.

Cuba was a pacesetter in Latin American television. Table 6.1 shows that as of December 1956 Cuba had 16 stations on the air, followed by Mexico (nine) and Venezuela (10).[1] Cuba had seven stations under construction while Brazil had 13; Mexico, 11; and Colombia, 10. It appeared that other Latin American nations were catching up to Cuba's precocious start. As Table 6.1 also indicates, Cuba had the second largest number of television receiver units (275,000) in Latin America, behind Brazil (405,000).

Barletta's Broadcasting Operation

Unlike Gaspar Pumarejo and Goar Mestre, Barletta went directly into television without radio experience. While his Ambar Motors auto dealership remained the financial cornerstone of his business empire, he developed an interest in mass media.[2] In 1949, Barletta led a group of businessmen that purchased the prestigious, liberal daily *El Mundo.* In 1952, he led a group that purchased Union Radio TV, Channel 4. Although *El Mundo* and Channel 4 were separate enterprises, Barletta's involvement in both organizations had business advantages. Soon after going on the air, Barletta's television station launched a popular after-

Table 6.1. Television stations and receivers in Latin America, 1956

Country	Existing Stations	Planned Stations	Receivers
Argentina	1	6	90,000
Bolivia	0	1	...
Brazil	6	13	405,000
Chile	0	2	...
Colombia	6	10	50,000
Costa Rica	0	1	...
CUBA	**16**	**7**	**275,000**
Dominican Republic	2	0	7,000
El Salvador	1	1	1,000
Guatemala	2	0	8,500
Mexico	10	11	250,000
Nicaragua	1	1	500
Panama	0	2	2,000
Peru	0	3	...
Uruguay	1	1	1,000
Venezuela	9	1	100,000

Source: Abstracted from "TV Girdles the Globe," *Television Age*, May 20, 1957, 33–37, 73.

noon program from *El Mundo*'s newsroom called "El Mundo en Television" ("El Mundo on Television"). The station called upon the popular Gaspar Pumarejo—the man renowned for having brought television to Cuba—to host "El Mundo on Television."[3]

"El Mundo on Television" featured a summary of day's news, updating events since the morning newspapers. The program also featured commentaries by *El Mundo*'s reporters. Pumarejo strolled through the newsroom, microphone in hand, chatting with reporters about sports, business, politics, social events, entertainment and other topics. The second half of the program featured reporters on their "beats" in Havana interviewing people.[4]

The program received acclaim for its coverage of the 1952 U.S. presidential election. It carried the state-by-state vote counts before any other Cuban news media organization. Most Cuban media organizations had to wait for the Associated Press (AP) and what was then the United Press (UP) news wires to relay the vote counts. "El Mundo on Television" got the counts first by flying *El Mundo*'s noted political columnist, Carlos Lechuga Hevia, to New York. Lechuga rented a room in Times Square in the heart of the city's theater district where a moving-light display (sometimes called the "news zipper" because it zipped up-to-the-moment news across the building) flashed the election results over the building at 1 Times Square. As soon as Lechuga phoned the results to *El Mundo* headquarters, the numbers were reported on the television program.[5]

Alberto Vilar, who helped construct Cuba's first television station (Union Radio TV, Channel 4) in Pumarejo's personal residence in 1950, continued as program director at Channel 4 under the subsequent owners—Manolo Alonso (1951–1952), Barletta and his partners (1952), Angel Cambo and his partners (1952–1957), the Mestre brothers (1957–1960) and, finally, Castro government "intervention" (1960). He fled Cuba in 1960. Vilar said that Havana's major television broadcasters had distinctly different management styles.

Vilar described Pumarejo as impulsive. "The great showman" implemented new ideas with little thought.[6] He rarely relied on research, preferring his gut instincts. "He never believed in the survey," Vilar said. "He never trusted them. He made his decisions using his own judgment." Indeed, Pumarejo publicly challenged the ratings of the Cuban Advertising Association that repeatedly showed his programs behind those of CMQ.[7]

While Pumarejo rejected survey research, CMQ's Goar and Abel Mestre paid close attention to them and the reports from Radiocentro's research department. While Vilar admired Pumarejo for his "showmanship," he described the Mestre brothers as "professionals."[8]

Vilar said Barletta had an intimidating demeanor: "If you would come to Barletta with an idea, he would not listen. He had his own ideas. And to show you he was right, he would ask, 'How much money do you have in the bank?' And you might respond, 'A few thousand dollars.' And he would say, 'When you have the amount of money that I have in the bank, then you can come and give me advice.'"[9]

Barletta sold his shares in Union Radio in late 1952. The station then changed its name to Television Nacional. Barletta entered into another television venture, Telemundo, Channel 2. Soon after Telemundo started broadcasting on Feb. 18, 1953, Barletta began construction of an eight-station network to compete against the CMQ network. Telemundo had difficulty breaking CMQ's virtual domination of the ratings. The ratings reports usually showed CMQ with at least 20 of the top 25 programs. Telemundo would have two to four top programs. Television Nacional would have one or two.

Pumarejo Returns

After Pumarejo sold Union Radio in August 1951, he and his family took an eight-month vacation in Europe. While Pumarejo was overseas, Fulgencio Batista came to power in a military coup. After the coup, Alonso sold Union Radio's radio and television outlets to separate owners.

When Pumarejo returned to Cuba, he settled on a ranch in the outskirts of Havana where he and his wife raised chickens. But his wife recalled that Pumarejo was always talking about radio and television.[10] Many Cuban entrepreneurs, who looked upon Pumarejo as a radio and television guru, believed that Pumarejo had a gut understanding of radio and television operations. Trinidad, the president of RHC–Cadena Azul, met several times with Pumarejo at his ranch during this period to discuss having Pumarejo join his network in some capacity.[11] Trinidad's radio network was experiencing serious financial problems. Sponsors were threatening to take their programs elsewhere if Trinidad could not increase his network's ratings.[12]

Pumarejo and Trinidad never finalized plans for Pumarejo to join RHC–Cadena Azul. On April 29, 1952, Trinidad sold the financially racked network to a group of U.S. and Cuban businesspeople for $1 million (U.S.).[13] At the time of the sale, RHC–Cadena Azul consisted of 12 radio stations. It also held construction permits for six television stations.[14]

The last radio survey before the sale of RHC–Cadena Azul (conducted Feb. 3 to 17, 1952, in Havana and outlying municipalities) showed CMQ radio with a rating of 9.57, far ahead of second-place RHC–Cadena Azul, with 2.55.[15] The sale of the network must have disturbed many Cubans. Trinidad was a legendary figure in Cuban radio. A 1953 *Bohemia* magazine report described a heart-wrenching account of Trinidad's sale of the network:

> As [RHC–Cadena Azul's] ratings continued to drop, advertisers fled in disdain. With each report, the ratings were less and less and now the purse of "el Guajiro" ["The Peasant," Trinidad's nickname], that in the beginning appeared to possess magical qualities, was exhausted. Now that he had nothing to give, those that said they were his friends abandoned him. . . . Amado, saddened, became ill. He who always knew how to conquer could not tolerate defeat. He had no other recourse but to sell what remained of what was once "the most listened to station in Cuba" and go home. Those that saw him slowly descending the stairs of the Palace of Radio [the Cadena Azul building] for the last time turned away their faces so that he would not notice that they had seen him crying.[16]

Heading the group of buyers of RHC–Cadena Azul was Edmund A. Chester, a former executive with Columbia Broadcasting System (CBS).

Chester was no stranger to Latin American broadcasting. During the early 1940s, he was in charge of CBS's Latin American radio network, "Network of the Americas," which included the stations in the RHC–Cadena Azul chain and other stations in Cuba.[17] Before joining CBS, Chester was an Associated Press (AP) correspondent who covered Cuba during the Machado years and developed a close relationship to then Sergeant Batista.[18] He also wrote a highly laudatory book about Batista.[19]

Joining Chester in the purchase of RHC–Cadena Azul were Elliott Roosevelt, son of the late President Franklin D. Roosevelt, and a young Cuban businessman named Heriberto Hernandez. There was little doubt that the purchase was mainly a U.S. endeavor, with the Cuban businessman included to assuage Cuban nationalistic sentiments. The new owners promised to revitalize the once-great network and expand into television.[20]

RHC–Cadena Azul did not fare any better under new ownership. The network was purchased by a group of Cuban buyers in April 1953, with Pumarejo representing the buyers.[21] Pumarejo, appointed general manager of the organization, gave a pep talk to demoralized employees, promising no personnel reductions. He also vowed that the network would forge ahead with its television plans.[22] Despite Pumarejo's enthusiasm, the May 4 to 23 ratings report showed RHC–Cadena Azul with a rating of 1.72, behind CMQ's 9.24 and Radio Progreso's 3.56.[23]

The "School of Television"

Shortly before Pumarejo became general manager of RHC–Cadena Azul, he and several business associates began leasing one hour each evening over Television Nacional starting at 9:30 p.m. His "Escuela de Television" ("School of Television") variety program started airing on Jan. 3, 1953. Pumarejo hosted the program, assisted by Lolita Berrio. The program was simulcast over RHC–Cadena Azul radio.[24] To obtain the best talent, the program's scouts combed the island.[25] The program attracted diverse acts, such as singers, dancers, acrobats, animal acts and comedians. Amateur talent was unpredictable, and occasionally off-color acts appeared, as when a male comedian dressed as a nun danced the mambo.[26]

Advertisers liked having the popular Pumarejo personally endorse products. Sometimes it wasn't obvious when he was endorsing a product. He would casually light up a cigarette or pour beer for himself. When he would smoke a cigarette on the air, the camera would focus on the brand name of the package grasped in his hand. When he would pour beer into a tall glass, the camera would focus on the label.

Within four months after its inauguration, the "School of Television" had more than 3,000 applications from would-be actors.[27] The program consumed Pumarejo's energies, and he resigned his position at RHC–Cadena Azul in early February 1954.[28] Three weeks later, on March 1, RHC–Cadena Azul went off the air. One Havana television columnist wrote of the closing: "Cadena Azul Building looks like a ghost town. For the first time in nearly 15 years, Cadena Azul radio signal is off the air on 590 Kcs. Things don't look too bright either."[29]

After RHC–Cadena Azul closed, rumors spread about businesspeople who might purchase the network. One of them was Radio Progreso's Manolo Fernandez. When a Havana journalist queried Fernandez about his interest in RHC–Cadena Azul, he curtly responded: "Not interested."[30]

After selling RHC–Cadena Azul, Trinidad retired to a farm in Guanajay. He rarely appeared in public. In December 1953, *Bohemia* magazine conducted a rare interview with the reclusive Trinidad at his farm in which he left open the highly unlikely prospect of returning to RHC–Cadena Azul.[31] In August 1955, after months of poor health, the 61-year-old former tycoon committed suicide. His body was found hanging from a tree on his farm.[32]

Pumarejo Finds Success

Pumarejo had been a famous radio announcer in Cuba since the early 1930s. In 1950, he started Union Radio TV and became the star of the station. Not surprisingly, his "School of Television" over Television Nacional received a good deal of publicity in magazines and newspaper entertainment sections.[33]

The "School of Television" was so popular that in March 1955 the Telemundo network lured Lolita Berrio, Pumarejo's sidekick on the "School of Television," to appear with Mexican actor Carlos Amador to host a short-lived program that was "an identical copy of Gaspar Pumarejo's 'Escuela de Television.'"[34]

Barletta, meanwhile, was involved in negotiations with Pumarejo to bring Pumarejo's popular program to Telemundo. During the summer of 1955, Telemundo and Pumarejo signed a five-year contract to carry the "School of Television" on Telemundo. The program started airing over Telemundo on Aug. 1, 1955, Monday through Friday, 2 to 4 p.m., and again from 9 to 10:30 p.m. The deal was profitable for both men. Barletta had a national network of stations, but lacked programs. Pumarejo had programming, but lacked a chain of stations.[35] The program was an immediate success. When the Cuban Association of Radio and Television Writers handed out their awards in 1955, Pumarejo was named best television host ("animador").[36]

As the "School of Television" grew in popularity, Pumarejo needed better facilities than those available at Telemundo, which lacked even air conditioning. He purchased his own equipment and a theater and hired technicians to produce his program. With the new theater-studio, Pumarejo could accommodate a large studio audience. The only thing Pumarejo continued to require from Barletta was his television signal. In March 1957, Pumarejo renegotiated a new contract with Telemundo. His evening programming now ran from 8 p.m. to midnight.[37]

"School of Television" became the general name for Pumarejo's blocks of programs. He scheduled Cuban versions of programs he had seen during his travels to the United States. These included "Queen for a Day," in which Cuban housewives won prizes, and "This Is Your Life," where people had their life stories recounted by friends and family members.[38] Pumarejo also created a version of the American game show "The $64,000 Question," in which contestants could win up to $4,000 per program over 16 programs. The U.S. program paid one lump $64,000 prize. In the Cuban show, contestants, dressed in academic caps and gowns, answered questions posed by Pumarejo dealing with Cuban history, sports, North American cinema and astronomy.[39]

Although CMQ-TV continued to carry the top-rated programs, some Pumarejo shows occasionally received high viewership. But Pumarejo's program ratings tended to fluctuate more than those of CMQ because he relied on publicity stunts to increase ratings that were difficult to sustain. For example, on some of "The $64,000 Question" programs he featured famous sport and entertainment personalities as contestants. On others he awarded unusually large prizes. In June 1958, to celebrate the first anniversary of the program, he awarded individual prizes of up to $32,000.[40] On another occasion, Pumarejo vacationed to Cuba's Varadero beach resort, taking his cast with him. The Varadero program featured Pumarejo in beach attire while actors and actresses performed under palm trees, by the pool side or on the boardwalk.[41]

By 1957, Pumarejo was having some success chiseling away at CMQ's domination. The August 1957 ratings report showed "Queen for a Day" with a rating of 38.5, tied for third place with a CMQ program. All the other top-10 programs were on CMQ. Other "School of Television" programs in the top 50 included the children's program "Pumarejo y sus Amigos" ("Pumarejo and His Friends") and "The $64,000 Question."[42]

But after the attention-grabbing summer programs, CMQ recaptured its domination in the fall. Eight of the top 10 programs in fall 1958 were on CMQ. The other two were on the Mestre brothers' second network, Cadena Nacional, which the brothers put on the air in early 1957. Pumarejo's "Queen for a Day," earned a respectable number 20; "Cumpleanos de Pumarejo" ("Pumarejo's Birthday Party"), number 27; "Pumarejo and His Friends," number 33; and "The $64,000 Question," number 40.[43]

Pumarejo's "Hogar Club"

The success of the "School of Television" gave Pumarejo the resources to launch another successful spin-off enterprise. He raised money from financial backers (mostly advertisers) to launch the "Hogar Club" ("Home Club") on Feb. 2, 1956. The "Home Club" was literally a "club," where members, mostly housewives, paid $1 monthly dues.[44] "Members" were feted with sponsors' product samples during parties and entertained by leading actors in theaters. They also had the opportunity to participate in raffles and win prizes, ranging from umbrellas to European vacations, mink coats or cash.

Some club activities were broadcast over the "School of Television" to promote the club. But the "Home Club" was technically a separate entity from Pumarejo's television venture. Within days after inaugurating the "Home Club," Pumarejo was deluged with thousands of letters from housewives inquiring how they could participate in club activities.[45] Within two years after its inception, the "Home Club" had an estimated 170,000 to 200,000 members.[46]

During February 1957, Pumarejo rented the Grand Stadium in Havana for a highly successful concert called "Fifty Years of Cuban Music." "Home Club" members were entertained by dozens of performers representing several generations of Cuban musicians.[47] In the summer of 1957, Pumarejo announced that he was investing $1.5 million to build six apartment houses. Once every month a fully furnished apartment would be awarded to a club member in a raffle carried over the "School of Television."[48]

A number of critics objected to the proliferation of raffles, of which Pumarejo was the undisputed leader.[49] To participate in the raffles, it was necessary to purchase some product to obtain an entry form. As one Cuban radio and television writer noted: "There are so many contests going on that you don't know what kind of soap or toothpaste to buy. Two major soap companies have a contest going on where one can win from a lottery ticket to a house furnished and all. 'Just send in your empty boxes to, etc.' is the slogan you hear on radio and TV."[50]

Liberace in Cuba

In the pursuit of higher ratings, Cuban broadcasters featured famous foreign talent. During the summer of 1956 alone, actors such as Argentine Libertad Lamarque and Mexican Ernesto Hill Olvera, a blind organist, appeared on CMQ-TV and Pumarejo's "School of Television." Television Nacional (Channel 4 in Havana) arranged for Mexican Carmela Reyes to appear, while Pumarejo signed Mexican "Lucho" Gatica to an exclusive contract. In one of his unrivaled publicity stunts, Pumarejo had Gatica on stage before "Home Club" members. Pumarejo turned to Gatica and said, "Turn around, Lucho," and Gatica was surprised to see his mother. Supposedly unknown to Gatica, Pumarejo flew the entertainer's mother to Cuba. She ran to hug her startled son. Gatica and his mother were crying, as were reportedly many of the mostly female members of the audience.[51]

On one well-publicized occasion in August 1956, Pumarejo arranged for the famous American pianist and entertainer Liberace to be his guest. Pumarejo had been trying to arrange Liberace's visit ever since he inaugurated the "Home Club." He paid Liberace $10,000 for three "Home Club" performances, an enormous sum for that time.[52]

In the past, CMQ-TV gained attention by showcasing such popular American stars as Cab Calloway, Louis Armstrong and Josephine Baker. Baker's appearances on "Caberet de Josephine Baker" ("Josephine Baker's Caberet") led to a regular spin-off program called "Caberet Regalias" ("The Royal Caberet") that remained among the top programs even after Baker left the show.[53]

In his usual flamboyant style, Pumarejo carried Liberace's arrival in Havana's Rancho Boyeros International Airport over the "School of Television." Three pianos were arranged at the airport, where popular Cuban pianists joined Liberace in a set of musical scores.[54]

After his airport appearance, Liberace and his brother, George, paid a courtesy call on President Batista.[55] Pumarejo then toured the entertainer around Havana. The pianist was photographed at night clubs with show girls and famous Cuban entertainers. One Havana society page editor noted that wherever Liberace went "he was greeted, oddly enough, by a band playing the Cuban and American national anthems as if he had been a visiting dignitary traveling in an official capacity."[56]

Two years later, Pumarejo scored another triumph. During late

August and early September 1958, Pumarejo arranged Spanish actress Sarita Montiel's visit to Cuba. Montiel was one of the most popular performers in Spanish-speaking nations. She received $25,000 for her 10-day visit.[57] For weeks prior to her arrival, Pumarejo promoted Montiel's visit over the "School of Television," even though she never appeared on the program.[58] As with Liberace, she performed exclusively for "Home Club" members in rented theaters. Pumarejo escorted Montiel and her husband, U.S. film producer Anthony Mann, to night clubs and scheduled interviews with local journalists.[59]

The "Home Club" and the "School of Television" were immensely popular and profitable. The successes were achieved by having Pumarejo's two partners run the business operations, freeing Pumarejo to concentrate on what he did best—entertaining. As Alberto Vilar, Pumarejo's program director at Union Radio TV, said:

> Pumarejo was a genius! . . . He sat down in front of a desk before the cameras and talked with no planning whatsoever. He would eat his meals over the air. Whenever he would eat certain foods on the air, it would become a fad, and everyone would eat the same foods. It was amazing the things Pumarejo could do. The only problem with Pumarejo was that he was a very poor businessman. He did not make money until he was allowed to act. [Eduardo] Caballero and [Manuel] Llerandi [Pumarejo's financial backers] controlled the business end. They wouldn't let him [Pumarejo] get involved in the business.[60]

Pumarejo's success was noticed by U.S. talk show star Jack Paar, who befriended the Cuban showman during one of his visits to Havana. During the summer of 1958, Pumarejo appeared as a guest on the "Jack Paar Show" in the United States. Paar introduced Pumarejo as "the number one video personality in Cuba." But, as one American television trade publication noted, to American viewers Pumarejo was "a stocky, ordinary-looking man whose friendly face sports a brush mustache and a pair of dark-rimmed glasses. . . . The physical appearance of Pumarejo [as he's known on the Cuban airwaves] caused little excitement in this country. What did lift a few eyebrows and possibly start some contractual grumbling was Mr. Paar's surprise comment that Pumarejo earns $400,000 monthly."[61]

Broadcasting Self-regulation

By the late 1950s, Cuba's television entrepreneurs were willing to spend almost any amount of money and engage in ever more risque

6. TV COMES OF AGE

programs to increase ratings. Although the techniques to increase ratings were reaching new heights, the quest for higher ratings in Cuban broadcasting was not a new phenomenon.

Since the 1930s, Cuban businesspeople were disturbed by false news reports on some small radio stations alleging outbreaks of people falling ill and even dying from tainted foods and pharmaceutical products. At one level the sensational reports were to increase ratings. At another, they were tacit acts of extortion. The stations made a point of identifying the brand names of the products. Many companies viewed this as extortion—an implicit message to purchase advertising or otherwise be the subject of these reports. Some businesspeople responded by banding together, refusing to advertise on stations that employed unfair advertising practices. This action eventually led to the formation of the Cuban Advertising Association. Members of the Association organized and agreed to withhold advertising from stations that engaged in slanderous news reports. While the embargo sometimes broke down as advertisers competed against each other to sponsor popular programs, the advertisers' unified approach to what they regarded as unfair advertising proved effective often enough to impress upon Association members their power as a consolidated force.[62]

The Association later flexed its muscle to influence matters of taste and propriety on radio by advocating the creation of a self-regulatory radio agency—the Commission on Radio Ethics (CER, La Comision de Etica Radial), which was created on Feb. 17, 1947. When television came to Cuba a few years later, the organization was renamed the Commission on Radio and Television Ethics.[63] Advertisers encouraged self-regulation because they were concerned about public complaints of sex and violence in broadcasting that sullied the image of program sponsors and advertisers as well as the media.[64]

The Ethics Commission was formed with the consent and participation of some leading broadcasters who had their own reasons for the establishment of the Commission. For example, Goar Mestre championed the creation of the Commission. He believed that self-regulation might stave off possible Cuban government censorship in the future.[65] Although the Commission was ostensibly independent of the government, the government supported the creation of the Commission and suggested it might intervene to enforce the Commission's rulings. As a report in *Carteles* magazine in 1949 noted: "Is this organization official? No, even though it is assisted by the government, it still remains a private entity."[66]

The Commission was the brainchild of four men: Juan Jose Tarajano, a lawyer, president of the Radio Screenwriters Association, and an announcer and writer at CMZ, Cuba's educational station operated by the Ministry of Education; CMQ's Goar Mestre; Radio Progreso's Manolo Fernandez; and Jose Manuel Viana, vice president of advertising at Sabates (the Cuban subsidiary of Procter and Gamble) and later president of the Cuban Advertising Association. Others, such as the well-known program producer Luis Aragon, also contributed to the creation of the Commission.[67] Tarajano became the commissioner general in charge of the Ethics Commission.[68]

A Matter of Taste

As a nongovernment agency, the Ethics Commission did not have the authority to impose fines or order programs from the air. But its "suspensions" still carried authority because Cuba's most important advertisers agreed to withhold advertising revenue from suspended programs.

The Commission's observers monitored programming and investigated complaints of violations.[69] Regulations concerned the portrayal of religion, marriage and the family, prostitution, sexual relations, profane language, torture, suicide, illnesses and physical defects. The Ethics Commission did not concern itself with news programming, fearing that this would be a violation of freedom of the press.[70]

During the summer of 1950, the Commission demanded that RHC–Cadena Azul eliminate references to risque subjects in three programs. Owner Amado Trinidad refused, claiming that the Commission's actions interfered with his independence. An angered Trinidad threatened to take all programming off the air and fill his schedule with religious music rather than yield to the Commission.[71] Only after the head of public relations at Tropical beer, a major advertiser on RHC–Cadena Azul, intervened and spoke with Trinidad did RHC–Cadena Azul reluctantly yield to the Ethics Commission's demands.[72]

Another incident occurred during the summer of 1952 over Union Radio, when the organization was owned by Luis J. Botifoll and Jose Luis Pelleya. A popular singer known as Clavelito (Miguel Alfonso Pozo) instructed listeners to place a glass of water on top of their radios while he sang. The water was warmed by the hot tubes inside the sets. Clavelito told listeners that if they drank the warm water they could solve their physical and emotional problems.

The Ethics Commission demanded that Clavelito cease his claims, which it felt dealt with occult issues.[73] For several weeks, Clavelito fought the Commission's decision. Meanwhile, Clavelito's program soared in the ratings.[74]

Union Radio co-owner Pelleya said that the Ethics Commission was pressuring the network to make Clavelito discontinue his faith healing claims. "But we were never worried," Pelleya said. "In those days, the only thing that would get your station closed was if you started yelling and screaming against Batista."[75]

The Ministry of Communications did in fact intervene on behalf of the Ethics Commission and ordered Clavelito's program (but not the station) off the air.[76] Although the Ministry had closed another station the same day for airing a political commentator's criticisms of the Batista government, the Ministry was inundated by protests over the action against Clavelito's program and hardly a bleat was registered over the closure of the other station.[77] Clavelito's program, with his water-on-the-radio routine, were back on the air after 24 hours.

The Ethics Commission, meanwhile, continued its pressure on Clavelito. It was not easy for the Commission to get advertisers to adhere to the Commission's rulings in the case of Clavelito's highly rated program. During the controversy, Clavelito visited Tarajano at the Ethics Commission office to explain his case. Clavelito said that he had studied the writings of Sigmund Freud and Uruguayan Constancio Vigil, both of whom believed that people's problems could be traced to their minds. Tarajano said he was stunned to hear Clavelito declare that he really believed his routine could heal the sick.[78] Pelleya, however, said that Clavelito spoke many times about how he could work miracles through faith healing. People with a variety of maladies visited the self-professed healer of the sick in his studio. In some cases they at least claimed they were cured by their faith in Clavelito.[79]

In 1953, CMQ-TV's "Royal Cabaret" came under the scrutiny of the Ethics Commission. Tarajano objected to a troupe of female dancers "in bathing-suit-like garments, adjusted very tightly and with low necks. The dance movements were occasionally inappropriate and exaggerated."[80] Since Goar Mestre was a vocal supporter of the Ethics Commission, CMQ tried to avoid contentious public arguments with the organization and yielded to the Commission's decision.

Pumarejo and the Ethics Commission

Pumarejo frequently contested the Ethics Commission's sanctions. Writing in 1989, Tarajano, who had several acrimonious clashes with Pumarejo, contended that Pumarejo publicly defied the Commission because he felt empowered by his connections with the Batista government: "He [Pumarejo] was dominated by an obsession to compete against CMQ and believed that he was able to obtain an advantage in his support with the assistance of the government of Fulgencio Batista."[81] For his part, Pumarejo complained that it was Tarajano who enjoyed the protection of various government agencies. Pumarejo also charged that Goar Mestre's broadcast organizations were not as closely scrutinized by the Ethics Commission as Pumarejo's "School of Television."[82]

During April 1956, the Ethics Commission cracked down on female impersonators in comedy routines. The Commission believed that the portrayals encouraged homosexuality and what it regarded as perverted sex. Havana night club acts frequently featured female impersonators in suggestive comedy skits. At the time of the ruling, several programs were indicted, including a CMQ-TV program. One program cited was Pumarejo's "School of Television," in which Uruguayan comedian Herbert Castro portrayed a female character known as "Pirula." Pumarejo balked at withdrawing Castro's comedy skit.[83]

Minister of Communications Ramon Vasconcelos contacted Tarajano and asked the Ethics Commission to relax its rule against female impersonators. Vasconcelos noted that Cuba had a tradition in theater of female impersonators. Eventually, Tarajano conceded that the contexts of the impersonation had to be considered.[84]

Two months later, Pumarejo appeared on the "School of Television" and announced that he would refuse to comply with the Ethics Commission's sanctions against an acrobatic act in which the woman allegedly revealed too much cleavage and a comedian used off-color humor. Pumarejo maintained that he was a victim of a "conspiracy," and noted CMQ's connections to the Ethics Commission. Pumarejo also challenged Tarajano to debate the Commission's suspensions of his acts with him on his television program. Tarajano accepted the offer.[85]

The two men did not have a face-to-face encounter. Instead, Tarajano made his statements from CMQ's studio. "School of Television" technicians set up a monitor in their studio to carry Tarajano's remarks. Split-screen coverage was used to show each man's reactions to the other's remarks. The public debate between the two men was so contentious that to capture the flavor of the controversy the transcript, which was recorded in *Bohemia* magazine, is being quoted in some depth. Tarajano began by reading a prepared statement:

> The director of the "School of Television" has presented himself as a victim of conspiracies . . . and he has put in doubt the honor of this organization by bringing its members to an absurd round table, trying to erect himself as

an arbiter of the destiny of Cuban television. We are going to answer the director of the "School of Television" without trying to testify to our morality. . . . He does not speak the truth when he claims that the Commission of Ethics was created by the CMQ circuit. The system represents a system of self-censorship that by happy coincidence is freely and spontaneously supported by announcers, radio broadcasters, writers and Cuban "publicitarios" [publicity people, including advertisers]. What is truly lamentable is that the director of the "School of Television," at every instance, has refused to cooperate with the Ethics Commission: in Union Radio, in [RHC-]Cadena Azul [when Pumarejo was president of the organization] and in his present programs.[86]

When Tarajano finished, Pumarejo responded:

Dr. Tarajano repeats on this occasion, as he has on many occasions . . . that I am involved in promoting official censorship of Cuban television and radio. And just as children are told "There is the bogeyman," we are told "There is official censorship." Many times in the past the CMQ Circuit has obtained the support of prestigious institutions in its plans and proposals, all attending to consolidate its dominion and to become the owners and masters of Cuban radio and television. But by dint of repeating "There is the bogeyman," even if the bogeyman does not come, the child still continues believing in the bogeyman.[87]

Pumarejo also argued that the Mestre brothers' Channel 7 in Havana, which primarily aired foreign movies and television programs, violated moral standards every day:

Please, Dr. Tarajano, have you never tuned into Channel 7? Do you not know how common it is for Mexican movies to have cabaret scenes with a "rumbera" [a sensual dancer or dance scene] in close up, with movements that can qualify as indecent with much more foundation than [the act of] our comedian Milos Vardes? Have you not seen the . . . many movies they show that I would declare unfit for minors or adults? . . . I assure you, Dr. Tarajano, . . . serenely and calmly, that I will not carry out those sanctions, because neither you nor the Commission will encounter strength—private or official—that can demand of me the fulfillment of a punishment that I do not deserve.[88]

Two days after the sensational encounter, Vasconcelos invited Tarajano and Pumarejo to his office. As in many earlier disputes between the Commission and broadcasters, there was no resolution. Although Pumarejo agreed to refrain from airing suggestive sex, he also claimed the acts never contained sexual content or innuendo in the first place. Each man left Vasconcelos' office claiming his side had prevailed.[89]

"Rocandrolicos"

While the Batista dictatorship attempted to silence political criticisms, it also displayed a prudish side under Minister of Communications Vasconcelos. On Feb. 13, 1957, Vasconcelos barred rock and roll music from radio and television, charging that the "Rocandrolicos" promoted "postures and movements considered frankly immoral."[90] At the time, only two television stations, channels 2 and 10, both operated by Barletta, carried a rock and roll program. The program featured teenagers who danced to live bands.[91]

Shortly after Vasconcelos announced his decision, an announcer at the rock and roll program interrupted the music to read a protest.[92] The government and Havana newspapers and radio stations were deluged with citizen complaints about the ban. Under pressure, Vasconcelos rescinded the order after the stations agreed to remove several dance steps that he described as "degrading."[93] The program celebrated the lifting of the ban by bringing teenage dependents of U.S. Embassy officials to the studio to demonstrate the latest dances in the United States.[94]

The incident with the rock and roll program, as with the earlier episode with Clavelito, demonstrated the popularity of television entertainment programming. Both of these incidents occurred during the Batista dictatorship, when stations were closed and commentators were frequently silenced for political criticism. While government actions against political criticism were condemned by a political elite, the general public only vigorously protested the actions against popular entertainment programs. What's more, public pressure often succeeded in getting the government to acquiesce. Imagine what could have been accomplished if the public had protested the government's actions against the political criticism?

CHAPTER 7
Batista's Legacy of Censorship

The 1952 Cuban presidential campaign was about to get under way when, in August 1951, Ortodoxo Party leader Eduardo "Eddie" Chibas committed suicide on his Sunday evening CMQ radio program. The dramatic incident threw Cuban politics into disarray. It was almost certain that Chibas would have been his party's presidential nominee with a good chance of victory.[1] Upon Chibas' death, Pardo Llada was the most charismatic Ortodoxo leader. But Pardo Llada, who just turned 27 a month earlier, was too young to lead the party. Roberto Agramonte Pichardo became the party's leader and, later, announced his presidential candidacy. Public opinion polls in late 1951 showed the Ortodoxos and Autenticos about even while Fulgencio Batista's United Action Party trailed far behind.[2]

Young Ortodoxo leaders, raised on Chibas' fiery rhetoric, railed against Batista and Autentico candidate Carlos Hevia. As always, lame-duck President Carlos Prio Soccaras was also a target of the Ortodoxo's venom. While Jose Pardo Llada and Luis Conte Aguero were the two most prominent Ortodoxo radio commentators, Fidel Castro, a little-known Ortodoxo member, also took to the airwaves to lash out against Batista, Hevia and Prio.[3]

Like many young Ortodoxos, Castro saw the power vacuum created by Chibas' death as an opportunity to advance his career. He convinced Agramonte to make several minutes of the Ortodoxo's Sunday evening program available to the party's young members on occasion. During these broadcasts, Castro himself frequently represented the young Ortodoxos.[4]

With Chibas dead, Batista felt confident that he could seize power in a coup d'etat with no credible opposition figure with the moral authority to challenge him.[5] Batista launched his coup during the early morning of March 10, 1952, three months before the scheduled election. The relatively bloodless coup took 77 minutes to succeed. Only two soldiers at the Presidential Palace died. Prio found asylum in the Mexican Embassy. He fled Cuba a few days later. Batista appeared on nationwide radio after the coup and explained that he overthrew the government because President Prio was planning his own coup to thwart the election and remain in power. Batista also announced that, because of the "national emergency," he was dissolving all political parties, imposing press censorship and suspending constitutional rights for 45 days. It was the first of many such on-again, off-again suspensions of civil liberties that Batista would announce throughout his presidency.[6]

The Ortodoxo Party had built its reputation on political honesty. Although the Autentico governments of Ramon Grau San Martin and Prio, which preceded Batista, were rife with corruption, both administrations generally respected human rights and democratic processes. The Ortodoxos always had access to radio and other media during the Grau and Prio administrations to criticize the government in power. The coup made Batista the leading foe of the Ortodoxos. While Pardo Llada and Conte Aguero used their microphones to attack Batista, and frequently experienced censorship of their programs for their temerity, Castro grew so disillusioned by the coup that he soon turned to violence.

Batista's Censorship

The day after the March 10 coup, Minister of Information (Propaganda) Ernesto de la Fe summoned representatives from Havana's radio and television stations to the Presidential Palace. CMQ's Abel Mestre attended, both as the representative of Cuba's largest radio and television network and as head of the Cuban Federation of Radio Broadcasters. De la Fe told Mestre that for the next 45 days during the state of emergency, radio and television stations were "free" to broadcast their own views and opinions, as long as they did not make their microphones available to private individuals.[7]

De la Fe's command was both artful and devious. It left the impression that the broadcasters were free to broadcast as they pleased, when in fact they enjoyed little freedom at all. Unlike the outspoken commentators, who had little to lose for their temerity, commercial broadcasters could not afford to be suspended a single day unless they were willing to lose substantial profits. In the past, commercial Cuban radio stations portrayed themselves as objective carriers of a spectrum of opinions. By carrying various political commentators, they claimed, they were performing a public service. They emphasized, however, that the commentators' views did not necessarily reflect the stations' views. De la Fe's command making radio and television stations responsible for all opinions carried over their outlets effectively silenced criticism of the government over the large radio outlets.

One Havana station, CMCH–Radio Cadena Habana, ignored de la Fe's warnings. On March 14, it permitted Pardo Llada to denounce the coup. The station was immediately occupied by government soldiers.[8]

For Batista, press censorship was a quick and simple way to deal with a complex problem. Batista repeatedly apologized for censorship, claiming that he was compelled by the national crisis following his coup and canceled election to impose censorship. Even in his memoirs, written in exile after Castro came to power, Batista bemoaned that he was forced to take "exceptional measures" against the press:

> Let me add a few words and a few memories concerning journalism. I have always felt devoted to the members of this profession. . . . Unavoidable duty made me adopt exceptional measures, authorized by the Constitution, during dire emergency, but we never resorted to the measures provided by law against those newspapermen who defamed me and my administration. . . . It is sufficient to take a quick glance at what journalism and the press were like during the era of the 10th of March Revolution [Batista's 1952 coup] and see what they have become under the Communist terror.[9]

There is reason to suspect that the severity of censorship depended upon the censor assigned to each media organization. Clarence W. Moore, who, with his brother, Carl, founded the English-language *Times of Havana* in 1956, said that even during censorship his newspaper did not unduly suffer. He described the censor assigned to the *Times* as a "nice fellow who often sipped coffee with newsroom staffers." On only one occasion, when the newspaper attempted to report about mothers of Batista's torture victims, did the *Times* have a story completely removed.[10]

Cuba's political radio commentators vehemently denounced Batista and press censorship. While the major radio outlets did not carry their protests, for fear of being shut down, some small stations were willing to risk carrying the commentators. For example, on Dec. 17, 1952, the Ministry of Communications closed CMCA–Radio Mambi for 10 days after a commentator broadcast a false report that the police chief of Havana was removed from office. The ministry then suspended Cadena

Oriental de Radio commentator Jose Pardo Llada and CMBQ–Radio Continental commentator Primitivo Rodriguez, each for 15 days, after they criticized the closure of Radio Mambi.

The U.S. Embassy in Havana, which monitored press freedom in Cuba, noted that with the exception of an "expected bleat" from the Communist newspaper *Noticias de Hoy,* not one Cuban newspaper protested the closure of Radio Mambi and the actions taken against the commentators who protested the closure.[11] According to a restricted U.S. Embassy dispatch, CMQ's Goar Mestre told Embassy officials that he was "privately" telegraphing his protest of the "arbitrary closure" to President Batista. Mestre argued that while there was no excuse for the false reports, "we must fight for certain procedures, and we don't think it is right for the government to march in and shut down a station. We are frankly deeply concerned because we see certain trends in this action."[12] The fact that the usually outspoken Mestre felt he had to "privately" communicate his displeasure indicated the cautious manner in which Cuba's commercial broadcasters responded to Batista's censorship.

On March 10, 1953, Radio Mambi was silenced again. The government closed the station for 24 hours after it reported that police had fired upon students protesting the first anniversary of the Batista coup. The closure of Radio Mambi led to a series of protests by various radio commentators, each of whom, in turn, was suspended by the government. Once again, Pardo Llada and Rodriguez were among the commentators who were suspended. In addition, Armando Garcia Sifredo of Onda Hispano Cubano radio and Guido Garcia Inclan, the director of COCO, had their broadcasts suspended for four days.[13]

In addition to earning the enmity of Cuba's broadcasters, Batista's censorship also reinforced credence to rumors of government oppression. For example, in August 1953 the propaganda ministry disseminated approved news reports stating that the Roman Catholic Archbishop of Havana had been injured during a fall. Ordinarily, this would not have been a major news story. The censored Cuban media reported the "facts" about the primate's accident, just as they had been instructed. But rumors spread that the archbishop had been tortured by Batista agents. As a report in an American newsmagazine noted: "Perhaps it remained only for the President to take his choice of two morals: (1) if the story was true, censorship evidently did not keep Cubans from learning it; (2) if the story was false, censorship obviously led many Cubans to believe it."[14]

When censorship was in force, it was vigorously implemented. But when it was lifted, the commentators returned to the air to level their charges against the Batista government. Frequently this led to another round of government censorship. Santiago Rey, a minister in Batista's cabinet, said that with almost 40 years retrospect Batista's error was his "softness" and unwillingness to impose complete censorship. "They [members of Batista's government] were all soft," Rey said. "They allowed what no real dictatorship or oppressive government would allow. These commentators were allowed to speak badly about the government."[15]

CMQ'S Response to Censorship

Although the government effectively silenced criticisms over the major broadcast outlets, Goar Mestre continued to criticize the Batista government during his many trips abroad. On March 22, 1952, the 3,800-member Inter-American Association of Broadcasters (IAAB), the main broadcast media "watchdog" organization in the Western Hemisphere, convened in Panama City, Panama, for its annual meeting and denounced the Cuban government's restrictions on the broadcast media. The IAAB cabled a telegram to Batista stating that "the people of the Americas have their eyes fixed upon Cuba, confident that all media for dissemination of thought will continue freely to fulfill their lofty mission." The telegram was signed by a host of leading broadcasters from North America and Latin America, including the IAAB's president, Goar Mestre.[16]

Goar and Abel Mestre had different approaches to dealing with government censorship. Goar Mestre had an internationalist perspective. His frequent business travels abroad brought him in contact with broadcasters in the United States, Canada and Latin American nations several months each year. Goar believed in a unified, regionwide approach by Latin American broadcasters in dealing with dictators.[17]

Abel Mestre, on the other hand, expressed little faith in international organizations. He believed in dealing with Batista through "quiet diplomacy." As the president of the Cuban Federation of Radio Broadcasters, he often met with Batista in the Presidential Palace to register his protests "in a dignified manner." Abel Mestre was also president of the National Association of Industrialists, representing the interests of Cuba's business community.[18] "We were dealing with a dictator here," Abel Mestre said, "and a very proud man. He would listen to us, but he did not like to be intimidated."[19]

Abel Mestre was frequently annoyed by delegations of foreign broadcasters who came to Cuba at Goar's request to demand that

Batista abolish restrictive press policies. Abel Mestre believed that this tactic only undercut his efforts at diplomacy and infuriated Batista. His gingerly approach to dealing with Batista's censorship might have kept the island's stations operating, but it also left the impression that Cuba's broadcasters were kowtowing to Batista. One censored Cuban newspaper account described the broadcasters' reactions after the March 10, 1952, coup this way: "The representatives of the broadcasting stations expressed their satisfaction with the treatment they had received and the guarantees that they enjoyed at all times during the crisis. . . . Abel Mestre, on behalf of the broadcasting stations, declared that they would carry out the constructive work on behalf of the nation and that he was grateful for the confidence in them which General Batista had displayed."[20]

In contrast to this press account, Abel Mestre described Minister of Information de la Fe, whom he negotiated with after the coup, as "a hell of an unreasonable man whom you couldn't talk with."[21] Mestre said that the 36-year-old politician, six years his junior, would lecture him like a schoolchild.[22] Before becoming the youngest member of Batista's Cabinet, de la Fe worked as a journalist at a half dozen newspapers and was involved in more than 20 highly publicized duels with leading politicians whom he criticized in the press, including Anibal Escalante, editor of the Communist *Noticias de Hoy,* and Rolando Masferrer Rojas, editor of the Batista organ *El Tiempo.*[23] The ambitious de la Fe left his ministerial post in 1954 to host a thrice-weekly 15-minute radio program in which he became the Cuban counterpart of Red-baiting U.S. Sen. Joseph McCarthy. In his program, de la Fe promised to "uncover Communists in their lairs, pull them out by the hair and hold them up to the light so that the public may see them." De la Fe even irked his old boss Batista by charging that "Reds" had infiltrated the Batista government.[24]

CMQ'S News and Public Affairs Programs

After the Batista coup, news programming took on special importance. CMQ-TV's newscast, "Noticiero CMQ," occasionally appeared among the top-rated programs in Cuba. The Mestre brothers met with both considerable success and controversy in public affairs programming with "Ante la Prensa" ("Before the Press" or "Meet the Press"), in which a panel of prominent journalists grilled leading politicians. The program, which went on the air in 1951, was described by Goar Mestre as "an outright copy of the NBC program" in the United

States with the same name.[25] The format was so popular that it was copied by other Cuban television stations and networks.[26]

On CMQ's version of "Meet the Press," three or four journalists posed penetrating questions to government officials. The program was moderated by Harvard-educated Dr. Jorge Manach Robato, a respected Cuban man of letters.[27] During Manach's frequent absences from "Meet the Press," the program was moderated by other intellectuals, such as Luis Alejandro Baralt and Francisco Ichaso, or CMQ's news director, Nicholas Bravo.[28]

The appearance of the intellectual Manach on television illustrated the academician's view that the broadcast media could be used to promote education and culture. During the early 1930s, when Manach was a member of the faculty of the University of Havana, he gained nationwide attention as the host of the educational radio program "University of the Air," which aired over CMBZ.[29] The program was dedicated to "the art of living." Manach invited scholars and intellectuals to the program to discuss Cuban culture and history. During the 1940s, the program, again hosted by Manach, returned to radio on CMQ.[30]

The original "University of the Air" during the 1930s gained nationwide attention during the dictatorship of President Gerardo Machado y Morales (1925–1933), when all political criticism was censored and educational centers closed.[31] After the 1933 revolution that toppled Machado, Manach was appointed the Minister of Education by the provisional government. While at this post, Manach never realized his dream of establishing a Department of Culture with the goal of disseminating Cuban culture to all citizens.[32] Although Manach was associated with high culture, he made an effort to reach the general public through popular magazines and newspapers as well as radio and television. He proudly referred to himself as a "literary journalist."[33]

Manach was hired as CMQ's cultural director when the Mestre brothers ventured into television in 1951. The Mestres expected that Manach would confine his activities to the arts and culture, not politics. To the brothers' chagrin, "Meet the Press" caused a number of troubles with the Prio and, later, the Batista and Castro governments.[34] It was not unusual for Goar or Abel Mestre to be called into various ministries or even the presidential palace to account for criticisms leveled against the government by guests on the program. Cuban presidents found it difficult to accept the explanation that the comments of the guests on the program did not necessarily reflect CMQ's views.[35]

In late August 1952, Emilio Ochoa, president of the Ortodoxo Party, appeared on "Meet the Press" and called Batista a "dictator." Ochoa also predicted that Batista would be overthrown before the end of the year. He then urged members of the Ortodoxo's youth movement to march upon the Camp Columbia military barracks "to see if the soldiers would fire upon them." Interior Minister Ramon Hermida gave orders to have Ochoa arrested on charges of "conspiracy and inciting the people to rebellion."[36] Ochoa was arrested as he left CMQ studios that day. He was found guilty and fined $1,000 in September.

One of the biggest political conflicts on "Meet the Press" occurred in May 1953, when the Batista government jailed Ortodoxo leader Pelayo Cuervo Navarro after the former senator had appeared on the program and claimed that high-ranking Army officers were stealing funds from the national lottery. Cuervo Navarro was arrested by Military Intelligence Service (known by the Spanish acronym SIM) agents as he left CMQ's Radiocentro Building and charged with inciting rebellion, public disorder and contempt of the government.[37]

Army Chief Major General Francisco Tabernilla accused Cuervo Navarro with having made "slanderous imputations against the Army in an effort to confuse public opinion and alienate the loyalty of members of the armed forces."[38] As for CMQ, Minister of Information de la Fe declared that CMQ and Manach were partial toward opposition leaders and unfair to the government. De la Fe then ordered government ministers not to appear with Manach on "Meet the Press."[39]

In response to de la Fe's charges, CMQ issued a statement that it was suspending "Meet the Press" until the government "reconsiders" its decision. The CMQ statement noted that "presenting only one side of Cuban life would deprive the program of the democratic sense we want to have." The government ban was short-lived, and "Meet the Press" was soon back on the air.[40]

Support for Batista

Batista is remembered today as the quintessential Latin American dictator—coarse, cruel and unsophisticated. But this view of Batista was formed largely after the Castro revolution. During his rule, he enjoyed modest support even from some social liberals. Batista's equivocal and apologetic stand for his actions garnered him some support.

New York Times correspondent Herbert Matthews interviewed Batista on Oct. 16, 1953. Years later, Matthews would come to be wrongly viewed by many Cubans as a spokesman and even apologist for Castro's rebel cause.[41] Batista appeared to make a positive impression on Matthews, who wrote approvingly about Batista's promise to lift censorship and hold a free presidential election.[42] Matthews also praised

7. BATISTA'S LEGACY OF CENSORSHIP

Batista's willingness to accept criticisms from Cuban newspaper editors attending the Inter American Press Association (IAPA) conference in Mexico City: "He [Batista] gives the impression of complete sincerity and he harbors no grudge against eminent Cuban editors who went to the Mexico City conference last week and attacked him. The President's good intentions are generally recognized, but some of his advisers are suspected, and it is questioned whether he himself is popular enough to rule democratically today even if he tries to do so."[43]

As Batista promised, censorship was lifted on Oct. 24, 1953, to coincide with "Journalists' Day." Even with censorship lifted, the infamous "Law of Public Order No. 997" was still in effect. The law prescribed penalties for a range of offenses that included "disrespect," "false rumors," "defamation," and "calumny."[44]

In addition to Matthews, Batista also received praise from syndicated American columnist Drew Pearson. Pearson visited Cuba in September 1955 and was photographed in Cuban newspapers toasting Batista. While in Cuba, Pearson stayed in a luxurious penthouse at the expense of Amadeo Barletta, Jr., described by *Time* magazine as the "son of a rich Batista crony."[45] In his final column upon leaving Cuba, Pearson compared his visit with Batista to his visit with Cuba's hated dictator-President Machado a quarter century earlier: "This time a couple of guards lounged around a Coca-Cola vending machine inside a rear door. Not even an armed sentry paced outside. Inside, in the president's office, I found the man some Cubans call a dictator to be a genial, mild-mannered gentleman of about 50 with a command of the English language that put my Spanish to shame and eyes which poorly concealed a sense of humor that frequently confounds his cabinet."[46]

Cuba's broadcasters lambasted Pearson's defense of Batista. Pardo Llada charged that "our illustrious friend Drew Pearson has defrauded us."[47] When Pearson wrote that Batista ruled with only limited force, Conte Aguero, a popular radio commentator and columnist in *Diario Nacional,* wrote in his column that Pearson's observations were "too ridiculous to comment."[48] Several Cuban newspapers that carried Pearson's syndicated "Merry-Go-Round" column dropped it in protest.[49]

How could Matthews and Pearson be so apologetic about Batista's censorship? Matthews, after all, was regarded as a social liberal at the *Times* who had openly supported the rebel cause when he covered the Spanish Civil War.[50] Perhaps from an outsider's perspective, the censorship seemed benign. Complaints against censorship appeared to come from a group of intellectuals in journalistic circles, mostly in the print media. But, paradoxically, their ability to loudly protest their lack of freedom seemed to attest to their freedom. How else could the liberal

Cuban magazine *Bohemia* (Nov. 1, 1953) so openly defy censorship with a cover page showing a screaming newsboy and the words "Censored" across the cover? It was a classic Catch-22 situation.

Complete Censorship

On July 26, 1953, Castro and his rebel supporters attacked the Moncada military barracks at Santiago de Cuba. Even at this early stage in his rebel career, Castro understood the value of cultivating favorable publicity for his cause. Shortly before the failed attack, Castro made his way to Santiago to find Conte Aguero, by now a popular radio commentator on Radio Progreso. Castro wanted to inform his Ortodoxo colleague of the impending attack and ask him to coordinate propaganda broadcasts. Conte Aguero, however, was in Havana for the weekend.[51]

The attack, in which 100 rebel and government soldiers were killed, was a military defeat for Castro, but a propaganda triumph. Castro was arrested and jailed. The government immediately suspended constitutional guarantees, which included complete censorship of all mass media.[52] Government censors were assigned to newspapers, magazines and broadcast stations to review all copy before publication. There was nothing secretive about the imposition of censorship. The press reported the names of the censors assigned to various media organizations. When the decree was lifted, the press reported the bombings, terrorist attacks and protests that could not be reported when censorship was in force.[53]

Under public pressure to show leniency toward Castro, Batista pardoned Castro and other political prisoners on May 2, 1955. Batista hoped that the amnesty would be regarded as a goodwill gesture. Castro left for Mexico and founded his "July 26th Movement" (named for the July 26 Moncada uprising) rebel organization and planned the Cuban revolution.

Criticisms against the government persisted. Batista responded by suspending constitutional guarantees and imposing censorship. By the mid- and late 1950s, government censorship of the broadcast media was so severe that even Abel Mestre, who had long disagreed with his brother Goar's tactic of publicly assailing government censorship, openly criticized the censorship in his capacity as president of the Cuban Federation of Radio Broadcasters.[54]

In 1956, Castro and a small cadre of his followers landed the 62-foot-long yacht "Granma" in Oriente Province. They formed a rebel army with volunteers from the countryside. Castro led hit-and-run attacks against government troops and installations. In response, the government instituted martial law and censorship to keep the rebels from gaining popular support. Batista's harsh response to the Castro threat only chiseled away at what little public and press support that Batista had.

During the early part of 1956, Castro was not yet the dominant rebel figure in Cuba. The Batista government had to contend with a number of would-be revolutionaries intent upon liberating Cuba from dictatorial rule. Perhaps the most famous was Aureliano Sanchez Arango, the Minister of Education during the Prio government. Batista ordered his agents to capture and torture suspected Sanchez Arango supporters and force them to disclose their leader's hiding place.[55] But the clever Sanchez Arango eluded capture.

By late 1956 and early 1957, Castro's rebels had established a stronghold in the Sierra Maestra hills. With surprising success, the rebels had attacked government military installations. Castro's name started to appear with some regularity in the Havana press. The government linked Castro to bombings, sabotage incidents, assassinations of government officials and growing unrest in the countryside. But it was not until *New York Times* journalist Herbert Matthews published his exclusive interview with Castro in the Sierra Maestra in February 1957 that Castro became the leading rebel figure and singular threat to the Batista government. The interview demonstrated that, contrary to the government's assertions, Castro had not been killed by government troops and that he has established a foothold in the Sierra Maestra.[56] Former CBS executive Edmund Chester, employed as Batista's public relations counselor at the time of the Matthews interview, denounced the interview as a fake.[57]

Before the Castro interview, Batista was making efforts to curry public opinion and demonstrate his commitment to freedom of the press. When the Inter American Press Association (IAPA) held its annual convention in Havana in October 1956, the Batista government went to great lengths to convince the IAPA that the Cuban press enjoyed press freedom. Many Cuban editors were permitted to openly express disagreement with the government. At the close of the meeting, the IAPA issued a report condemning government restrictions against the press in six Latin American nations, but not Cuba.[58]

After the IAPA left Cuba and Matthew's interview with Castro was published, the Batista government launched a new crackdown on press criticisms. Censorship became so severe after 1957 that the media could no longer even mention that their reports were censored. Some Cuban broadcasters tried to inject innuendos into their reports that the news was censored. For example, Manolo Iglesias, CMQ's popular news announcer, who usually ended his 11 p.m. program with the phrase "That's all the news," started attaching a sarcastic addendum: "That's all the news, as you well know."[59]

Iglesias was arrested by Batista's secret police in September 1957 in connection with his role in underground, anti-Batista activities. He was given 24 hours to leave Cuba. He made his way to Mexico, where he offered his services to the July 26th Movement. The Movement sent him to Venezuela to serve as an announcer at Radio Continente, a commercial station whose powerful signals could be clearly received in Cuba.[60] A few weeks after Iglesias' hasty escape from Cuba, Cubans were surprised to hear Iglesias on the air at his regular time, announcing that from now on his broadcasts could be heard over Radio Continente: "This is Manolo Iglesias, the voice of freedom, speaking to you from Radio Continente in Caracas. Tonight, and every night at this hour, I will bring you the truth about our beloved Cuba."[61]

CMQ had carried the program of Batistiano commentator Otto Meruelo since the mid-1950s (Meruelo paid for the air time). Iglesias and Meruelo kept a running feud with each other in their back-to-back programs.[62] After Batista fled Cuba, the Cuban Association of Radio and TV Critics (CARTV) gave Radio Continente an award for "outstanding services rendered to the people of Cuba in their fight for freedom."[63] At about the same time, Meruelo received a 30-year prison term from a military tribunal for his service to the Batista government.[64]

Batista's crackdown on press freedom and civil liberties caused a rift between Cuba and the United States. The U.S. Embassy in Havana was alarmed by vitriolic editorials in Batistiano newspapers maligning U.S. officials. Since the editorials were permitted during a period of government censorship, the U.S. government interpreted these editorials as sanctioned Cuban government commentaries. This might have been a mistake, since even Batistiano newspapers maintained varying degrees of independence from the government. A classified memo from the Embassy to the Department of State described the editorials in the following way: "It would appear that the government's attitude is motivated by a combination of vindictiveness and disappointment, since the government had apparently formed the mistaken opinion that the policy of the United States was one of full support for the present regime."[65]

The U.S. Embassy was particularly distressed by editorials in Havana's *El Tiempo* about the U.S. ambassador to Cuba and the Secretary of State. Embassy documents described Rolando Masferrer Rojas, the owner and director of *El Tiempo,* as "one of the most completely corrupt, vicious and unscrupulous men in Cuba. . . . He maintains his own private 'army' of goons, which is completely independent and not subject to control by any regularly constituted armed forces and frequently 'assists' those forces to maintain law and order."[66]

A Subversive Radionovela

The Batista government crackdown on political criticism from 1957 to Batista's hasty flight from Cuba on New Year's Eve of 1959 was intense and unrelenting. Newspapers and radio stations had to be alert to journalists and commentators who might cause their employers trouble by criticizing the government. The censorship was interfering in the news media's daily business operations.

For the most part, newspapers and radio stations kept an eye on political commentators, naturally suspecting that if trouble would arise, it would come from them. But Cuba had a long tradition of subtle political commentary in fiction that found a place in radionovela (radio soap opera) scripts. Ironically, one fictional program that indirectly lambasted Batista was on a network reputed to be secretly owned by the dictator, CNC (Circuito Nacional Cubano).[67] Management was apparently unaware of the veiled messages inserted in the scripts by anti-Batista writers.

The program "El Dictador de Valle Azul" ("The Dictator of the Blue Valley") started airing over CNC in late 1957. It starred Rolando Leyva as the rebel leader Taguary, who, with his group of men, roamed the Blue Valley and helped the people fight the valley's evil dictator in each episode.[68] The comparisons with the dictator Batista and the rebel leader Castro were unmistakable. The government's failure to recognize the satire only made the government appear inept as well as tyrannical.

The Legacy of Repression

It is interesting to note that for all of Batista's repressive actions, including tortures, so much criticism was directed against Batista's censorship of the press. Perhaps this was because the effects of censorship were so apparent to the public. The once vibrant—and perhaps reckless—Cuban news media had been intimidated into silence.

When censorship went so far that *Bohemia* magazine discontinued publishing its popular "Seccion en Cuba" ("Cuban Section"), the most widely read part of the magazine, Cubans realized the full extent of press censorship.[69] While the serious and respected *Bohemia* lost circulation as a result of censorship, the humor magazine *Zig Zag* witnessed increased sales. *Zig Zag* thrived during this period because government censors had difficulty interpreting the cartoons' jabs against the government.[70]

Castro himself deserved some credit for publicizing censorship under Batista and making censorship a salient concern. While Batista was imposing media crackdowns, Castro, from his Sierra Maestra stronghold, was promising complete freedom of the press after the revolution.[71] Castro was also carefully cultivating the good will of foreign journalists, such as Matthews.[72] During May 1957, CBS newsman Robert Taber, accompanied by his crew, ventured into the Sierra Maestra and broadcast a documentary on Castro.[73]

Meanwhile, Cuban journalists complained that their U.S. counterparts were getting all the "scoops" because of the restrictions on the local press. On June 8, 1957, the Provincial Collegium of Journalists (the Professional Organization of Journalists) charged that Cuban journalists in Oriente Province covering rebel activities were hindered by the government, while "U.S. correspondents and photographers enjoy all kinds of facilities."[74]

Within Cuba, Castro earned the support of influential political radio commentators. Castro sent messages to Conte Aguero through a secret agent identified by the battle name of "Lt. Hernandez," knowing that Conte Aguero would communicate these messages to the Cuban people. Conte Aguero said that, according to these messages, Castro wanted to "solve the national situation through the wide, wide path of disinterest and grandeur."[75]

In late February 1958, Castro publicly declared, through a communication with Pardo Llada, that he wanted to speak with a coalition of Cuban newspaper journalists in the Sierra Maestra mountains "so that I may tell the people of Cuba through them [the journalists] what they're [the Cuban people] interested in knowing about our attitude at this decisive moment."[76]

The Batista government attempted to silence news about Castro, with little success. In January 1958, 25,000 copies of *Bohemia* were seized by authorities because the issue featured an article about Castro. Some issues that had made been circulated were reportedly snatched from customers' hands. Issues of the humor magazine *Zig Zag* also were also confiscated for reporting about Castro.[77]

During March and April 1958, *Bohemia* correspondent Agustin Alles Soberon became the first Cuban reporter to interview Castro in the Sierra Maestra. He was followed by scores of other Cuban journalists who trekked to the hills to interview the rebel leader.[78]

Castro also allowed the popular Pardo Llada to accompany his rebel troops during the last four months before the overthrow of Batista.[79] Looking back on his short stay with Castro's forces some 30 years later, Pardo Llada said he was not sure why he was allowed in the Sierra Maestra. Pardo Llada hoped to be in charge of the rebel's propaganda radio station, but Carlos Franqui was in charge of Radio Rebelde.[80] Only after Batista fled Cuba and Castro came to power did the Fidelistas use the charismatic Pardo Llada's propaganda skills to solidify Castro's power.

Radio Rebelde was inaugurated on Feb. 24, 1958, boldly claiming to represent an alternative government: "This is Radio Rebelde! Transmitting from the Sierra Maestra, in the Free territory of Cuba."[81] Franqui, regarded at the time as one of the staunchest Communists in the Sierra Maestra, would later say after his defection that he sought to open Radio Rebelde to a variety of views: "I had an idea that radio was a collective voice of the revolution, so I didn't allow the Communists that arrived in the Sierra like Luis Mas Martin and Carlos Rafael Rodriguez to speak on the air. Likewise, I didn't allow Pardo Llada, who arrived at the end of the campaign practically as an exile, to use the radio as a political instrument."[82]

The Fidelistas' radio propaganda campaign from the Sierra Maestra also included popular Cuban radio and television stars who made their way to the rebel encampment to promote the rebel cause over Radio Rebelde. Stars such as Ricardo Martinez, Jorge Enriquez and Guillermo Perez, whom most Cubans thought of as entertainers, not politicians, became news readers for Radio Rebelde and denounced Batista.[83] Perhaps the most famous was Violeta Casals, an actress who regularly appeared on Gaspar Pumarejo's "Escuela de Television" ("School of Television").[84] After Batista fled Cuba, Casals was lauded as "the feminine voice of Radio Rebelde."[85]

While Castro led a coordinated campaign to win the support of Cuban and foreign journalists and promised freedom of the press in the post-Batista era, Batista continued his crackdown on the press and all dissent. Batista's censorship was so unpopular that one of the first press-related actions taken by the newly installed Castro government was to end all pre-publication censorship and arrest all persons who served as censors in the Batista government.[86]

CHAPTER 8
The Precarious Years

*By the late 1950s, Batista's continued hold on power seem-*ed uncertain. The government suffered embarrassing defeats and hit-and-run military attacks. Batista responded to the pressure as he had done in the past—by intensifying censorship to suppress embarrassing news. A presidential decree, issued on Jan. 15, 1957, stated that censorship was needed because "fires in sugar plantations and acts of sabotage and terrorism against private property, public services, business establishments and public schools made suspension of guarantees necessary."[1]

Under the censorship, the Cuban media often refrained from mentioning Castro's name. Even Cuba's advertising industry was intimidated. During late 1957, an advertisement for a U.S. wristwatch that appeared in three Cuban newspapers caused a minor sensation because the bearded model resembled Castro. The company carried the same advertisement in 95 countries. Although the Cuban government did not respond to the advertisement, the watchmaker's Cuban distributor removed it from Cuban newspapers and magazines.[2]

Despite the censorship, a new twice-weekly afternoon English-language newspaper called *The Times of Havana* debuted in the crowded Havana newspaper market in February 1957. Publisher Clarence Moore, who also published the *Cuba Petroleum News Digest,* hoped the *Times* would offer a liberal alternative to the conservative *Havana Post,* a 59-year-old English-language daily.[3]

Many businesses retrenched in the face of censorship and political instability.[4] The broadcasting industry, however, offered the public escape from reality. Some broadcasters, ironically, experienced growth during this politically tumultuous period. By all accounts, Cubans were enthralled by "the give-away programs of TV and radio and in the coupon and label clipping of manufacturers' products which return prizes ranging from toys and lottery tickets to automobiles, apartment houses or TV sets."[5] In addition, Cuban radio and television networks were attracting some of the most famous stars in Latin America and the United States.[6] In the United States, the American Federation of Radio and Television Artists, alarmed by the trend of U.S. entertainers such as Jack Paar and Steve Allen broadcasting their programs from Cuba, demanded that networks that sent performers and technicians to the island must provide workers with $300,000 in life insurance.[7]

In Havana, broadcast magnates Goar Mestre and Gaspar Pumarejo reacted differently to Cuba's volatile political climate. Outwardly, Pumarejo seem unperturbed. He invested in a daring economic venture to bring color television to Cuba. After Batista fled, Pumarejo was accused by the new government of having unjustly profited through his connections with the Batista government.

Mestre reacted to the precarious political situation in two ways. First, he used his prominent position as one of Latin America's most renowned broadcasters to denounce Batista government censorship during his numerous business trips abroad. A second and more practical approach by Goar Mestre to the volatile political situation was to invest money overseas in case he would lose CMQ.

Television for the Provinces

During the final days of the Batista dictatorship, a group of businessmen in Camaguey, about 350 miles from Havana, planned to start Cuba's first television station in the island's interior that was not part of a Havana-based network. The station went on the air several months after Batista fled Cuba.

Television Camaguey, Channel 11, started airing programs in Camaguey on March 10, 1959, three months after Batista fled Cuba.[8] The 2,000-watt station was officially inaugurated a month later. At the time, Camaguey had 165,000 people and 15,000 television receivers.[9] Both CMQ and Telemundo relayed their Havana programs to "repeater" stations in Camaguey, but neither carried unique programming for the province.[10]

Antonio Milla Espinosa, co-owner of the Milla and Cebrian advertising agency in Camaguey, believed that there was a market for a local station in Camaguey. With his partners, Juan B. Castrillon, the owner of La Voz de Camagueyano radio station, and Manuel Barreiro, a lawyer, Television Camaguey, S.A., Milla rented a three-story building and invested $200,000 for equipment in March 1958. Because of equipment delivery problems, the station did not go on the air until a year later.

Milla, the president of the company, conceded that Television Camaguey could not compete against CMQ and Telemundo's lavish entertainment programming and quality news productions. But it could offer distinctive local entertainment and news. Of Television Camaguey's staff of 39 employees, about nine or 10 were in the news department at any time. The station carried one-hour news programs at noon, 6 p.m. and 10 p.m. It also had its own van and camera crew cover local news.[11]

Borrowing from the "round table" programs common on Havana television stations, Television Camaguey also aired a program called "Panel de Prensa" ("The Press Panel"), moderated by Juvenil Adan.[12] Occasionally, notable Havana journalists such as Agustin Tamargo and Jose Pardo Llada, when in Camaguey, appeared on the program.[13] Television Camaguey also featured a variety program called "La Corte de la Felicidad" ("The Court of Happiness"), based on the successful amateur-variety program formula established by Gaspar Pumarejo's "Escuela de Television" ("School of Television"). The program was hosted by Alfredo Vivar.[14]

Since money was always a problem at Television Camaguey, the station also carried a good deal of free promotional films supplied by foreign embassies.[15] Still, the station could count on famous entertainers from Havana to appear on the station gratis when they were visiting Camaguey. Even Mexican and Argentine actors with contracts in Havana night clubs and radio and television stations were sometimes persuaded to appear when they were in the province. Milla said, "We had to beg a lot. We didn't have much money, but we received a good deal of sympathy."[16]

Color Television

In addition to the plans to start the island's first provincial television station, the last days of the Batista dictatorship also featured the first color television station. The station was launched by the indomitable Pumarejo.

In 1956, Pumarejo obtained the rights from the Ministry of Communications to broadcast over Channel 12, incorporated as Tele-Color, S.A.[17] He then raised $1 million from a number of business partners to launch what was billed as the first "all-color" television station

8. THE PRECARIOUS YEARS

in the world. Stations in the United States that carried color programming were broadcasting black and white programs during certain hours.

The station's transmitter was placed atop the newly constructed 30-story Havana Hilton Hotel, across from the CMQ's Radiocentro Building. Channel 12's studio was on the first floor. The station was equipped with a 10-kilowatt remote-control transmitter, two cameras, two 16-millimeter projectors, one 35-millimeter projector, a 58-foot-high "standing wave" antenna installed on the 30th floor and a master control room on the third floor.[18] The station had test patterns and some programming on the air by December 1957. It began broadcasting regular programming on March 19, 1958.[19]

For Pumarejo, getting Cuba's first color television station on the air must have given him the same satisfaction as when he debuted Cuba's first television station seven years earlier. The feat brought him publicity and perhaps a chance to beat his business enemy, Goar Mestre.

For years, CMQ-TV had hinted that it might bring color programming to Cuba. In 1954, Manolo Cores, CMQ's executive vice president of programming, told a Havana television writer that a major obstacle preventing CMQ from expanding into color was not the cost of the equipment, but the lack of color receivers in Havana: "We could have color TV equipment in Cuba in a few months, but what would we do with it? How many advertisers would spend their money in a way of publicity that lacked its main objective, that is to reach the public? . . . I believe that four or five years will elapse before sufficient color sets will be in the market that will warrant any investment by our advertisers."[20]

Rather than invest in color television, CMQ had opted to stake its future in videotape technology. In 1956, the Ampex Corp. in the United States developed an experimental VTR (video tape recorder) for television stations to record live programs onto magnetic tape for later use. The video copies required no film processing. Another advantage was that the VTR tapes could be erased and reused. Particularly important, the videos were of such high quality that viewers could not distinguish them from live productions. By contrast, the existing "kinescope" technology of filming programs from special monitors required processing and yielded grainy recordings. CMQ ordered a VTR from Ampex Corp. By the time that Ampex was ready to ship the device in 1958, the political situation in Cuba was so risky that CMQ did not take delivery.[21]

When Pumarejo announced his decision to start broadcasting in color, there were only 509 color television sets in Cuba, including units in stores and on promotional display in Esso service stations. At the time, a 21-inch color set sold for about $700 in Cuba, about twice that of a black and white unit.[22] Even in the United States, where some stations were broadcasting part of the day in color, color television was not a great success. Pumarejo responded to the critics by reminding them of similar criticisms when he started Union Radio TV: "As for the arguments about the lack of technicians, the difficulties of installations, operation and repair—we have been listening to such talk since the days when black and white television was introduced in Cuba seven years ago. And now it's a solid Cuban industry."[23]

Pumarejo met with RCA President David Sarnoff during his visits to New York. Sarnoff apparently encouraged Pumarejo to start a color television station.[24] Pumarejo told a Havana journalist that Sarnoff told him that the reason Americans were slow to purchase color television sets was because there was so little color programming available. Rather than wait for the number of sets to increase to the point where it was financially feasible to broadcast color programs, Pumarejo decided to broadcast color programs to promote the sales of color sets. Pumarejo decided to go into color television in a big way—with an "all-color" station broadcasting 20 hours a day from 6 a.m. to 2 a.m.[25]

Actually, RCA's problems with color television in the United States were more complex than the public's unwillingness to purchase sets. The Federal Communications Commission had approved a standardized color system developed by RCA, the parent company of NBC, in 1953. The first color programs were broadcast by NBC during the 1954–1955 season. At that time, NBC was broadcasting 12 to 15 hours a week of color programming. But the other American networks refused to broadcast color programs because RCA held most of the important patents on color-compatible equipment. They did not want to spur growth in a color system that would benefit their competitor. Even as late as 1960, there were no color programs on CBS and ABC.[26]

Noting Pumarejo's meeting with Sarnoff, CMQ's Abel Mestre speculated that Sarnoff might have had his own reasons for persuading Pumarejo to start a color television station. With a color station in Havana, Mestre said, Sarnoff could show American stations reluctant to invest in color technology that even a small Caribbean island was broadcasting color programs.[27] Abel Mestre scoffed at the idea of establishing color television: "Color TV was certainly not one of the things that we were worried about. This was happening in 1957, 1958. Hell, we had so many problems that I didn't think that anybody in his right mind would invest money in Cuba at this time. We were worried as hell. The political situation in Cuba was very dangerous."[28]

Clifford W. Slaybaugh, RCA's manager of worldwide sales, who sold radio and television equipment to both the Mestre brothers and

8. THE PRECARIOUS YEARS

Pumarejo, believed that Pumarejo was in a race to beat CMQ to the air with color television. As for whether Pumarejo had "beaten" his enemy Goar Mestre by getting color television on the air, Slaybaugh said: "I'm not sure that he [Mestre] was caught with his pants down. He didn't want to do a half-ass job, if I may say so. It takes a lot of planning to get color broadcasting on the air. It's an operation of great magnitude."[29]

For all Pumarejo's efforts, the station was plagued by sound and transmission problems.[30] The programming was remarkably similar and amateurish, combining color films with voice-over commentaries. Programs such as "Social Life," featured films of banquets, weddings and testimonials, while "Sports Life" showed sports footage supplemented with commentary. Renowned historian Hermino Portell Vila hosted "International Day," in which he provided political commentary to accompany film footage from around the world. "Doorways to Havana" aired footage of events in the capital and famous people arriving and departing Havana, filmed at Rancho Boyeros Airport.[31]

Channel 12 received some kudos, if not high ratings, for its commitment to news and public affairs programming. The popular Jose Pardo Llada occasionally appeared in round table programs interviewing prominent politicians. The station showed color films of fires and accidents and other breaking news stories. The color processing required three or four hours, sometimes putting the station at a competitive disadvantage. Perhaps more worthwhile were the color feature film segments made by Channel 12 correspondents in Miami, Madrid, New York and Mexico City.[32]

One Havana entertainment columnist wrote of the programming: "Pumarejo better do something about improving the programs of his 'all color' Channel 12. The quality of the pictures shown is pretty bad and interviews being made by some of the boys are 'just terrible.' Makes one wonder if it's worth while buying a color set to see 'this.' How about it?"[33]

Carlos Castaneda who, with Lisandro Otero, hosted a noon newscast at Channel 12, said that there were rumors Pumarejo had acquired money from the Batista government to start the station. Pumarejo, however, had never taken public stands on political issues. In addition, few people accused Channel 12 or any of Pumarejo's enterprises of being an outright Batistiano organ that propagandized on Batista's behalf. Still, many Cubans were suspicious as to how Pumarejo raised the capital to start a color television station while the nation was in political turmoil.[34]

Pumarejo, meanwhile, was as popular as ever among his fans. Some Hogar Club members organized as the Committee of Lisa (a neighborhood in the city of Marianaw) and, without authorization, purchased advertisements in newspapers and magazines claiming that Pumarejo was a candidate for senator. Perhaps suspecting that the organization was not comprised of fans but of foes trying to embarrass Pumarejo by linking him with the Batista government, Pumarejo unsuccessfully attempted to locate the group's members. Pumarejo purchased signed, full-page advertisements denying he harbored political ambitions or was associated with any political stands: "I maintain friendly relations with personalities and very prestigious figures from the political world and the government as well as different sectors of the [political] opposition."[35] During a speech before the Cuban Association of Radio and TV Columnists (CARTV), Pumarejo said that he was "a radio and TV man with no political connections."[36]

Castaneda said that Pumarejo had established relations with wealthy people and advertisers in Cuba over the years whom he could have turned to for money. In particular, businessmen Eduardo Caballero and Manuel Llerandi, the main financial backers of Pumarejo's "Escuela de Television" ("School of Television") and "Hogar Club" ("Home Club") operations, were willing to fund Pumarejo's enterprises. Pumarejo continued to operate "The School of Television" and the "Home Club" while he was in charge of Channel 12.[37] The rumors of secret assistance from Batista continued to haunt Pumarejo after Fidel Castro came to power.

Goar Mestre's Foreign Ventures

For Goar Mestre, government censorship became so severe during the final days of the Batista dictatorship that Mestre went into self-imposed exile from September 1957 to February 1958. In exile, he traveled throughout Latin America and the United States to protest a Batista decree that Mestre asserted had "converted [Cuban] broadcasters into mere puppets of the government."[38] While in exile, he wielded his influence with foreign broadcasters and the Inter-American Association of Broadcasters (IAAB) to press the Batista government to lift the restriction.[39] Mestre returned to Cuba after an IAAB delegation had met with Batista in 1958 and persuaded the dictator to withdraw the decree.

Upon his return, Mestre was so disgusted with the incessant censorship that, despite the protestations from his brother, Abel, he clandestinely funneled about $150,000 to Castro through supporters over the next few months.[40] As Goar Mestre explained: "We saw this Robin

Hood. And we said, 'Let's support this guy, maybe he's honest.' This is where we made our great mistake, and we paid dearly for it."[41]

While there is no way to verify Goar Mestre's claim that he gave money to Castro, it was not unusual for wealthy Cuban entrepreneurs to send the rebel leader financial support. During the last months of the Batista government, many Cuban bankers and entrepreneurs secretly donated money to Castro's rebels.[42] Mestre said he sent money to Castro not out of any admiration for the rebel leader but because the censorship and political climate was making normal business operations impossible.[43]

At the same time that Mestre was protesting the unbearable political situation inside Cuba, he was also preparing for a worse-case scenario by investing in broadcasting ventures overseas. The overseas investments proved to be valuable after his Cuban media empire was confiscated by the Castro government in September 1960.[44]

Regardless of the political situation in Cuba, Mestre might have invested abroad as part of his normal business operations. By the mid-1950s, Goar Mestre had joined an elite club of well-known Latin American broadcasters which included Emilio Azcarraga of Mexico, Genaro Delgado Parker of Peru and William Phelps of Venezuela. These entrepreneurs saw broadcasting as a regionwide venture that transcended national borders.

As early as 1954, CMQ-TV entered into a contract with the Ponce de Leon Broadcasting Corp. in San Juan, Puerto Rico, for the construction of WAPA-TV, Channel 4.[45] The Mestre brothers acquired 20 percent of WAPA's shares, the maximum the Federal Communications Commission (FCC) permitted foreigners to invest in U.S. broadcasting outlets. With partial Mestre ownership of WAPA, the Mestre brothers brought popular talent to the Puerto Rican station, including two of Cuba's most popular comedians under contract with CMQ, Leopoldo Fernandez and Mimi Cal.[46] CMQ lent money to local entrepreneurs and former U.S. district attorney Jose Ramon Quinones, the U.S. owner of WAPA, to purchase shares in the station, so in fact the Mestre brothers exercised more leverage over the station's operations than was reflected by their 20 percent ownership.[47]

In 1957, Goar Mestre founded Television Interamericana, S.A. (TISA), a company that distributed dubbed U.S. movies and some Latin American films throughout Latin America.[48] Mestre invited three other Latin American broadcasting entrepreneurs to join him in TISA—Phelps, owner of Radio Caracas Television in Venezuela; Azcarraga, owner of Mexico's largest radio and television networks; and Angel Ramos, owner of WKAQ in Puerto Rico.[49] Mestre preferred to own film production companies rather than stations because Latin American nations had laws restricting the ownership of stations to nationals, but little or no restrictions on film production companies.[50]

With the exception of the Puerto Rican venture, Abel Mestre did not join his brother in foreign media ventures. The eldest brother, Luis Augusto, died in 1958. After fleeing Cuba in 1960, Abel Mestre settled in Miami and scorned the idea of foreign investments in broadcasting: "I have always been the type of person who believes that radio and TV should be owned by the people who live in the country. I don't think that radio and TV is something to be exploited by foreigners."[51]

TISA sought to expand commercial television into Colombia by providing programming to a group of local investors. TISA's Colombian venture proved to be a challenge. Television was established in Colombia shortly after dictator Gen. Gustavo Rojas Pinilla came to power in 1953. It was organized under the State Office of Information and Press, directly under the presidency. Although Rojas Pinilla was ousted in 1957 and Colombia became a democracy, regulations concerning television ownership remained in effect. As a result, there was a government monopoly on television.[52]

The U.S. networks were investing in television throughout much of the region at this time. But they avoided Colombia, seeing it as a hostile business environment and a risky financial investment.[53] The Colombian government looked askance at Latin American broadcast entrepreneurs such as Mestre, Azcarraga, Ramos and Phelps, viewing them as Latin American versions of U.S. network entrepreneurs.[54]

Despite the negative attitude of the Colombian government toward foreign investment, Mestre persuaded his partners in TISA to expand into Colombia. He felt that the U.S. networks' views about Colombia were shortsighted. He was certain that there was a large audience for commercial television in Colombia.

It happened that at this time the Colombian government planned to expand government television throughout the nation. But the government lacked the financial resources to establish a television system.[55] As a "goodwill gesture," Mestre convinced his partners in TISA to provide the government television monopoly with $30,000 worth of equipment and the promise of more to follow. The money was offered with the understanding that the equipment was to be used only for educational programming. In the event that the government used the money and equipment for commercial programming, according to the contract, TISA would be reimbursed for its expenses.[56] As Mestre said of TISA's goodwill gesture in a broadcasting industry publication: "TISA believes in give and take, not just take."[57]

TISA's efforts proved unsuccessful. Colombia did not develop commercial television until 1965, when businesswoman Consuela de Montejo, who had worked for the McCann Erickson advertising agency, successfully bid for the first television concession and established Teletigre. With the financial assistance of the American Broadcasting Company (ABC), she brought North American filmed programs to Colombia. She was so successful that when de her contract expired in 1970, powerful political and business forces in Colombia conspired against her renewing the contract.[58]

Mestre's Television Empire in Argentina

After Fidel Castro came to power in 1959, Goar Mestre, fearful that CMQ's assets would be confiscated, secretly established television production companies in Argentina and Peru. To conceal his dealings in Argentina, he would fly from Havana to Miami, and then from Miami to Buenos Aires.[59] These ventures were in partnership with investors in the respective nations and the Columbia Broadcasting System (CBS) in the United States. Also in 1959, Mestre created Goar Mestre & Associates, a Panamanian-based company, to offer television management services.[60]

As Mestre described Argentina at this time, the country was a television market waiting to be served. Primarily because of the influence of former President Juan Domingo Peron, broadcasting developed along a completely different direction in Argentina than most other Latin American nations. Since 1951, Argentina had only one government-operated television station, Radio Belgrano–TV, Channel 7. Although the state owned the broadcast media, they were primarily subsidized by advertising. Even after the overthrow of Peron in 1955, the government continued its ownership of the broadcast media.[61]

The first serious steps toward privatization of Argentina's broadcast media occurred in 1959. The government licensed three television stations to broadcast in the Buenos Aires vicinity. All three had ties to one of the U.S. television networks. With the assistance of CBS and Time-Life, Inc., Mestre hoped to establish Argentina's first privately operated television station. As in Cuba, Mestre's plan to be "first" in privately operated television was dashed. Compania Argentina de Television, Channel 9, went on the air several months before his station.[62]

Legally, Mestre was never involved in Argentine television broadcasting, only television production. Argentine law required television stations be owned by Argentine citizens. He skirted this law in Argentina and elsewhere in Latin America by owning film production companies that provided exclusive programming to stations and networks. In Argentina, Mestre joined in partnership with CBS, Time-Life, Inc. and several Argentine entrepreneurs to form the Proartel (Producciones Argentinas de Television) production company.[63] Proartel also purchased Argentine films, claiming to have acquired up to 90 percent of the country's total production from 1937 to 1955. Finally, Proartel set up dubbing studios. The first foreign program to be dubbed was the American Western series "Rawhide."[64] Eventually, the company expanded to provide programming to a dozen stations throughout Argentina, including two government-owned stations.[65]

In Argentina, Mestre's wife, Alicia Martin Mestre, a native-born Argentine citizen, acquired controlling interest of Rio de la Plata TV, Channel 13, in Buenos Aires. Proartel became the licensed supplier of programming to Channel 13, which went on the air on Oct. 1, 1960.[66]

It was ironic that Mestre should have found success in Argentina. During the late 1940s, Mestre was *persona non grata* in Argentina when, in his capacity as president of the Inter-American Association of Broadcasters (IAAB), he had personally attacked the Peron government and accused it of muzzling the Argentine broadcast media.[67]

Mestre's second Latin American base was in Peru. Starting Oct. 1, 1959, Mestre and his partners inaugurated the Pantel production company in Lima. Pantel supplied all the programming for Panamericana Television, Channel 5, and four other Peruvian stations. Mestre and his American partners at CBS sold their shares of Pantel to local entrepreneurs just before the production company was among several media organizations confiscated by the revolutionary government of Gen. Juan Velasco Alvarado in 1968.[68]

From his base in Argentina as head of Proartel, Mestre worked in partnership with U.S. and Venezuelan investors in 1964 to establish Proventel, a television production company in Venezuela. Proventel provided programming to Cadena Venezolana de Television (CVTV), Channel 8, in Caracas, part of a five-station network.[69] The Venezuelan venture proved to be more challenging than his past foreign enterprises. Unlike his Argentine and Peruvian ventures, where there was little competition and no established television industry, Caracas had two stations supplied with U.S. programming, Channel 2 (Radio Caracas TV, with NBC ties) and Channel 4 (Venevision, with ABC ties).[70] Adding to the stiff competition, CVTV's transmitter was poorly situated, resulting in bad reception. The station lost $13 million before Mestre and his partners sold the station in 1967.[71]

A Meeting with Franco

Another attempt by Mestre to expand into television abroad, this time in Spain, did not get beyond the proposal stage. In 1962, through a business connection established by CBS president William S. Paley, Mestre visited Spain with Merle Jones, president of CBS International. The two men traveled to Spain with the intention of establishing a joint Proartel–CBS television film distribution company. After a series of long interviews with Manuel Fraga Iribarne, Spain's minister of communications and tourism, Fraga Iribarne arranged for Mestre and Jones to meet with Generalissimo Francisco Franco. The scheduled 15-minute interview with Franco appeared to go smoothly and lasted 45 minutes. Franco was pleased to hear that Proartel had access to dubbed versions of his favorite U.S. program, "Perry Mason."[72]

The evening after the interview, Mestre received a call at his hotel from Fraga Iribarne saying that the meeting went well and it was likely that Franco would approve the deal. Then Fraga Iribarne requested a favor from Mestre and Jones. He said that CBS newsman Walter Cronkite was in Spain shooting a program for his documentary series, "Twentieth Century." In fact, Cronkite interviewed Franco shortly after his meeting with Mestre and Jones. Mestre and Jones were not even aware that Cronkite was in Spain.

Fraga Iribarne asked Mestre to ask Jones to use his influence with CBS and Cronkite to make the program favorable to Franco and Spain. Mestre told Fraga Iribarne that he would talk with Jones. But even as he put down the telephone, Mestre knew that the minister's request would cause difficulties. In Latin American business dealings, it was common to request favors after granting favors. From Fraga Iribarne's view, there was nothing unusual in his request to influence Cronkite's program. But the U.S.-educated Mestre also knew that in the United States the news and management aspects of television were separate and staunchly defended their independence. He knew that NBC's news department would be angered by a request from management to change the program in any way.[73]

As expected, Jones was shocked by the request. Jones suggested that Mestre explain to Fraga Iribarne that it would be impossible to honor the request. But Mestre felt that it was not worth trying to explain the situation to Fraga Iribarne. Instead, Mestre suggested giving Fraga Iribarne the impression that Jones spoke with the news department and tried to influence the coverage of the program:

I said that two things can happen here. If the program is favorable to Franco, we're in. If the program is unfavorable to Franco, we're out. Now, if we tell him that we can't do anything, we're out from the beginning. So why don't we play the 50 percent chance that we have and pretend that we're going to do something and if we fail we're out. But who knows what the program can say. He [Jones] became very concerned. I think that he was disgusted with me at such a proposal. And he communicated to Fraga Iribarne that he wouldn't attempt to influence the program. And Mr. Fraga Iribarne wouldn't have anything to do with us. And you know what? When the program ["Twentieth Century"] came out, it was favorable to Franco anyway.[74]

Mestre's collaboration with CBS in Argentina was followed by other U.S. network ventures into Argentina. NBC and ABC each established contracts to supply programming to stations in Buenos Aires.[75] But NBC and ABC's ventures in Argentina, like elsewhere in Latin America, were not as profitable as the networks had hoped, and NBC soon withdrew from the Argentine market.[76] As one NBC executive said of his network's Latin American television ventures during the late 1960s and early 1970s: "We simply overestimated the market. . . . For a while everyone thought it was a new frontier. We quickly found out it wasn't."[77]

Mestre said that the failures of the U.S. networks in Latin American television should not be attributed to market miscalculation. He argued that the U.S. networks failed to provide Latin Americans with Latin American cultural programming. "The Americans failed to realize that television here is a different animal from television in the United States," Mestre said. "People in Argentina don't mind the occasional American program, but what they really like are shows with local flavor."[78]

Wherever he traveled throughout Latin America and expanded into television, Mestre was a fervent advocate of government non-intervention in television. When Mestre was interviewed in 1969 by U.S. journalism scholar David Manning White for *Television Quarterly* magazine, he restated his well-known position in favor of private ownership and operation of television. Mestre also used the interview with White to criticize government-operated Channel 7 in Buenos Aires. Although Channel 7 was government-owned, it depended upon commercial advertising and competed against Channel 13 and other privately owned stations:

[T]he present government, which has done such a wonderful job of really fostering private enterprise, has not been consistent to the point of applying this philosophy and this policy to the government television station. . . . Nevertheless, the Channel 7 operation has lost hundreds of millions of dollars and the only comforting thing from this experience, and this is very

8. THE PRECARIOUS YEARS

important in our [Latin American] countries, is that once again it has been eloquently proven that private enterprise can do things better than the government.[79]

On Aug. 1, 1974, Mestre's Argentine holdings were confiscated by the government of Isabel Peron. "It was like in Cuba all over again," Mestre recalled, "even worse."[80] In 1983, with a democratically elected government in Argentina, 71-year-old Mestre made a failed bid to go into Argentine television again. In partnership with a group of Argentine entrepreneurs, Mestre sought to convert Argentina's largest motion picture company into a television production center called Teleinde (Teleproducciones Independientes S.A.).[81]

CHAPTER 9
Castro Comes to Power

*Batista had spent New Year's Eve 1959 at the Camp Co-*lumbia military barracks receiving reports about the deteriorating political situation. At a little past 2 a.m., he boarded a DC-4 aircraft for the Dominican Republic. As the plane bearing the dictator lifted off the airfield, what would later be known as the "pre-Castro" era came to an abrupt end. Many Cubans, including the island's broadcasters, hoped that the republic would return to the laissez faire democracy that existed before Batista's 1952 coup.

After Batista's downfall, Cubans of every class recounted how they had always despised the hated dictator. Once a sense of normality returned, Fidel Castro and his rebels marched triumphantly into Havana and were hailed as liberators. In February 1959, Castro was appointed prime minister. Manuel Urrutia Lleo, a respected judge, became provisional president. Free elections were promised and, for a short while, it appeared to many Cubans that there would indeed be a return to business as usual.

Cuban and U.S. businesspeople alike sought to curry favor with the popular new government, purchasing advertisements in the semiofficial government newspaper *Revolucion* and proclaiming support for the new regime.[1] For their part, Cuban broadcasters recounted their contributions to Batista's downfall and their tribulations during his regime. Many had their licenses suspended for airing critical reports. Others were imprisoned or exiled. While the broadcasters' stories of their struggles against Batista were often based in truth, *New York Times* correspondent Charles Friedman warned that the accounts were often exaggerated: "It is questionable how many of them [broadcasters] helped the rebel movement. As years pass, no doubt the number will grow phenomenally.

Long after the revolution of 1933, Cubans who were small children then were boasting of having manned the barricades against the dictator Machado."[2]

Speaking at a convention of international broadcasters in the United States a few weeks after the revolution, CMQ's Goar Mestre expressed relief for the end of "seven miserable years, during which we were harassed, persecuted and annoyed by the government."[3] He also said that CMQ experienced difficulties during the days after Batista's flight, but "came through very nicely, along with other Cuban broadcasters who took an impartial position."[4] Mestre said that CMQ lost an estimated $100,000 (U.S.) in commercial revenue during the three days while rebels occupied CMQ studies. He added, however, that he was gratified by CMQ's role in "letting people stay at home and watch the revolution on TV instead of going out in the streets."[5]

Neither Mestre nor most broadcast owners were in their stations during the morning hours when Batista fled Cuba. The highly lauded coverage following Batista's flight was the work of station employees. Mestre's comments about enduring advertising losses seemed inappropriate in the context of the revolution. He said his naive remarks reflected his enthusiasm over Batista's flight.[6]

Commercial radio and television's role in the revolution was that of an information provider. During the last days of 1958, Cubans were glued to their radio sets. The country was rife with rumors of a coup d'etat, and "every traditional indication, based on decades of Latin American history, pointed to the imminent downfall of the government."[7]

Cuban radio and television also served as a stabilizing agent during crisis. Station managers were keenly aware of the retribution killings and rampant crime in 1933 after the collapse of the Machado dictatorship.[8] Major stations voluntarily withheld reporting rumors of Batista's flight.[9] Even after the stations received confirmation of Batista's departure, they continued to withhold the information until authority could assert itself.[10]

While some small radio stations reported Batista's flight, these reports were not taken seriously while the big radio and television outlets continued to broadcast their usual programs. The first credible report of Batista's retreat came from Telemundo's political reporter, Carlos Lechuga. He made the announcement and then launched into a denunciation of Batista. Journalists John Dorschner and Roberto Fabricio attributed the celebrations in Havana's streets over Batista's departure to Lechuga's announcement: "After that [Lechuga's announcement], there was no doubt that the rumors were true. The streets became a stage for celebration, a singing and chanting and waving of banners."[11]

Cuban broadcasters were praised for maintaining calm during the crisis.[12] For example, at Gaspar Pumarejo's color television station the announcement of Batista's flight and its implications were explained by *Chicago Tribune* reporter Jules Dubois, a respected journalist in Cuba.[13]

After Batista's aircraft left Cuba, Major Gen. Eulogio Cantillo, head of the Army, withheld announcing Batista's departure for nine hours.[14] Upon announcing Batista's departure, Cantillo invited members of the Cuban Press Bloc (the newspaper association) and the Cuban Federation of Radio and Television Broadcasters to Camp Columbia.[15] Miguel Angel Quevedo of *Bohemia* and Sergio Carbo of *Prensa Libre*, angered over Cantillo's long silence about Batista's flight, refused Cantillo's invitation.[16] CMQ's Abel Mestre, Radio Progreso's Manolo Fernandez and Radio Salas' Guillermo Salas were not sure why they were invited to Camp Columbia.[17] Abel Mestre suspected that they were invited to "bear witness to history."[18]

In Camp Columbia, Abel Mestre was privy to how the last bastion of Batista's military handled the crisis.[19] He was not encouraged. Mestre recalled: "I asked Cantillo, 'What do we do now? Can you suggest something?' And he said, 'No, I can't suggest anything. We will have to wait for Fidel Castro.' So then we knew that we were in a hell of big trouble."[20]

Civic Resistance Movement

While Cuba's top military leaders were locked in their barracks and fretting over how to deal with the crisis, Havana representatives of Castro's July 26th Movement, known as the Civic Resistance Movement (CRM), received word of Batista's flight hours before the official announcement and executed prepared plans for Castro's transition to power. The CRM, established in early 1957 as a fifth column for the rebel cause, consisted of middle and upper class professionals organized in secret cells.[21]

The propaganda arm of the CRM coordinated broadcasts to inform Cubans about the political situation and maintain order. For the conservative upper classes and businesspeople, many of whom were leery of Castro, the CRM's propaganda chief who appeared on CMQ-TV was a reassuring sight. He was Emilio Guede, a Havana advertising executive who was far from a wild-eyed radical.

"We were very aware that the public depended upon broadcasting," Guede said, "and we were careful about how we conducted ourselves. There were no police on the streets and we received reports that mobs of people had ransacked police stations and military headquarters and

9. CASTRO COMES TO POWER

took arms. The situation was out of control. We believed it was our job to maintain order."[22]

After meeting with CRM members, Guede, assisted by a university student named Vicente Baez, converted CMQ's studios into the heart of the July 26th Movement's information complex.[23] For the next three days, almost all of Cuba's radio and television stations were centered in the makeshift revolutionary network in the 10-story Radiocentro Building. Guede and Baez did not meet the Mestre brothers in CMQ. Some U.S. television reporters also used CMQ's facilities as their outpost, working beside the rebels. The news director of a Miami television station praised U.S. and Cuban coverage emanating from CMQ's facilities: "For the first time in two years, the Cuban people were getting uncensored news."[24]

Guede and Baez found CMQ's technicians eager to assist in airing the CRM broadcasts.[25] Guede's description was confirmed by Goar Mestre: "They [the CRM] never took over or commandeered the facilities of CMQ. They found everyone in the organization decidedly cooperative."[26] A few stations were not part of the revolutionary network. Radio Progreso was commandeered by another revolutionary organization, Directororio Revolucionario (Revolutionary Directorate), the only serious rival organization to the July 26th Movement.[27]

Citizens ranging from ordinary people to prominent businesspeople walked into CMQ's studios to express their opinions over the air about the national situation. Guede and Baez had no compunctions about refusing to give the microphones to certain speakers. For instance, one bitter young man wanted to talk about how he had been tortured by Batista's soldiers. Guede feared that the man's story would fuel public anger, so he talked the man into stating that this was not the time to seek revenge.[28]

The fear that Batistianos might escape justice became acute after news spread that the hated Rolando Masferrer Rojas, who headed his own private army and was responsible for atrocities in the countryside, had fled by yacht to Florida. Groups of vigilantes searched for Batistianos in hiding. Hospitals called CMQ to complain that mobs were stopping ambulances to ferret out Batistianos.[29] Guede aired announcements calling on citizens to permit ambulances to pass without hindrance: "We told them that it was better for Batistianos to get away than to have innocent people die."[30]

Guede also ordered militiamen to protect the *Diario de la Marina* building after learning that mobs were marching on the newspaper plant, as they had done to *El Tiempo,* operated by Masferrer. But Guede said that *La Marina,* though conservative, was not a Batistiano organ. He maintained that there was a place for *La Marina* in the new Cuba that would respect press freedom.[31]

Promises of Press Freedom

Castro, meanwhile, delivered broadcasts from the Sierra Maestra, in preparation for his advance into Havana. Among his many promises, he promised a return to freedom of the press. It was clear, however, that Batista supporters would not share the new freedom. Several Batistiano newspapers and radio stations were confiscated by on Jan. 1 and later converted into government organs.[32] These included the newspapers *Manana* (Jose Lopez Vilaboy, director, 55,000 circ.), *Pueblo* (F. Valdes Gomez, director, 28,000 circ.), *Ataja* (Alberto Salas Amaro, director, 32,000 circ.), *El Tiempo* (Rolando Masferrer, director, NA circ.) and *Alerta* (Ramon Vasconcelos, director, 10,000 circ.).[33]

Radio outlets associated with Batista were also confiscated. In most cases, the confiscations were of small stations. However, on Jan. 12, 1959, the government confiscated the 11-station Circuito Nacional Cubano (CNC) radio network. CNC had been allegedly acquired by Batista during the late 1950s, after the death of owner Jose Piedra.[34] In the provinces, the government confiscated Radio Mambi and Radio Ten-Ten.[35]

As part of its commitment to freedom of the press, the new government eliminated press subsidies. It also announced that it would bring charges against the last two ministers of the interior, under whose authority all censorship was exercised.[36] Evangelina de la Llera, chief censor under Batista, was arrested. Ernesto de la Fe, Batista's Minister of Information from 1952 to 1954, was also arrested and languished in La Cabana prison where he claimed that "all Cuban newspapermen and many foreign newsmen knew I was Batista's enemy."[37]

Press Criticisms of Castro

While the Cuban press generally supported the new government, there were criticisms. The criticisms often dealt with matters such as excessive zeal in administering social reform programs or pinning Castro down on the promised date for elections. Although there was no formal press censorship, with censors assigned to news organizations, the press treated Castro gingerly because he was immensely popular. Further, Castro was not afraid to wield his popularity to publicly criticize the press and intimidate it into silence.

In January 1959, Castro vented his rage against the humor weekly

9. CASTRO COMES TO POWER

Zig Zag after it had published a cartoon portraying former Batista loyalists lining up behind Castro. The cartoon was sufficiently ambiguous to be interpreted as either an attack on Castro or on Batista supporters hiding behind Castro's popularity. Castro threatened to lead a public boycott against the magazine. *Zig Zag* immediately refrained from carrying cartoons that could be interpreted as critical of Castro.[38]

It was relatively easy to intimidate the domestic press into submission. Overt government censorship was not needed. As a 1960 report in U.S. magazine *TV Guide* observed: "There is not much suppression of the news and views by the Castro government. But commentators and writers censor themselves, for the most part."[39] It was more difficult to intimidate the foreign press. The government responded with indignation against the foreign press' portrayal of the public trials and executions of Batista henchmen as "bloodbaths." The men being tried en masse in the Havana Sports Palace before jeering crowds were among the most hated men in Cuba.[40] In at least one case, an execution was delayed until dawn so that photographers could photograph the administration of justice in better light.[41]

Although Cuban media coverage of the trials were largely uncritical, there was no dispute about the quality of the television coverage. As the *TV Guide* report also noted: "Cuban coverage of special events is superb. It's generally pooled broadcasting, with all stations carrying the same rally or pubic function, using live cameras on the ground and even two or three in helicopters."[42]

As part of the government's "Operation Truth" campaign to show its side of the Cuban story to Cubans and the world audience, the morgues were opened and Cuban television carried scenes of disinterments of mass graves of victims shot, burned or buried alive. Testimonies were recounted of torture by scorching feet, mutilating bodies and extracting fingernails.[43] Castro himself appeared as a prosecution witness against an accused Batista henchman, delivering a four-and-a-half hour harangue against the doomed man.[44]

New York Times journalist Herbert Matthews defended Castro against the criticisms from the foreign press. He published an article entitled "Journalism and Its Responsibilities" in which he criticized U.S. press coverage of the executions for contributing to deteriorating U.S.–Cuban relations.[45] *Chicago Tribune* correspondent Jules Dubois also supported Castro. Not surprisingly, the Cuban government lionized Matthews and Dubois as the best U.S. journalists.[46] While Matthews would remain loyal to Castro, Dubois would grew disillusioned and become one of Castro's most fervid foreign press critics.[47]

Sins of the Past

Scholars of Cuban news media have frequently referred to the "corruption" and "irresponsibility" of the pre-Castro media. Cuban broadcast scholar John Spicer Nichols described the Cuban broadcast media prior to Castro as "seedy, censored, venal puppets of government and industry."[48] Marvin Alisky, a longtime observer of the Latin American press, wrote that Batista employed "subsidies and bribes more than censorship, and his system flourished as painless control until his ouster on Dec. 31, 1958."[49]

The practices of press subsidies and bribes during the Batista haunted the news media after Castro came to power. Lists of newspapers and journalists that had accepted bribes and subsidies were distributed in Havana during the first days after the revolution. A partial list appeared in *Revolucion*. The U.S. Embassy in Havana obtained the list, which indicated that the Batista government was paying $217,300 each month to Cuba's newspapers and journalists. According to the list, *Informacion* was receiving the most—$24,000 a month. Payments to individual journalists ranged from $100 to $2,000 a month.[50]

According to the Embassy report, with the exception of the magazine *Bohemia* and the newspapers *Prensa Libre* and the English-language *Times of Havana,* all major print media had accepted subsidies. The list did not include broadcast media.[51] The Embassy's charge d'affaires predicted that the new government would continue to subsidize the press:

> What the revolutionary government is going to do about the press subsidy is still not known. Here again—as in the case of gambling—the government finds itself caught between wanting to stop the practice which runs contrary to the principle of a free press and the economic reality that if it is not continued, many of the dailies in Havana will fold with all the attendant problems of unemployment in this important sector. In the end, the government will probably take the course of least resistance: swallow the principle and continue the subsidy in some form.[52]

Press subsidies under Batista took many forms, including covert support of government organs and overt payments to independent newspapers to publish educational and cultural supplements. *Informacion,* for example, openly received government assistance, "in the name of culture," to publish thick inserts dealing with social and cultural events. The inserts contained high-quality photographs (up to 24 pages on Sundays) printed on a rotary press.[53] After the revolution, the various hues of the subsidies did not matter. Simply having accepted subsidies from the hated Batista government was enough to be labelled a Batistiano organ.[54]

Carlos Todd, the anti-Communist columnist of *The Times of Havana,* doubted *Revolucion*'s claim that the list of subsidized newspapers and journalists had been "found" in the Presidential Palace. He asserted that the publication of the list was part of a conspiracy by the government to discredit the press:

> The method of discrediting the press . . . was subtly carried to a fine art. It is true that newspapers accepted subsidies. They had been doing so under every single government in years past. They had to, in order to exist. . . . Certainly some newsmen were sold out to Batista & Co. That is irrefutable. All of them? That is something else again. . . . Today, the whole press stands condemned as a fraudulent group of people who were completely sold out to Batista. If the whole press of Cuba had been totally bought by the dictatorship, exactly why was censorship instituted? . . . One question. Who subsidizes *Hoy?* Another: Does *Revolucion* make money exclusively from its meager advertising?[55]

Todd earned a reputation as one of the "most direct, honest and irreverent" critics of Communist influence in Cuba.[56] During this early stage in the revolution, when Castro was immensely popular, Todd was largely alone in savaging the government. Conservative businesspeople who hoped to deal with Castro—including Todd's uncle, sugar magnate Julio Lobo—unsuccessfully tried to convince Todd to curb his anti-Communist rhetoric.[57]

Todd's question concerning the financing of *Noticias de Hoy* (Today's News) and *Revolucion* was a legitimate one. The newspapers claimed to be independent of the government. Yet both newspapers had been given the facilities of confiscated newspapers. *Hoy* was the mouthpiece of the Communist Party, if not the Castro government. During the early months of the Castro revolution, some observers believed *Revolucion* might develop into an independent voice. Although there was no question that *Revolucion* supported the Castro government, one observer wrote that "it is clear that the editors (of *Revolucion*) were trying to formulate a distinctive approach which was not merely an echo of Fidel Castro."[58]

Carlos Franqui, *Revolucion*'s editor, clandestinely published the newspaper in his house during the late 1950s. After being given *Alerta*'s facilities after the revolution, Franqui traveled to the United States and Europe, touring *The New York Times* and other newspapers while purchasing equipment for his new plant. He denied he was a Communist and that *Revolucion* was a government mouthpiece: "This plant is the property of the government, and although we sympathize with the government we feel that a newspaper should be independent and not a member of the government."[59] But *Revolucion* never developed into the independent newspaper that some hoped and thought possible.

Background to Subsidies

The question of government press subsidies had been a matter of public debate among Cuban intellectuals during the years following the 1933 revolution. Many well-meaning liberals maintained that press subsidies were needed to sustain a healthy democracy and encourage debate about political issues.[60]

The elected governments of Ramon Grau San Martin (1944-1948) and Carlos Prio Soccaras (1948-1952) had practically institutionalized press subsidies. Their motives, however, were not to encourage debate and public education. Instead, the Grau and Prio governments found that while they could not muzzle the press they could tame it through the use of subsidies.

Many newspapers became dependent upon government subsidies for their existence.[61] In 1935, Havana, the center of Cuba's newspaper industry, had 15 daily newspapers, with circulations ranging from 2,500 to 43,000. This number included three specialized business newspapers, an English-language newspaper for U.S. businesspeople and tourists and three Chinese-language newspapers for Cuba's sizable Chinese community.[62] The island had a Yiddish and Spanish-language weekly, *Havaner Leben-Vida Habanera,* serving Cuba's "Jewish Colony" from 1932 to 1960.[63] For a three-year period during the early 1930s, there were two weekly newspapers serving the Jewish Colony.[64]

Several Havana newspapers that received subsidies—such as *El Mundo, Diario de la Marina* and *Informacion*—were regarded as among the best in Latin America.[65] When Castro came to power in 1959, Havana, a city of about 850,000, had 16 daily newspapers.

Once the subsidies had created more newspapers than the city could profitably sustain, it became almost impossible for a newspaper to survive on circulation and advertising alone. There was no way to withdraw the system of subsides without newspaper shutdowns, unemployment and the impression that the government was trying to silence press criticism. Some entrepreneurial publishers created "fly-by-night publications . . . just to get in on the gravy."[66] As an indication of Cuba's newspaper-rich environment, Table 9.1 shows daily newspapers

Table 9.1. Daily newspaper circulation in Havana, 1930-1958

	Year Established	1930	1940	1950	1958	Appeal
			(in thousands)			
Advance	1933	..	18**	25**	27**	General
Alerta	1935	..	12**	10**	10	General
Ataja	1957	..	..	..	32	General
Commercial	1916	8**	..	..	..	Business
EL Commercio	1886	8*	..	..	..	Business
El Crisol	1934	..	78*	30*	35**	General
Diario Espanol	1907	4*	..	..	..	Business
Diario Finanzas	1934	..	5*	..	..	Business
Diario de la Marina	1832	75*	28*	41*	62*	General
Diario Nacional	1954	..	..	..	NA	General
La Discussion	1911	NA	84*	11*	..	NA
Evening News	1912	2**	..	..	..	English
Excelsior	1921	NA	NA	NA	52*	General
Finanzas	1933	..	..	5*	15*	Business
Heraldo Commercial	1917	NA	11*	11*	..	Agriculture
Heraldo de Cuba	1911	45*	..	..	..	General
Hoi Men Kong Po	1913	NA	4*	..	..	Chinese
El Imperial	1916	60*	..	..	..	General
Industria y Comercio	NA	..	..	1*	1*	Business
Informacion	1932	..	54*	35*	52*	General
Luz	1933	..	NA	25*	..	General
Man Sen Yat Po***	1920	NA	10	10	3	Chinese
Manana	1939	..	NA	49*	55*	General
El Mundo	1901	45*	19*	22*	27*	General
Noticias de Hoy	1938	..	18*	27*	..	General
Noticiero Mercantil	1935	..	3*	..	..	Business
El Pais	1921	NA	95	65	66	General
Post	1898	14*	10*	7*	13*	English
Prensa Libre	1941	..	..	60	95	General
Pueblo	1937	..	13**	NA	28	General
Telegram	1922	7**	..	..	..	English
Tiempo en Cuba	1950	..	..	NA	NA	General
Wah Mon Sion Po	NA	..	50**	NA	NA	Chinese

Source: Abstracted from Editor & Publisher Year Book (New York: Editor & Publisher), data from volumes from the respective years. Circulation figures should be regarded with suspicion because only El Mundo in 1958 was subject to an independent audit.

Numbers without stars = all day.
*Morning.
**Evening.
***Published by the Kuomintang Nationalist Party.
NA = Data unavailable or the newspaper was not published that year.

in Havana and their reported circulations from 1930 to 1958.

By the time Castro came to power, a few large newspapers reported circulations in excess of 70,000.[67] Circulation figures should be regarded with suspicion because only *El Mundo* (27,000 weekdays and 40,000 Sunday in 1958), thought to have one of the largest circulations, was audited by the independent Audit Bureau of Circulations (ABC).[68] Clarence Moore, publisher of *The Times of Havana*, said he knew of Havana newspapers claiming circulations over 75,000 that sources in the newspaper industry told him were really about 10,000 or 20,000.[69]

In addition to press subsidies, low-paid journalists were placed on government payrolls by government officials. As Alisky wrote: "A reporter assigned to cover the Ministry of Education worked a five-day week. On Saturdays he would moonlight as a public relations counsel for the Education Ministry for a free-lance salary. The chances of his writing adverse stories about the ministry he advised were zero."[70]

Defending Press Freedom

In addition to having accepted government subsidies, the Cuban press had another weakness that could be exploited by the Castro government to mute press criticism. The Cuban press did not display the North American "libertarian" journalistic tradition of defending press freedom in principle by vehemently denouncing the confiscations of Batistiano newspapers. The "libertarian" tradition can perhaps be best summed up by the phrase, "I disapprove of what you say, but I will defend to the death your right to say it."[71]

U.S. journalists were dumbfounded by the Cuban press' pusillanimous response to the confiscations of Batista newspapers and radio stations. Typical of American journalists' responses was that of Edwin C. Stein, managing editor of the *New York Journal-American:* "The strange thing there was that four Batistiano dailies had been confiscated on Jan. 1, 1959, without a word of protest from the independent newspapers—startling action by a supposedly democratic government and startling lack of reaction by the free press."[72]

Among Cuba's Spanish-language dailies, *Informacion* was nearest to the "typical" U.S. newspaper in editorial content, appearance and ideology. Angel Fernandez Varela, *Informacion*'s editor, took pride in the newspaper's "objectivity." He also pointed to the newspaper's long, thin columns of international stories (mostly news service reports) and noted how they gave the newspaper the appearance of the *Wall Street Journal.* Fernandez Varela insisted that *Informacion* and other commercial newspapers protested the confiscations of the Batistiano newspapers. He conceded, however, that the protestations were hardly a ringing defense of press freedom: "It's one thing to speak up, and it is another thing to speak up in a hard-hitting way. We could have kept hitting and hitting against this if we wished. But we didn't. We said it was wrong and dropped the matter. Everybody thought that this was a particular problem with Batista and the people related to Batista, not the big ones [newspapers] that were independent."[73]

Even if the Cuban press had denounced the confiscations of Batistiano newspapers, it is unlikely that a libertarian argument would have won over many Cubans. Some of the Batistiano newspapers were operated by the most hated men in Cuba. For example, *El Tiempo*, operated by Masferrer, was turned over to the Communist newspaper *Hoy*. Masferrer, who also published a newspaper in Santiago de Cuba called *Libertad*, led a private army accused of numerous atrocities.[74]

Pressures on Broadcasters

During his rebel years in the Sierra Maestra, Castro's medium of choice for overriding the censored Cuban media was radio.[75] Through Radio Rebelde, Castro trumpeted his victories over Batista's military forces and promised to restore Cuba to democracy. Once in power, Castro preferred television. Television allowed him to project his dynamic personality and organize support for his programs. As Goar Mestre recalled:

> When Castro came into Havana we simply turned the television over to him lock, stock and barrel. He was in my office all the time. While he was in the hills as a guerrilla he had never realized the power of TV but, once he came to power, he quickly saw that this was one way to reach the Cuban people in their homes. Then you couldn't keep him off. He was the prime-time show. He never spoke for less than four hours, and his record was six hours and 15 minutes nonstop. He just chatted on and on, repeating himself, hammering home his points about social services, better education, no more corruption. He had the style of a star performer, with that big beard and olive-green uniform; all through he'd smoke away at his cigars and sip coffee and cognac.[76]

During the summer of 1959, Minister of Communications Enrique Oltuski traveled to Washington, D.C., and met with representatives of the Federal Communications Commission (FCC). FCC officials were concerned about Cuban government confiscations of broadcast media.

The 23-year-old Oltuski, a political moderate and a graduate of the University of Miami, assured the Commission's members that his government had no intentions of taking over Cuba's private broadcast media.[77] Oltuski asserted that the broadcast outlets that had been confiscated during the early days of the revolution were Batista organs. For all practical purposes, Oltuski argued, they were never privately operated stations. He noted that Goar Mestre, the island's leading broadcaster, was operating as normal. This, he said, was evidence of the government's "respect for the free enterprise system."[78]

To most observers, Cuba's radio and television stations remained as lively as they were before Castro. Perhaps the best indicator of their vibrancy was the barrage of mind-numbing commercials—not something one would expect in an orthodox Communist state. As a 1959 *New York Times* report noted: "Cuban commercials have some originality but are merciless in their devastation of the viewer's nervous system. Lengthy, repetitious, noisy and often in bad taste, they blare out a spiel that would make even a Madison Avenue man shudder. The accent on sex stems from customs firmly entrenched on the island."[79]

Pumarejo Is Targeted

When Fulgencio Batista fled Cuba, Gaspar Pumarejo was in the United States purchasing equipment for his recently inaugurated color television station. Pumarejo, long rumored to have accepted financial support from Batista, returned to Cuba a few weeks later and faced a cascade of rumors about his close relations with the Batista government. During late February 1959, He appeared on Channel 12 with a leading revolutionary labor leader whom Pumarejo accused of spreading rumors about him. Pumarejo denied that he was in collusion with Batista. Home Club president Eduardo Cabellero even interjected himself into the interviews, adding: "Our position is very well defined at this moment of happiness in our motherland. Never did any of our ventures receive subsidies or political jobs from the previous government, from the lottery or any other department or para-state entity that many other private ventures benefitted from in our country."[80]

In a possible effort to avoid antagonizing the new government, Channel 12 drastically reduced its news programming in February 1959 and dismissed 15 newsmen. Rather than reduce friction with the government, this action angered the Cuban Newspaper Guild. The Guild called upon the government to investigate whether the station had violated the newsmen's rights.[81] Meanwhile, as Pumarejo had trouble paying his bills and employees' salaries, his workers reportedly besieged him and demanded to know why he lavished so much money on his color television venture and in bringing foreign talent such as Liberace, Lucho Gatica and Sarita Montiel to Cuba over the past year.[82]

With suspicions mounting against Pumarejo, he left Cuba in early March. A few weeks later, Pumarejo's Channel 12 (Tele-Color, S.A.), "Escuela de Television" ("The School of Television") and the "Hogar Club" (The "Home Club") were confiscated.[83] The government produced records indicating that Andres Domingo y Castillo, Batista's press secretary, owned about $40,000 in Channel 12."[84] The Cuban government viewed color programming as an extravagance. Programs over confiscated Channel 12 were broadcast in black and white. The government gradually reintroduced color programs again in 1976.[85]

Carlos Todd of *The Times of Havana* was no admirer of Pumarejo, describing him as "a fat, jolly man of dubious morals."[86] Todd also described Pumarejo's colleague, Otto Sirgo, who frequently hosted "The School of Television," as a "one time honorary SIM [Batista's secret police force] member."[87] Nevertheless, Todd argued that the confiscations of Pumarejo's businesses fit Todd's conspiracy theory that the Castro government was discrediting private media with the ultimate aim of taking over all mass media:

> The channel was intervened by the government when it was found out that Andres Domingo y Castillo, Batista's fair-haired boy, owned 40,000 pesos worth of stock [a Cuban peso was about equal to a U.S. dollar]. With this excuse, the government moved in. It seems to be a fait accompli that the remaining stock holders, who may or may not have had anything to do with Batista, will sell out and the state will take over the channel as its very own medium of propaganda.[88]

The government appointed Gabriel Casanova Salum Nasser the "intervenor" to manage Channel 12. Casanova continued to air much of Channel 12's same entertainment programming.[89] But the station also carried programs featuring ugly allegations against Pumarejo. Casanova headed televised discussions with former station employees who described their former boss as a swindler and lecher. Todd described the round tables as "nauseating":

> The most conservative adjective that could be employed to describe what went on then was nauseating. Anyone who claims that there is only good in mankind should have seen that program. Accusations, foul epithets, insults and filthy aspersions of every kind were used against the owner of Channel 12 by the very same people who sang his praises two or three

weeks before. Pumarejo's sex life was discussed over the air waves. One woman, who accused her fellow workers of submitting, if unwillingly, to Pumarejo's advances, set herself up as the pillar of virtue that was holding up the moral structure of the TV station. It went on for hours of acrimony, unsubstantiated charges, scandalous accusations and uncontrolled ravings. Casanova Salum Nasser raised not a finger in protest.[90]

Some Channel 12 employees protested Casanova's scurrilous programs. Casanova had to lead the programs against Pumarejo himself because no one on the news staff would. Historian Hermino Portell Vila, the station's commentator on international affairs, was fired after he protested the treatment of Pumarejo. Casanova hired new employees whom Todd described as "young Communist liners."[91]

While Pumarejo was out of the country, executives in his three companies remained in Cuba and were vilified. Sirgo, vice president of "The Home Club" and a regular replacement for Pumarejo on the "School of Television," was charged with swindling $333,000 from 200,000 "Home Club" members.[92] Sirgo protested that he was vice president "only in name" and that his income from Pumarejo was compensation for his acting.[93]

Sirgo and club treasurer Eduardo Caballero were briefly jailed. Ironically, after having been publicly humiliated, Sirgo resumed his career in television in the grand Pumarejo tradition. He incorporated as "Espectaculos Otto Sirgo, S.A." ("The Spectacular Programs of Otto Sirgo, Inc.") and began contracting blocks of time to air entertainment programs over the Telemundo network. Sirgo arranged for some of Cuba's most famous stars to appear on his programs.[94] Telemundo needed Sirgo's programming. When Pumarejo fled Cuba, his "School of Television" programs over Telemundo went off the air and Telemundo's ratings plummeted.[95]

While Pumarejo and his colleagues were being vilified inside Cuba, radio commentator Jose Pardo Llada aired a transatlantic telephone interview with Pumarejo from Spain. Pumarejo said that he would return to Cuba, clear his name and reclaim his properties:

> I was never involved in politics. Nor am I swindler or a liar. I am a Cuban actor, and I protest against the lies that a group of angry schemers are saying about me. . . . I am not an enemy of the revolution. I proudly experienced the friendship of Fidel Castro, and I am sincerely grateful for what he has done for Cuba. I have faith and put trust in the Cuban people's longing for equality and justice and the shining truth.[96]

Shortly after Pumarejo's interview with Pardo Llada, the Ministry

9. CASTRO COMES TO POWER

of Recovery of Stolen Property issued a surprisingly conciliatory announcement conceding that it had committed "errors" in confiscating Pumarejo's properties. The agency's secretary, Faustino Perez, said if his agency was unjustified in its actions, the matter would be corrected. But only a little more than 24 hours later, the agency announced, "That in general a few errors had been committed, but the confiscation was justified."[97]

In exile, Pumarejo journeyed throughout North America, Europe and Latin America, contracting time with television stations to carry his programs. He appeared on television in Miami, Peru, Guatemala, Spain and elsewhere. He finally established headquarters in Newark, New Jersey, hosting a 60-minute Spanish-language variety program. Once a week he flew to Puerto Rico to host a variety program on WAPA, Channel 4—a station that once ironically was partially owned by the Mestre brothers.[98] Because of ill health, Pumarejo returned to Puerto Rico two weeks before his death in 1975. He was 61.[99]

During his many travels, Pumarejo continued to criticize his old business nemesis Goar Mestre. During a trip to Peru in 1963, he charged that the now-exiled Mestre used his influence in Cuba to manipulate the Cuban ratings to exaggerate CMQ's programs and underreport those of the other stations. He also claimed that Mestre was responsible for driving RHC–Cadena Azul owner Amado Trinidad to suicide.[100]

CHAPTER 10
Freedom of the Press in Castro's Cuba

After coming to power in 1959, Fidel Castro reaffirmed his commitment to freedom of the press. The new government eliminated prior restraint and fired—and even jailed—the censors in the Batista government. At the same time, Castro was not afraid to criticize newspapers, radio stations and journalists whose reports he disapproved and accuse them of disloyalty. While some critics argued that Castro's condemnations of the news media had the effect of censorship by intimidating the press into silence, Castro's supporters responded that Castro was merely exercising his own freedom of speech.[1]

Starting in April and May 1959, several episodes of press harassment occurred. There was no evidence that Castro was behind these incidents. But they were the prelude to eventual government confiscations of Cuba's print and broadcast media.

In April 1959, *El Mundo*'s respected columnist Juan Luis Martin, a fervent anti-Communist, was arrested and held incommunicado. He was not charged with any offense. Martin was released two weeks later without explanation. Cuba's journalistic community remained silent about the incident. Only *The Times of Havana,* which confirmed the rumors from *El Mundo* staff, carried a one-column description of the arrest.[2]

In one of the more bizarre forms of press harassment, officials at the Ministry of the Treasury proposed legislation in May 1959 to tax people whose names appeared in newspaper social pages, known as the "cronicas." Anyone who wanted to be regarded as important in Cuba's class-conscious circles had their weddings and parties reported in the cronicas. It was an open secret that favorable coverage in the cronica's could be purchased, and one notorious *Diario de la Marina* "cronista" (social page writer) was reported to have made a "banker's living" from his job.[3]

The cronicas had become an institution in Cuban society. A young Fulgencio Batista, like other aspiring Cuban politicians, purchased coverage in the cronicas. Batista earned kudos during the 1933 revolution for siding with student revolutionaries in toppling the tyrant Gerardo Machado. He was determined to remain in the public eye and succeed in politics. Batista, who came from a humble background, had several obstacles to overcome. An orphan raised by Quakers and a onetime cane field laborer, he was disparagingly referred to as "el Negro" because of his dark complexion. This put him in bad stead with Cuba's class-conscious and race-conscious upper crust.[4]

According to the proposed society-page tax, people whose names appeared in the cronicas would be taxed $1 for each adjective used to describe them. They would also be taxed $5 per column inch for individual photographs and $10 per inch for group photographs. The tax was to be collected by the newspapers, which could pocket 10 percent of the revenues for their collection services.[5]

The tax legislation was never enacted. On June 5, Treasury Minister Rufo Lopez Fresquet withdrew the proposal following a barrage of complaints. The legislation might have been the act of zealous government officials intent on disparaging the upper classes and bourgeois press. But the audacity of the proposal shocked Cuban editors and publishers.[6] Lopez Fresquet would later defect Cuba and denounce Castro. While in Cuba, however, he reportedly had ambitions to become president and, "in the eyes of some, lost his head while serving as minister of the treasury and came to exaggerate his own importance."[7]

During this time, CMQ, like most media organizations, experienced a series of labor-management disputes. What was particularly disturbing to CMQ's Mestre brothers was that the government appeared to encourage labor dissension. In one major incident, Cainas Milanes, the president of the National Association of Cattleman, spoke from CMQ-TV's studio and objected to the government's agrarian reform program. The cattlemen were among the largest landowners in Cuba and stood to lose property by the proposal to restrict individual landowners to 3,300 acres.[8] While Milanes spoke, a message briefly appeared on the screen in favor of agrarian reform. The Mestre brothers were infuriated by the unauthorized announcement. A technician took it upon himself to insert the message. The employee was reprimanded. But Abel Mestre suspected government involvement because CMQ received several pleas from government officials to show leniency.[9]

In another episode, the Minister of Labor met with Abel Mestre and pressed him to sign a new contract with CMQ employees. CMQ signed an accord shortly before the revolution. The new contract presented by the minister offered back pay to employees who missed work to fight against Batista's forces. Mestre said that it was impossible to know which workers were absent to battle Batista. He refused to sign the contract.[10]

"There were lots of these little incidents going on at the time at CMQ," Abel Mestre said. "There appeared to be a pattern which I do not think we fully understood at the time. We suspected that many of them [the employees] were working with the Fidelistas. We couldn't say for sure. But our investigations indicated to us that certain segments in the government encouraged them."[11]

With these incidents, Goar and Abel Mestre suspected that they might lose their properties. Shortly after Goar Mestre fled Cuba in March 1960, he told a reporter for the U.S. trade publication *Advertising Age* that he "had already seen the handwriting on the wall—not as early as I would have liked—but by early 1959."[12]

A President Falls

By mid-1959, some officials in Washington feared that Castro was leading Cuba on a Soviet-Communist path. The belief was that while Castro "might" not be a Communist, those close to him were—particularly his brother, Raul, and his colleague, Ernesto "Che" Gueverra.[13] Discussion among political pundits concerned whether Cuba was "going Communist." As Paul Bethel, the U.S. press attache in Cuba, observed, "Communism was more than an important issue in Cuba by July of 1959; very little else was talked about."[14]

On April 2, 1959, Castro arrived in Washington and appeared on the U.S. television program "Meet the Press." The interview program was carried live on Cuban television. The U.S. journalists who grilled Castro pounded away at the issue of Communism. Castro responded angrily against what he viewed as the U.S. journalists' patronizing questions that his government was infiltrated by Communists: "The Communists simply have a newspaper *[Hoy]*. Why raise the ghost of Communism simply because the Communists are not being persecuted? . . . When the government begins by closing one newspaper, no newspaper can feel safe."[15]

Castro's response reflected his position regarding attacks against Communism. While Castro said that he was not a Communist, he maintained that the Communist Party, like other parties, had a right to participate in the government.

With the debate as to whether Castro was a Communist, events shedding light on Castro's attitude toward Communism were closely monitored. On July 2, 1959, Castro gave a speech warning that it was "not entirely honorable" to attack the Communists.[16] On July 13, President Manuel Urrutia Lleo, a respected anti-Communist, gave the last of three interviews to CMQ-TV commentator Luis Conte Aguero in the Presidential Palace. In the interviews, Urrutia criticized the Communist Party.

Conte Aguero, a leading anti-Communist spokesman, hoped that the interviews would strengthen Urrutia politically. He advised Urrutia before his third interview that the most politic approach would be to praise Castro while attacking Communism.[17] According to Urrutia's account, he had contemplated resigning the presidency during at least three occasions because of his political ineffectiveness and figurehead status.[18] Many of Urrutia's supporters, including Conte Aguero, urged him to remain in the government and defend the anti-Communist cause.

During this last televised interview with Conte Aguero, Urrutia followed Conte Aguero's suggestion to attack the Communist Party and praise Castro. Despite rumors of differences between Castro and Urretia, Urretia said that he and Castro "are on the same road."[19]

Conte Aguero asked Urrutia to respond to charges in the Communist press that Urrutia was disloyal to the revolution because of his criticisms of the Communists. Urrutia responded by questioning the loyalty of the Communists:

> If it be disloyalty to Russia, they are wrong, because never have I proffered loyalty to Russia. Now, if that be disloyalty to Cuba I think it would be difficult for them to prove it. . . . Read *Hoy* and you will notice that most of the paper is devoted exclusively to defending the interests of the Soviet Union. . . . Thus I say and declare, here and now, on my own responsibility, that the Communists in Cuba want to create a second front against the Cuban revolution. . . . I reject Communist support and I think that true Cuban revolutionaries ought to reject it openly because there is no reason for two fronts in Cuba.[20]

Carlos Rafael Rodriguez, editor of *Hoy,* charged that Urrutia's remarks violated Castro's position that to attack the Communists was "not entirely honorable."[21] Castro responded to Urrutia's remarks on July 17 by resigning as prime minister, citing an irrevocable rift between himself and the president.

That same day, Abel Mestre received a telephone call from his secretary while he was at lunch in his regularly frequented restaurant. He was informed that Raul Castro, head of the military, was waiting to meet with him in his office. When Mestre returned to his office, Raul Castro informed him that Fidel Castro was going to speak over CMQ that evening, and to prepare the studio for his arrival.[22] "It was not unusual for us to get ready for Castro with little notice," Mestre said. "There were armed soldiers outside the building, but I did not think this was unusual. I thought they were checking the place for Castro's safety. We had no idea that Castro was preparing to purge Urretia from the government."[23]

In a four-hour speech that ran into the morning of the next day, Fidel Castro accused Urrutia of making statements "bordering on treason" and creating an anti-Communist hysteria: "I am not a Communist, and neither is the revolutionary movement communistic, but we are not Communist just to fawn on foreign powers. What is the reason for raising the phantom of Communism? To persecute the Communists? Here we do not persecute anybody. I have respect for all ideas and beliefs. . . . Do we persecute Catholics or Rotarians or [the conservative daily newspaper] *Diario de la Marina*."[24]

Noting press reports that Urrutia purchased a $40,000 "mansion," Castro referred to Urrutia's luxurious life-style and $10,000-a-month salary. Castro and other Cabinet members voluntarily accepted reduced $700-a-month salaries while Cuba was experiencing economic problems. Castro said that he could tolerate Urrutia's life-style. "The really serious thing," Castro said, "was Urrutia's stand against Communism and charges that Cuba was laying itself open to a 'second front.'"[25]

Ironically, the story about Urrutia's "mansion" was exposed by anti-Communist columnist Carlos Todd of *The Times of Havana,* a supporter of Urrutia. After the story appeared, Urrutia brought libel suits against Todd and *Avance* writer Bernardo Viera, who repeated the story. Urrutia did not deny the report but claimed that the story inferred that he earned his money through dishonest means.[26]

In addition to drawing attention to Urrutia's life-style, Castro also noted that Cuba's former commander of the armed forces, Major Luis Diaz Lanz, had recently fled Cuba and was testifying before a U.S. Senate subcommittee on the influence of Communism in Cuba. Pointing to the bad international press that Cuba was receiving, Castro said that "the next day in the international press news services we find ourselves accused by none other than the president of the republic."[27]

As Castro continued his diatribe, a crowd gathered outside the Presidential Palace demanding Urrutia's resignation. Urrutia hurriedly assembled the Cabinet and tendered his resignation shortly before midnight while Castro was still on the air. Urrutia was escorted out of the Presidential Palace and placed under house arrest. He eventually found asylum in the Venezuelan Embassy.

While still on the air, Castro was handed a note informing him of Urrutia's decision to resign the presidency. This gave Castro the pleasure to publicly announce Urrutia's resignation. A new provisional president in line with Castro's position toward Communism was named the next afternoon. Less than a week later, Castro resumed his position as prime minister. With the anti-Communist Urrutia purged from power, talk about Communist infiltration of the Cuban government persisted both in Cuba and in the United States.[28]

The U.S. Response

With increasingly tense relations between the United States and Cuba, Paul Bethel, the U.S. press attache in Havana, approached Cuban broadcasters with a plan to report the U.S. position directly to the Cuban people.[29] This was a risky gambit. If it were known that a member of the U.S. government was working with Cuban broadcasters, Castro could charge that the Americans were meddling in Cuban affairs. As for the broadcasters, they faced the possibility of being labeled spies and anti-revolutionaries.

Bethel, who dealt with Abel Mestre, wrote: "We found Sr. Abel Mestre more than ready to cooperate. This was important because both Abel and his brother Goar enjoyed considerable prestige in Cuba and the Inter-American Association of Broadcasters."[30]

CMQ news director Nicolas Bravo suggested that a "dignified appearance" by U.S. Ambassador Philip Bonsal, who spoke fluent Spanish, on CMQ-TV's "Meet the Press" might be successful in communicating the U.S. position.[31] When Bethel approached Bonsal with this plan, Bonsal was leery. He became more reluctant when he learned that the program required him to fend questions from a panel of journalists. Bonsal feared that a hostile panelist might raise the touchy issue of U.S. imperialism.[32] Despite assurances from Abel Mestre that the journalists would not be antagonistic, Bonsal rejected the offer.[33]

Later, Bethel suggested the production of a series of television and radio programs designed "to show the Communists to be the traitors that they were, and to identify them with Batista."[34] Bethel's attempt to link leading Communists in the Cuban government to Batista was by no means far-fetched. Despite Batista's anti-Communist rhetoric, he was a pragmatic politician who had struck numerous political alliances with the Communist Party in the past. Batista had won the Communist Party's backing during his successful 1940 presidential campaign.

With the assistance of the U.S. Information Service, Bethel received background reports on leading Communist officials who collaborated with the Batista government during the 1940s. He also requested a budget from the United States Information Service to partially defray CMQ's production costs. The State Department, however, was uneasy about potential accusations of the United States meddling in Cuban affairs. It rejected the plan. In his memoirs, Bonsal wrote that if his plan was implemented, it "might have obviated the need for the Bay of Pigs invasion."[35]

Press Wars

In late 1959 and early 1960, several Cuban newspapers that judiciously criticized government actions were condemned by Castro during his marathon speeches. Castro's condemnations were followed by attacks in government media organs, such as *Hoy* and *Revolucion* and the scathing radio denunciations of Jose Pardo Llada. Carlos Franqui, editor of *Revolucion,* claimed that Pardo Llada's broadcasts were of great importance in Castro's aggrandizement of power after the revolution: "If we have to share historical responsibility, I think Fidel Castro could have existed without my presence. I don't know if he could have existed without Pardo Llada."[36]

For Havana's newspapers, being assailed by Castro, or the unofficial voice of Castro through government organs, portended danger. Ritual public burnings of magazines and newspapers accused of anti-revolutionary inclinations were becoming commonplace. While being attacked by Castro involved risk, it also had rewards. Newspapers that responded to Castro's criticisms quickly sold out, with some vendors charging as much as a dollar an issue.[37]

During the summer of 1959, the government laid the legal foundation for the confiscation of industries that illegally profited during the Batista years. Article 24 of the Fundamental Law permitted the Ministry of Recovery of Stolen Property to confiscate the holdings of industries and individuals who had accepted gifts, favors and subsidies from the Batista government.[38]

In the following months, Castro accused several newspapers with having secured subsidies from the former government. At the request of several Cuban newspapers, the Inter-American Press Association (IAPA) investigated the charges. The IAPA was and still is a "media watchdog" organization comprised of management-level newspaper journalists in North American, Latin American and Caribbean nations.[39] During the inquiry, IAPA president Alberto Gainza Paz of Argentina received photocopies of canceled checks from Batista government agencies made out to some of the newspapers. The checks arrived "by pure coincidence" from an anonymous source.[40]

Despite the canceled checks, the IAPA concluded that Cuban newspapers were not compromised by Batista. Gainza Paz explained that it was accepted practice in previous Cuban governments for agencies to pay newspapers to carry government advertising, edicts and listings of public works. While Gainza Paz said that the payments were not equivalent to bribery and no quid pro quo of favorable news coverage was expected, he added that he personally disapproved of the practice.[41]

The investigation also determined that the Cuban newspapers enjoyed press freedom to the extent that they could publish without prior government review. The IAPA, however, warned that "the propaganda machinery of the Castro revolution is ready to attack and disparage those who dare to criticize the measures and acts of government. The equivalent of censorship could be accomplished easily if agitated mobs attack newspaper plants or instill fear of physical damage or even death."[42]

The IAPA criticized government restrictions against press freedom everywhere in Latin America, the Caribbean, Canada and the United States. Most governments accepted these accusations, refuting them but rarely engaging in public debates with the IAPA. Perhaps because of Castro's commitment to press freedom as a cornerstone of the revolution, the government felt obliged to challenge the IAPA's charges. During the IAPA's annual convention in San Francisco in 1959, the government-appointed editor of *Diario Nacional* engaged in fervent floor debates with IAPA members and defended Cuba's policy toward the press.[43]

When press subsidies were withdrawn by the Castro government, newspapers were forced to rely on circulation and advertising revenue. But many businesses and industries that traditionally supplied the newspapers' advertising revenue were experiencing their own woes. Swank department stores that once accounted for pages of newspaper advertisements and supplements drastically reduced their advertising expenditures. There was little demand for their imported luxury items during these lean times.

While newspapers suffered during this period, radio and television continued to prosper. They relied heavily on soap, tobacco and beer advertising—basic goods not seriously affected by the weak economy.[44]

Aggravating the situation for Cuba's newspapers, the government provided them with little or no official information.[45] This put them at a competitive disadvantage to official and semiofficial government newspapers.[46] Finally—and perhaps most importantly—many journalists and graphic arts workers openly favored the government in government-press disputes. Newsroom employees framed their relations with their employers in class terms—the publishers were the wealthy oppressors while the workers were the oppressed laborers.

The Coletillas

Professional journalistic organizations became increasingly militaristic and passed resolutions calling upon their members to append statements of disapproval to news stories that they believed were anti-revolutionary. These statements, known as "coletillas" (little tails), took several forms and typically read: "The contents of this newspaper do not conform to truth nor to the most elemental journalistic ethics."[47]

To publishers, the coletillas represented an act of insubordination. When newsroom employees refused to obey publishers' demands to withdraw the coletillas, the police were sometimes called. The police usually refused to interfere in what they viewed as internal labor-management squabbles, even when the disputes came to fisticuffs.[48]

The first coletilla appeared in *Informacion* in early January 1960.[49] A few days later, another appeared in *Avance*.[50] *Avance*'s publisher, Jorge Zayas, decided to fight the coletillas. Zayas wrote a front-page message in the Jan. 18 issue warning readers that the coletillas reflected the views of discontented workers, and that the edition did not necessarily represent *Avance*'s views. Journalists and graphic arts workers countered with their own message, stating that the public should not be deprived of the opinions of the newspaper's laborers.[51] The newspaper, in effect, had become a forum in which labor and management aired their differences. Zayas, fearful of retribution for challenging the coletillas, took refuge in the Ecuadorian Embassy later that day. That evening, Castro devoted more than two hours of his five-hour speech to "the sordid, shameful" history of *Avance* and its publisher.[52]

On Jan. 21, Zayas arrived in Miami. That same day, the Ministry of Recovery of Stolen Property announced that it was confiscating *Avance*.[53] The government appointed a four-person committee of "intervenors" to operate *Avance*. Fearing that anti-Communists would attack the newspaper, the government assigned soldiers to protect the plant.[54]

Although Zayas was portrayed as a traitor by the Cuban government, among members of the U.S. journalistic community he was depicted as a defender of press freedom. He was appointed the IAPA's regional vice president of Freedom of the Press Committee for the Caribbean.[55] He also started publishing a series of syndicated columns in *The Miami Herald*.[56] In his columns, Zayas wrote that there was no longer any doubt that Castro was a Communist.[57]

Inside Cuba, a few Cuban newspapers cautiously questioned the government's actions against *Avance*. Agustin Tamargo, who wrote a daily column in *Avance,* was disappointed by the newspapers' timid response. "This is a page in the history of Cuban journalism that is a real shame," Tamargo said. "The editors of the papers didn't show any solidarity. They thought that maybe they could escape the persecution of the government. Every time a newspaper fell, they avoided saying anything."[58]

After Zayas fled Cuba, coletillas continued to appear with increasing regularity.[59] Responding to IAPA criticisms against the coletillas, the Havana Reporters Association issued a response asserting that coletillas represented an expansion rather than a diminution of freedom of the press:

> If to such wire stories and articles Cuban newspapers and graphic arts workers add an explanation at the end, this cannot be interpreted as a restriction or limitation on freedom of expression, but rather a wider application of such liberty of expression in which newsmen and graphic arts workers can also express their opinions in addition to the publisher.[60]

To avoid coletillas inserted into their papers, many newspapers relied on wire service stories to report Cuban news. After the Zayas episode, coletillas were expanded to include news agency reports that journalists and graphic workers believed unfairly criticized the Castro government. The coletillas were followed by a predictable series of events. Publishers and editors protested the coletillas and engaged in public disputes with their employees. The publishers and editors were then criticized in *Revolucion, Hoy* and Pardo Llada's radio broadcasts. The disputes ended with the confiscations of the newspapers. The number of privately operated daily newspapers in Cuba dwindled from 17 when Castro marched into Havana in January 1959 to four in April 1960. Meanwhile, the government of China announced that it was planning to publish a Chinese-language daily for Havana's 30,000 Chinese-Cubans that would represent the voice of the People's Republic of China.[61]

Among Havana's four remaining daily newspapers in April 1960, *Diario de la Marina* and *Prensa Libre* addressed political issues and criticized the government. *El Crisol* consisted largely of sports and crime news.[62] *Informacion,* which prided itself on its "objectivity," refrained from taking political stands.[63] The weekly English-language *Times of Havana* eagerly threw itself into the debate. But its influence was so minimal among average Cuban citizens that Cuban officials largely ignored it.

During May 1960, fights inside *Diario de la Marina* between management and workers over coletillas led to the intervention of the newspaper (May 11). The takeover of the 128-year-old *La Marina,* the oldest existing daily in Cuba, met with little public outcry because it was too far to the political right for most Cubans. During Cuba's War of Independence, *La Marina*'s editorials favored the Spanish; during the Second World War, it favored Fascist movements; during the postwar era, it favored the United States.[64]

Before the intervention of *La Marina,* publisher Jose Ignacio Rivero anticipated that some disgruntled journalists and printers would claim that most workers rejected *La Marina*'s editorial policies. To counter this action, Rivero planned to publish the names of 318 of the paper's 450 employees who were willing to sign a letter in support of *La Marina.* The newspaper was intervened during the early morning hours on the day when the letter was to be published.[65] The day after the intervention, a crowd chanting anti-American slogans held a symbolic funeral celebrating the death of *La Marina.*[66] Rivero fled for safety in the Peruvian Embassy. He was later awarded the IAPA's Hero of Freedom medal.[67]

Any attempt by the government to intervene against *Prensa Libre* posed a problem. It was the most widely read daily in Cuba. Sergio Carbo, *Prensa Libre*'s director, was a member of the revolutionary generation of the 1930s that toppled dictator Machado. The paper, founded by Carbo in 1941, criticized Batista before the revolution and refused to accept Batista government subsidies. An early supporter of Castro, *Prensa Libre* was generally considered progressive, although Carbo had become more conservative in recent times.[68]

Only after *Prensa Libre* came to the defense of *La Marina* was it vulnerable to intervention. In its last editorial as an independent newspaper, *Prensa Libre* ran a scathing denunciation of the employees who usurped *Diario de la Marina*'s editorial powers through coletillas, calling them "jackals of journalism."[69] *Prensa Libre* was intervened on May 16.

Three months after the takeover of *Prensa Libre, Revolucion* took control of *Prensa Libre*'s modern facilities.[70] But Carlos Franqui, *Revolucion*'s editor, whose signed editorials whipped up public sentiment against *Prensa Libre* and other newspapers, grew disillusioned with the Castro government. He left Cuba in 1968, expressing regret for the downfall of *Prensa Libre*. But Franqui did not regret the demise of *La Marina:* "*Prensa Libre* was scrupulous in its editorial policy, but its staff made mistakes because they did not understand the situation. Nor did we. *Revolucion* wanted to argue the issues, but we certainly did not want our opposite numbers to vanish—with the exception of *La Marina*. . . . I always hated *La Marina;* it had defended [Spain's Francisco] Franco and Fascism in general. It was the mouthpiece of the sugar interests, and the church hierarchy—always pro-Spain and anti-Cuba."[71]

The Last Newspapers

El Crisol closed on June 4, 1960, citing "economic difficulties."[72] *The Times of Havana* ceased publication in early November 1960 with little fanfare. The English-language newspaper, read mostly by Cuba's "American colony," experienced few labor problems. It simply could not afford to operate in the inhospitable business climate and with Americans leaving the island.[73] After closing the newspaper and returning to the United States, publisher Clarence Moore appeared before the Florida Bar Association and blamed the United States for driving Castro to the left. The paper's former chief columnist, Carlos Todd, who fled Cuba a month before Moore, harshly criticized his former boss for this analysis. Todd claimed that Castro alone was responsible for the crackdown on human rights in Cuba.[74]

By the time *Informacion*, the last commercial newspaper, ceased publication in December 1960, its demise was a fait accompli.[75] For more than a year the staid newspaper had seen advertising revenues dwindle. To survive, *Informacion* kept raising its newsstand price and reducing the number of pages. The newspaper, which at the start of the Castro revolution was sometimes 100 pages on Sundays, was reduced to half as many pages by the summer of 1960.[76]

An official decree, issued by the Ministry of Commerce on Oct. 4, 1960, limited Cuban dailies to 16 pages on weekdays and 24 on weekends. The stated intent was to reduce Cuba's reliance on imported newsprint, which had to be purchased with U.S. dollars because most countries refused Cuban currency. *Hoy* and *Revolucion* accepted these restrictions as their patriotic duty.[77] The Cuban government, meanwhile, was trying to promote domestic newsprint production from sugarcane. Cuban newspapers disliked sugarcane newsprint because it absorbed too much ink.[78]

Officially, *Informacion* folded because of economic and labor-management problems. But editor Angel Fernandez Varela traced

Informacion's troubles to the government: "Labor was responsible for our troubles. Laborers were inspired and planted by the government, that's for sure. But the appearance was given that our problems were labor problems with no government intervention whatsoever."[79] In January 1961, the Roman Catholic magazine *La Quincena*, the last independent medium of any sort, ceased publication.[80]

Coletillas were uncommon—but not unknown—in the broadcast media. John A. Lent, a scholar of Caribbean mass communications, reported incidents of coletillas in critical radio commentaries.[81] Goar Mestre said that CMQ never experienced a broadcast coletilla.[82] It might have been that only small radio outlets experienced coletillas, and only infrequently.

A U.S. Department of State report noted an incident of a coletilla in the broadcast media on March 7, 1960.[83] Commentator Arturo Artalejo Fernandez, of Radio Capital Artalejo in Havana, suspended his commentaries on his program "Con la Manga al Codo" ("With Sleeves Turned up to the Elbow") when an announcer came on the air after his program and stated that Artalejo's remarks "did not conform to the truth."[84]

Pressures on the Foreign Press

During late 1959 and early 1960, foreign correspondents who wrote critical stories about Cuba experienced harassment. *Miami Herald* correspondent James Buchanan was imprisoned for allegedly attempting to assist a Cuban fugitive escape the island. He served 13 days in jail before being released with a 14-year suspended sentence.[85]

There were other incidents of foreign reporters being briefly detained.[86] But government arrests of foreign journalists were infrequent. The government claimed that the Cuban people—not the government— independently acted against foreign correspondents who published lies and distortions about Cuba. Even if this were true, the government contributed to the animosity against the foreign press. Castro berated critical foreign reporters by name and whipped up public opinion against them.[87]

Chicago Tribune correspondent Jules Dubois, an early supporter of Castro, supposedly suffered the wrath of the Cuban people. During the days after the revolution, Dubois led a failed campaign to have *New York Times* journalist Herbert Matthews, another Castro supporter, appointed U.S. ambassador to Cuba. Dubois wired cables to Vice President Richard Nixon and other high U.S. government officials praising

10. FREEDOM OF THE PRESS IN CASTRO'S CUBA

Matthews for his indirect role in the liberation of Cuba and noting the respect Matthews enjoyed among the Cuban people.[88] Like other U.S. correspondents once enamored of Castro, Dubois started criticizing the disintegration of press freedom and other freedoms in Cuba.

In response to his critical reports, the Barber's Union of Pinar del Rio passed a resolution declaring Dubois "an undesirable customer." It instructed its members to refuse to give Dubois shaves or haircuts if he ever visited the province. The Union of Hotel and Restaurant Workers refused to serve Dubois or operate the elevator lifts for him.[89]

Dubois intensified his criticisms against Castro, adopting the rhetoric of the anti-Communists.[90] In late October 1959, Castro denounced Dubois as an enemy of Cuba during one of his marathon speeches. After the speech, Dubois had to be rescued from a mob. The *Chicago Tribune* later announced that it was replacing Dubois with another correspondent.[91]

CHAPTER 11
The Great Debate over Communism

Political commentators censored under the dictatorship of Fulgencio Batista experienced a new sense of freedom in 1959. Cuba's leading commentators were schooled under the late Eduardo Chibas, the founder of the Ortodoxo Party who committed a dramatic over-the-radio suicide in 1951 as he railed against widespread political corruption. The commentators looked forward to returning to their microphones and denouncing their enemies. As *New York Times* correspondent Charles Friedman wrote:

> No sooner had Premier Fidel Castro's bearded warriors chased out Fulgencio Batista then the long-suppressed broadcasters burst into action. ... The taboo on political programs imposed by Batista had the same effect as if he had taken away from the Cubans their beloved beans and rice. Smoldering in protest, they had to knuckle under. The alternative was jail or worse. The way things were going, one could easily have joined the society of martyrs. As the new government took over, the industry sighed happily. Ace commentators warmed up vocal organs and practiced arm waving for a return of free speech.[1]

Jose Pardo Llada and Luis Conte Aguero, both disciples of Chibas, were Cuba's most prominent commentators after the Castro government came to power. Their broadcasts after the revolution, independent of any party affiliation, "served as a clearing house for protest and as an important center of agitation."[2]

During the last four months of 1958, Pardo Llada was with Castro's rebels in the Sierra Maestra hills. With his trademark oversize dark glasses and lisp, Pardo Llada had been a fixture in Cuban radio for the past 15 years. He returned to Cadena Oriental de Radio in 1959, where he worked during the years before the Batista coup. His new program was from 1 to 2 p.m. every day. Pardo Llada's longtime friend and Ortodoxo colleague, Max Lesnick, had a 12:30 program that preceded his.[3] Because of their support for Castro, both men were described in the U.S. press as Castro cronies who spewed out unending litanies of "American imperialism and monopolists."[4]

Conte Aguero returned to Cuba in January 1959 from self-imposed exile in Argentina. He had established a reputation as an author, radio commentator, newspaper columnist, poet and Castro's semiofficial biographer. After the Castro revolution, Conte Aguero became a leading anti-Communist spokesman on his noon to 12:30 daily program over Radio Progreso. When CMQ's Abel Mestre asked him to host a daily television program from 1:30 to 3 p.m., he gladly accepted the offer while continuing his radio program. After his Radio Progreso program, he drove to CMQ's Radiocentro Building for his television program, "Hablar con Conte Aguero" ("Speak with Conte Aguero"). Conte Aguero said he maintained this hectic schedule of daily radio and television programs because he viewed the broadcast media as "vehicles" to promote his anti-Communist cause.[5]

Pardo Llada and Conte Aguero both claimed to vigorously support Castro's revolution and oppose its enemies. But Castro's ambiguous stance toward Communism left room for the two commentators to distinguish themselves. Conte Aguero took an aggressive stand against Communism, accusing Cuba's Communists of being more loyal to the Soviet Union than to Cuba. Pardo Llada, on the other hand, supported Castro's view that there was a place for the Communist Party in the "Grand Coalition" of new Cuba.

Emilio Ochoa, the president of the disorganized Ortodoxo Party, expressed disgust at Pardo Llada and Conte Aguero for abandoning the party and seeking political power on their own. "All these people—Pardo Llada, Conte Aguero, etc.—believed that the revolution was wonderful and that they were going to be Gods in Cuba."[6]

CMQ's Relations with Castro

After the revolution, relations between Castro and CMQ started on the wrong path. Castro was abruptly cut off the air during his first appearance on CMQ-TV's "Ante la Prensa" ("Meet the Press") program after he had spoken for two hours.[7] After experiencing Castro's wrath, CMQ's Mestre brothers never cut Castro off the air again.[8] Feeling that they did not know enough about Castro, they made inquiries to discover who they might hire as an announcer to explain what was happening inside the government. Their inquiries led them to Conte Aguero. As Abel Mestre said:

> When Fidel came to power and Batista fled Cuba, we had no one at CMQ—commentators or journalists—who had good connections with any of the Fidelistas. We were eager to establish such connections. It had been mentioned to us that Conte Aguero had very good relations with Castro and even wrote a book about Castro. And then I spoke with him and asked him to be a commentator on CMQ. And there is no question whatsoever that from the beginning he was fundamentally in favor of what Fidel Castro stood for and was doing, up until a certain point.[9]

After Conte Aguero joined CMQ, Abel Mestre had several meetings with Conte Aguero in his office regarding whether Castro was a Communist.[10] Conte Aguero kept reassuring the skeptical Mestre that Castro was not a Communist. The commentator, however, expressed reservations about the men surrounding Castro.

"La Coubre" Explosion

Pardo Llada criticized Conte Aguero over the radio as early as July 1959, when Conte Aguero encouraged President Manuel Urrutia Lleo to denounce anti-Communism over Conte Aguero's CMQ television program. Urrutia's temerity in attacking the Communists, egged on by Conte Aguero, resulted in a clash with Castro in which Urrutia was forced to resign and later take refuge in a foreign embassy. Despite the disastrous consequences of the Urrutia affair, Conte Aguero continued to denounce Communist influence in the government.

The debate over Communist influence became more acute after the French munitions ship "La Coubre" exploded in Havana Harbor on March 4, 1960. Eighty-one men, including 27 Cuban dockworkers, died in the explosion. The 4,300-ton freighter exploded while workers were unloading Belgian-supplied weapons. The next day, Castro led the funeral procession for the dockworkers. He delivered a stinging oration, accusing the United States of bombing the ship. Although the cause of the explosion was never discovered, an investigation by the ship's owners found no evidence of sabotage.[11]

Pardo Llada appeared on the radio the day after Castro's speech and repeated Castro's assertion of U.S. complicity in the explosion.[12] Comparing the explosion with an historical incident that many Cubans regarded as the most egregious example of U.S. imperialism in Cuba,

Pardo Llada likened the explosion of "La Coubre" with the explosion of the U.S.S. "Maine" in the same harbor in 1898.[13] The United States cited the "Maine" explosion to justify its intervention in Cuba's War of Independence against Spain.

Astonishingly, Pardo Llada also claimed to have unearthed "new evidence" of the United States' role in the sinking of the "Maine." His proof was the testimony of a 75-year-old man. The man said that when he was 13 he saw U.S. officers running to the harbor minutes before the disaster because he said they knew the ship would explode. The man also said that years later he had taken part in the salvaging of the "Maine" and uncovered evidence indicating a bomb was planted inside the ship by the Americans.[14]

Times of Havana columnist Carlos Todd reported that during normal times Pardo Llada's remarks would have been laughable. However, he added that "it is not laughable when you realize that there are many minds in this country that have been prepared to accept unconditionally any statements by men of Pardo's stamp."[15]

The anti-Communists joined the nationwide mourning for workers killed in the explosion, but they avoided making reference to the sensitive issue of U.S. participation in the calamity.[16] With the hostility directed against the United States, many Cubans who had once supported the United States remained silent about accusations of U.S. involvement in the explosion of "La Coubre."[17]

The government organized a fund-raising drive to assist the families of Cubans who had died in "La Coubre" and purchase weapons from foreign governments. Conte Aguero lent his support to the drive. He stood beside a large glass container outside CMQ's Radiocentro Building and thanked people as they dropped off their donations of money or jewelry. When people donated religious objects such as crucifixes, Conte Aguero, a devout Catholic, made religious remarks, such as "The cross is the symbol of eternity" or "God is our real monarch." According to Conte Aguero, these references to God upset the Communists, who intensified their attacks against him.[18] It was at this time that Conte Aguero launched what he called his "noble campaign" to warn Castro that the government was being undermined by Communists.[19]

A "Noble Campaign"

Conte Aguero launched the first salvo of his "noble campaign" on March 22, 1960. In a speech to the Havana Lions Club entitled "Karl Marx against Jose Marti," Conte Aguero claimed that the views of Cuban martyr Jose Marti (who died fighting the Spanish during Cuba's War of Independence in 1895) were opposed to Marxism.[20] Conte Aguero also claimed that Communists were subverting the revolution. He said he felt compelled to speak up and support the anti-Communist cause by "persuading those who were beginning to lose their perspective under the barrage of cheap Communist tactics to remain firm in the ranks and posts."[21]

As Conte Aguero recalled the Lions Club speech, the audience broke into cheers. Tears streamed down their eyes. Even the hired help joined in the applause.[22] While there were cheers, there were also challenges. *The New York Times* reported jeering and charges of "Yankee lackey."[23] From Conte Aguero's perspective on the podium, the jeers were drowned by the applause.[24]

The speech received wide attention. It was reprinted in several newspapers, including *Diario de la Marina* and *Prensa Libre*. *Revolucion* described the speech as an attempt "to murder the Cuban Revolution."[25] When Pardo Llada went on the air the next day, he described the speech as "divisionist."[26] Pardo Llada also accused Conte Aguero of being an agent of U.S. newsmagazines, newspapers and wire services, which he said were stirring world opinion against Castro and Cuba.[27] Max Lesnick, who knew both men since their early years in the Ortodoxo Party, said he tried to bring the two together. But they would not meet. Events had gone too far for reconciliation.[28]

On March 24, 1960, Conte Aguero appeared on CMQ-TV and charged that Communists were infiltrating the government. He also promised that he would read an open letter to Castro over the air the next day. As promised, Conte Aguero read the letter on Radio Progreso, warning Castro of unnamed Communists in the government. He said he would read the letter again on his CMQ television program later that day. He concluded his radio program by announcing that he would soon retire temporarily from radio and television "to write and mediate" and await Castro's response.[29]

Pardo Llada appeared on the air at 1 p.m., a half hour after Conte Aguero's radio program concluded. He said that Conte Aguero should either be expelled from the country within 24 hours or shot.[30] Pardo Llada also said that while "not all anti-Communists are traitors, all the traitors are anti-Communists. . . . I would rather be a sincere Communist than a lackey of the Yankees."[31]

When Conte Aguero's driver pulled up to CMQ's Radiocentro Building that day, hundreds of demonstrators were outside, some supporting and some opposing Conte Aguero.[32] Although he had been warned that demonstrators would be there, he was shocked by the size of the crowd. He said that he wanted to get out of the car and make his way into the studio to read his letter to Castro on television. But the crowd was so threatening that his driver stepped on the accelerator and sped away.[33]

From the fifth floor window of the Radiocentro Building, Goar and Abel Mestre and several CMQ executives watched the crowd threatening Conte Aguero and blocking his entrance into the building. The brothers instructed their news director to write an editorial for the evening news condemning the "provocation against Conte Aguero." Meanwhile, an announcer appeared on the air in place of Conte Aguero and described the events that had occurred outside the Radiocentro Building.[34]

Goar Mestre felt endangered. He was the public persona of CMQ. Now he feared that his association with CMQ put him in danger.[35] Mestre left the building through a production studio and made his way to his car and drove home. Once home, Mestre emptied his safe of money and jewels and prepared to flee the country with his family.[36]

That evening, representatives from the Ministry of the Treasury, accompanied by militiamen, entered CMBF-TV, Channel 4, the Havana station of the Mestre brothers' Cadena Nacional network. The Ministry served orders impounding the station's financial records. It claimed to have uncovered evidence that Batista had "substantial interests" in CMBF-TV. The Ministry was referring to the fact that Alberto Vadia, a contractor who did business with the Batista government, held shares of CMBF.[37]

It was no secret that Vadia had purchased 25 percent of CMBF in 1957.[38] Carlos Todd of *The Times of Havana* ridiculed the notion of Batista involvement in CMBF: "The reason for this drastic action is that Batista & Co. had a share in the intervened channel. It took somebody 15 months to come around to that conclusion, and come around they did at a most convenient time."[39]

Goar Mestre was at home packing in preparation for leaving Cuba when the phone rang. It was CMBF's program director, Alberto Vilar. Vilar recalled: "They [militiamen] were already in the building when I reached Goar on the phone. I asked Goar what we should do. He didn't seem surprised."[40]

"I was expecting something like this. That's why I wasn't surprised," Mestre said. "What could I tell him [Vilar] to do? I told him to get out of there and go some place and get drunk."[41] On March 27, Mestre boarded an airplane for New York with most of his family.

Vilar remained as program director at government-intervened CMBF-TV for two months before leaving Cuba. During the intervention, network programming was not much different than before. The only difference was that the network did not carry religious programming and some U.S. films with patriotic themes—such as John Wayne war movies.[42]

Conte Aguero had found a temporary hideout with friends. While in the house, he watched government officials on television denouncing him as an enemy of the revolution. On March 28, Fidel Castro delivered a four-hour speech. More than two hours of the speech were devoted to a denunciation of Conte Aguero. Castro denied that Conte Aguero was ever his friend.[43]

The next day Conte Aguero made his way to the Argentine Embassy, where he requested and received asylum. Before entering the embassy, he issued a statement: "When the Prime Minister twisted at will certain facts of my life to imply that there was dirt where there was only cleanliness, when I heard him term me vain, a pedant, a buffoon and a jerk after [once] having called me 'the most popular commentator in Oriente' and 'the young leader with the most prestige and intellectual capacity of the last republican period,' I felt pity for him."[44]

Government denunciations of Conte Aguero were now regular radio and television fare. Although these denunciations did not mention CMQ or Radio Progreso, which carried Conte Aguero's programs, there was a possibility that the Conte Aguero incident might be used to justify the seizure of the networks.

On March 31, Abel Mestre entered CMQ-TV studios and, just before the start of the "Meet the Press" program, told station workers that he would appear on the program alone that day. On the air, Mestre announced his and Goar's retirement from television "until the situation is clarified." It was not common knowledge then that Goar Mestre had already left Cuba.[45] When Abel Mestre referred to Castro's speech denouncing Conte Aguero, he pointed out that Castro "was kind enough to not involve us [CMQ] with the political views of that commentator [Conte Aguero], who was the main topic of that speech."[46] Mestre added:

> We want to say that it has always been our policy not to assume responsibility—outside of what the law requires—for the opinions mentioned by our guests and commentators. Besides being professional journalists, these commentators are citizens who have their own standards for looking at public issues. It would not be difficult for me to show that among the commentators at CMQ, they have displayed radically different views. . . . Here, all criticisms are heard, and we have always stated that our purpose is to air public opinion through live discussion as our program "Meet the Press" illustrates. Not even when the indefatigable Ortodoxo leader Eduardo Chibas had a show on our airwaves was it possible to label CMQ with his political views.[47]

On April 6, 1960, the Argentine Embassy secured safe passage for Conte Aguero to leave Cuba. Conte Aguero was escorted to the airport by the Argentine ambassador and a member of the Cuban Ministry of Foreign Relations. At the airport, he said that Communism in Cuba "has official authorization for all its villainy, even to putting in danger the lives of those who oppose it."[48] When Conte Aguero arrived in Miami, he brought with him letters from Castro addressing the commentator as "my brother" as proof that Castro at least once regarded the commentator as his friend.[49]

After Goar Mestre left Cuba, Abel Mestre remained in Havana to oversee CMQ's business affairs. Unlike his famous brother, Abel had shunned the public limelight and felt safe in Cuba. While he was able to move about freely, his activities were restricted after his and Goar's bank accounts were frozen, along with those of 400 other prominent Cubans.[50] Abel visited various government ministries and received a few sympathetic listeners, but no action was taken on his behalf.[51] After he appeared on "Meet the Press," the situation became dangerous and he fled the island on April 1.

Radio Progreso, which carried Conte Aguero's radio program, experienced severe labor problems after the Conte Aguero episode.[52] Co-owner Manuel (Manolo) Fernandez fled to Miami on June 10, leaving the network in the hands of his brother, Ovidio. Radio Progreso was intervened by the government on July 4, 1960.[53]

Within six months after the Conte Aguero episode, CMQ was confiscated by the government. Conte Aguero met with the Mestre brothers before launching his "noble campaign" over CMQ and warned them that his campaign might put CMQ in jeopardy. He praised the brothers for allowing him to continue.[54]

Was the Conte Aguero episode responsible for the takeover of CMQ? *New York Times* correspondent Tad Szulc thought so: "The incident provided an excuse for the government to place its own trusted men in key positions at the CMQ Television Network, Cuba's largest, over which Senor Conte had spoken."[55] Abel Mestre, however, said that CMQ was already experiencing difficulties, including labor problems, before the Conte Aguero episode.[56] He believed that CMQ would have been confiscated regardless of Conte Aguero's campaign.[57]

Pardo Llada Defects

Pardo Llada, long admired as an independent political broadcaster, earned a reputation as a Communist sympathizer and apologist for the

Castro government. He admitted that events had gotten beyond his control, and he felt uncomfortable with his reputation as a Castro lackey. Crestfallen, he defected in March 1961 while in Mexico on his way to Brazil, where he was scheduled to confer with Brazil's president on a diplomatic mission. In Mexico City, he declared: "I am breaking with Fidel Castro upon reaching the conviction that in Cuba it is no longer possible to maintain a position that is not in accord with the line of the Popular Socialist [Communist] Party and that any expression of independence, even in defense of the social program of the revolution, is considered a deviationist, divisionist or counter-revolutionary attitude. I leave Cuba in response to the command of my conscience."[58]

The Cuban government remained silent about Pardo Llada's defection for seven days. Finally, government-intervened *El Mundo* responded: "During seven days we have all but refused to believe the reality. But today we must recognize that Pardo Llada has gone over to the counter-revolution."[59]

Cuban government media launched a relentless tirade against Pardo Llada. *Revolucion* described Pardo Llada as a "traitor," "great deceiver rat" and a spy who "had sold himself to Yankee gold."[60] The staff at Cadena Oriental de Radio, Pardo Llada's primary broadcast outlet, issued a statement asserting that "the feeling of disgust is felt more profoundly by us because that worm has been deceiving us for two years through the most infamous farce since he used the fighting, revolutionary microphones of Cadena Oriental de Radio to launch his initiatives, and all of us, without a single exception, offered him our assistance and generous cooperation."[61]

While Cuban government media viciously attacked Pardo Llada, he received little sympathy outside Cuba. Historian Hugh Thomas wrote: "[Pardo Llada] defected to Mexico late in March, screaming 'betrayal' in the same voice as he had until then screamed 'imperialism.'"[62] A one-paragraph account about Pardo Llada's defection that appeared in *Time* magazine illustrated the negative image that Pardo Llada had earned in the U.S. press:

> Hitler had his [Josef] Goebbels and Castro his Jose Pardo Llada. If there was one sure thing about Pardo Llada, Castro's favorite and most poisonous radio commentator, it was that he was Cuba's number 1 opportunist. At the last possible moment, he switched from Batista's to Castro's side, and the venom he once, in Batista's pay, directed against Castro was now directed in Castro's pay against Batista. Last week he announced another switch in loyalties. He turned up at a Mexico City press conference, a defector from Castro, declaring that Communism had taken over Cuba and he could not stomach it.[63]

11. THE GREAT DEBATE OVER COMMUNISM

Lesnick, one of Pardo Llada's most vigorous supporters, said that the unfavorable portrayal of Pardo Llada in *Time* magazine and other U.S. news media represented "an American point of view."[64] As for *Time*'s assertion that Pardo Llada was once on Batista's payroll, Lesnick denied that Pardo Llada ever supported or praised Batista. Even Pardo Llada's critics conceded that he was never in collusion with Batista.

This alleged association with Batista, Lesnick speculated, might have been the result of Pardo Llada's brief presidential candidacy in 1958.[65] Once it had become clear that Batista would not permit fair elections, Pardo Llada withdrew his candidacy and called upon his supporters in the Nationalist Revolutionary Party to boycott the election. Nonetheless, his brief participation in the election might have been viewed as legitimizing Batista's claim of fair elections.[66]

Pardo Llada dismissed his presidential campaign as an unrealistic venture promoted by his friends: "My friends put me on the ballot. But it was a symbolic move. We didn't have a chance. Imagine. Fidel was already in the Sierra [Maestra], and he had already begun his fight. . . . But it really wasn't a presidential aspiration, but some friends who said 'Pardo for president' and came out with some posters. But it never went any further. There was no campaign. I left for exile in Spain and returned to enter the Sierra."[67]

As for the charges of being a Castro crony, a long record of radio speeches reprinted in *Revolucion* show Pardo Llada propagandizing on behalf of Castro. Pardo Llada conceded that at least during the early months of the revolution he enthusiastically supported the Castro government. Nonetheless, he maintained that he was an "independent" broadcaster who was never instructed what to say.[68]

After fleeing Cuba, Pardo Llada wrote his apologia entitled "I was a Fidelista," published in the Cuban exile publication *Bohemia Libre*. *Bohemia Libre* was the popular Cuban magazine *Bohemia* published by *Bohemia* publisher Miguel Angel Quevedo in exile.[69] Pardo Llada conceded in his *Bohemia Libre* article that he had become scorned as the "Minister of Hate" and "Castro's Goebbels."[70] An incident that obviously had some impact on him occurred in July 1960, when his car was riddled by machine-gun spray from a passing car. Pardo Llada was not hurt. Three months later the government announced that it had found and executed a man accused of the assassination attempt.[71]

Pardo Llada wrote in *Bohemia Libre* that even when he voluntarily attacked anti-Communists in his radio broadcasts, he was never in complete agreement with all government policies. He claimed that as early as February 1960, just before he launched a series of scathing denunciations against Conte Aguero, he got into an internal "cold war" ("guerra fria") with Communists in the government. He also wrote that he warned Castro that the Cuban public was becoming weary of doctrinaire Marxist media. At this time, Castro had not yet publicly announced that he was a Marxist and would not do so until December 1961.[72]

While Pardo Llada never named Conte Aguero in his *Bohemia Libre* article, he asked his readers to understand how he viewed the staunch anti-Communists such as Conte Aguero. Under a heading entitled "The errors of those who were not anti-Communists," Pardo Llada wrote that the anti-Communists were closely identified with the United States and its history of imperialistic domination of Cuba. Meanwhile, he wrote, certain Communist ideals appealed to people like himself. He claimed that between Communism and anti-Communism there was a third path exemplified by non-aligned political leaders of the day, such as Jawaharlal Nehru, Sukarno and Gamal Abdal Nasser.[73]

Many leading members of the Cuban exile community never forgave Pardo Llada for the relatively brief period of his career when he was a willing or unwilling Castro spokesperson. Over the years, however, Pardo Llada's image in the exile community has improved. Part of the credit can be attributed to his feisty daughter, Bernadette. In July 1991, Ms. Pardo, a television reporter at a Spanish-language station in Miami, interviewed Castro in Guadalajara, Mexico, during an Ibero-American summit conference. She became a heroine in the exile community when she confronted Castro with a letter the Cuban leader had written to her father in 1958 praising freedom of the press. After Ms. Pardo pressed Castro as to when he would permit press freedom in Cuba, Castro said that Cuba was not yet ready. Ms. Pardo recalled that during one point in the meeting, Castro stared at her and said: "You know? You look just like your mother."[74]

When interviewed more than 30 years after fleeing Cuba, neither Pardo Llada nor Conte Aguero would criticize each other. They met in Miami and elsewhere in Latin America on several occasions during the 1980s and had reached some understanding. As Pardo Llada said, "People like us who have been involved in political and revolutionary struggles, I believe that we forget and forgive."[75] Conte Aguero claimed that both men were now "brothers united in the fight against Fidel Castro."[76]

Both Pardo Llada, a drama student, and Conte Aguero, a lawyer, put great consequence on the power of oratory to move public opinion. Yet, the two men perceived themselves as having different broadcast styles. Pardo Llada described the difference between his and Conte Aguero's style in this way:

11. THE GREAT DEBATE OVER COMMUNISM

He [Conte Aguero] was a very good, lyrical orator, with certain tendencies to be florid. I don't say this to be critical. Some people are like this. Conte Aguero's oratory style still fascinates many people. I think that I have a communication style that is more direct, or perhaps more clear. I go directly to the story. I don't use those endearing terms that gave Luis such popularity and success.[77]

Conte Aguero described his style as rational and logical: "I always gave great thought to my words before I spoke. I made my arguments with logic. My words came from my heart. I did not yell or scream."[78]

Tad Szulc, the *New York Times* correspondent in Cuba during the Pardo Llada–Conte Aguero dispute, agreed that there were some stylistic differences between the two men, with Pardo Llada more caustic in his attacks and Conte Aguero more likely to embellish his speeches with colorful phrases. But he felt that "the differences were not all that great."[79]

The End of CMQ

Amadeo Barletta, the owner of the Telemundo television network and other properties, held onto his 30 businesses (the number varied because he bought and sold businesses) worth an estimated $40 million until February 1960. The government accused Barletta of tax evasion and profiting under Batista.[80] Considering that Barletta had long been suspected of Batista connections, it was surprising that he was able to hold his properties for so long.[81]

Barletta and his son were briefly placed under house arrest in Barletta's mansion across the street from Abel Mestre's house in a swank country club section of Havana. Barletta then made his way to the Italian Embassy, where he remained for 111 days before being allowed to leave for the Dominican Republic.[82] He made his way to Miami, where, like many other Cuban publishers, he published his newspaper, *El Mundo*, in exile.[83] Meanwhile, government-operated Telemundo was renamed Television Revolucion.

The confiscation of the Telemundo television network left CMQ with no effective competition. Ironically, while critics in the government complained about the "CMQ monopoly," the government helped CMQ virtually monopolize radio and television by eliminating CMQ's major competitors. Goar Mestre said that CMQ was making a profit until it was confiscated on Sept. 12, 1960. Mestre added, however, that "we knew that it was just a matter of time before they [the government] would come for CMQ."[84]

According to a State Department report, the confiscation of CMQ represented the first Cuban government expropriation of a broadcast medium in which the government did not even attempt to justify the takeover on the grounds of past Batista collusion.[85] Instead, the government maintained that CMQ was confiscated because of labor problems and because the Mestre brothers had abandoned their broadcast properties after fleeing Cuba.[86] The government appointed Gregorio Ortega, a writer for *Revolucion,* as "intervenor" of CMQ. Ortega kept most CMQ programming intact. One major change, however, was that the annual live television broadcasts of the U.S. World Series baseball games to Cuba were canceled and replaced with Cuban baseball games. No explanation was given for this change except "a new philosophy in the regime at CMQ."[87]

During April 1961, Itiel Perez, state director of Cuban television, attacked the now-exiled Barletta and Pumarejo for their Batista connections. Perez, however, did not accuse the exiled Mestre brothers of Batista connections. Instead, Perez accused the brothers of operating an organization that served the interests of the United States:

> [T]he organization of [the] Mestre brothers showed some independence as to official [Batista] policy. It aimed more or less at protecting the home and North American capitalist systems and political principles within the framework of the interests of these circles. It is possible to say that from the political point of view it followed the directives of the [U.S.] State Department, great North American monopolies and great industrial enterprises in Cuba.[88]

Although the Cuban government never formally accused the Mestre brothers of Batista connections, Pardo Llada did. The day after the confiscation of CMQ, Pardo Llada unleashed a vitriolic radio attack against the exiled Mestre brothers.[89] He accused the brothers of using their radio and television networks to undermine the revolution.[90] When questioned about his attack against the Mestre brothers, Pardo Llada dismissed the event as insignificant and stated that he couldn't remember the incident:

> Look, I don't want to have to defend myself against things that have been said about me. It was said that I pushed for intervention against CMQ and that I was responsible for what happened to *Diario de la Marina* and the Rivero family [that owned the newspaper]. I had absolutely nothing to do with all that because I was not the government. I was the man that spoke on radio. I had nothing personal against Mestre. I don't think I attacked him. However, I did attack *Diario de la Marina.* It was a matter of ideology. But

11. THE GREAT DEBATE OVER COMMUNISM

at the same time that I attacked it, I was good friends with the people there. But I would have nothing to do with the closing of any station or newspaper.[91]

Upon its takeover, the CMQ broadcast empire was consolidated into the official government broadcasting system, the Independent Front of Free Stations, known by the Spanish acronym FIEL. FIEL consisted of more than 100 radio stations and, with the takeover of CMQ, all 28 television stations in Cuba.[92]

FIEL had been organized by Ernesto "Che" Guevara with the assistance of Miguel Llanes, a leftist Chilean whom Guevara had brought to Cuba.[93] By May 1961, Castro had a regular Friday broadcast over FIEL.[94] FIEL also featured a number of well-known announcers who were thought to reflect the government line. They included Pardo Llada, Luis Gomez Wanguemert, Eddy Martin, Tony Fernandez and Max Lesnick.[95]

Pardo Llada said that he had nothing to do with the establishment of FIEL. But because of his close relationship with Gueverra, and as the most well known commentator on FIEL, he became closely associated with the network. Pardo Llada had recently accompanied Gueverra on a whirlwind tour through Africa, Japan, India and Israel, and it was widely believed that the popular commentator was Gueverra's propagandist or public relations advisor. In addition, Pardo Llada and Che were thought to share an affinity for Peronism (a philosophy of Latin American unity tinged with anti-Americanism espoused by then-exiled Argentine strongman Juan Domingo Peron). By the time FIEL was organized on March 20, 1960, Pardo Llada already felt uncomfortable with his close association with the Castro revolution:

> At first everything was the same as always. I was independent. But then began the confiscations of privately owned stations, and they created the FIEL network. Fidel decided that the broadcasts I was transmitting via Cadena Oriental de Radio should be transmitted over the [FIEL] network throughout the whole country. I was already almost broken with the revolution. Perhaps I wasn't a person whom they trusted because I was not a Communist, nor did I have any liking for the Communists, nor was I Fidel's slave. . . . When FIEL began operating, I was not involved [in its creation]. They didn't want anything to do with me.[96]

The Radio Swan Connection

One of the accusations that Pardo Llada made against the Mestre brothers in his Sept. 13, 1960, speech was that the CIA radio station, Radio Swan, had been "transformed into CMQ in exile."[97] While Pardo

Llada's description of CMQ as a CIA station was an exaggeration, it was not without substance. CMQ programming did indeed appear on Radio Swan. Abel Mestre admitted that much.[98]

Shortly after leaving Cuba, Abel Mestre incorporated CMQ in Tallahassee, Florida. Goar Mestre was not involved in CMQ in exile. Using the CMQ name, Abel Mestre started producing radio programs in a studio in Coral Gables, Florida, a swank section of Miami. The programs were shipped by air to stations throughout South America and the Caribbean for rebroadcast to Cuba. The stations featured news and commentary on the political situation in Cuba that were decidedly anti-Castro.[99]

Among the stations that aired the CMQ programs was Radio Swan, a 50-kilowatt AM station off the Honduran coast that was secretly operated by the CIA.[100] The CIA operated the station through a civilian front organization called The Gibraltar Steamship Corp.[101]

Abel Mestre said he received money from a number of his "friends" to produce the radio programs in Coral Gables from 1961 until 1967, when the financing dried up. Although he could not say for certain whether the U.S. government funded the programs, he suspected that at least some of the money came from the State Department. "It came from friends that we had," Mestre said. "It may be that these friends were close to the U.S. government. . . . Yes, it [the money] might have come from the U.S. government. I didn't know for sure. I was never specifically told so. They don't give you a receipt and tell you this comes from the State Department."[102]

CHAPTER 12
The Omnipresent Microphones

This book described broadcasting in Cuba before the Com-
munist government nationalized all mass media in the early 1960s. It might at first appear as if the story of Cuban broadcasting before Castro's ascent to power in 1959 was merely a prologue for the Castro era. But the plot and characters in the story of Cuban radio and television during the years preceding Castro were not merely the opening acts for some bigger act to follow. These men (for the most part, Cuban society did not include women in important positions during this time) shaped and influenced Castro-era broadcasting.

Pre-Castro broadcasting involved several major themes, including the alleged corruption of the broadcast media, the economic conditions in which the media operated, the political conditions in Cuba and issues related to freedom of the press.

Corruption

When scholars make passing mention of the people and broadcast media organizations in pre-Castro Cuba, they usually dismiss the media owners and their organizations as "corrupt" or "irresponsible."[1] The charges of irresponsibility stem from the media's escapist programming. The charges of corruption can be traced to the tradition of politicians secretly purchasing shares of radio and television stations. These practices were widespread before the Batista dictatorship. After the Castro revolution, however, the broadcast owners who were revealed to have received assistance from the Batista government were depicted as traitors and their assets were confiscated.

Economic Conditions

Cuban radio experienced rapid growth during the 1930s and 1940s. During the 1950s, television came to Cuba and quickly became a major media industry. The early development of radio and television was accomplished with little involvement or intervention by the Cuban government.

Wealthy businesspeople, some with U.S. financial backing, thrived in this environment. They constructed radio and television stations and networks that were the envy of Latin America. Many Cuban stations rivaled those of much larger nations in the region. One leading scholar of international broadcasting described pre-Castro Cuban radio and television as one of "the most freewheeling private commercial systems in the hemisphere."[2]

Not until dictator Fulgencio Batista's March 10, 1952, coup did Cuban politics thrust itself into the story of the island's radio and television systems. Batista implemented harsh censorship and virtually silenced all political criticism. Batista's military coup and subsequent harsh rule were the source of much public and media discontent.

Cuban broadcasters, like most other segments of Cuban society, warmly greeted Castro's seizure of power. They hoped that government-media relations would return to "normal," as conditions were before the Batista dictatorship. They were quickly disappointed.

The Castro government gradually shifted to a Marxist system which included government control of the press. The unstable economic and political climates created by the Castro government during 1959 and 1960 stunted broadcast industry growth. The Cuban broadcast industry that had prospered in the free enterprise climate before Castro could not survive the political and economic tumult created by Castro's revolution. Within two years after Castro's rise to power, all mass media would be in government hands. Had events taken a different path in Cuba, it is possible that Cuba might have developed Latin America's largest radio and television networks.

Political Conditions

The corrupt but democratically elected governments of Ramon Grau San Martin (1944–1948) and Carlos Prio Soccaras (1948–1952) frequently complained about what they perceived as unfair press treatment. While they occasionally engaged in obligatory suppression of Communist newspapers, mainstream, commercial media were permitted great latitude to discuss political issues and criticize the government.

A few radio stations leased time to political commentators. The station owners claimed that the commentators' views did not reflect the stations' management. The only ideology the owners subscribed to was free enterprise. Many politician-commentators gained popularity as a result of their clever use of the broadcast media.

Generally, Cuba's commercial broadcasting industry avoided embroiling itself in national politics. Even after Batista's coup, most broadcasters reluctantly accepted broadcasting restrictions with little protest. The broadcasters appeared more annoyed by the Batista dictatorship's incessant censorship, which hindered the Cuban broadcasting industry's financial growth, than any lofty moral concerns about human rights and personal freedom.

Freedom of the Press

Discussions about freedom of the press in pre-Castro Cuba usually concerned the print media. The stories of the travails of magazines and newspapers under Batista and Castro have become legendary and part of the Cuban political lore. Cuban print journalists portrayed their industry as a social institution that defended the public's "right to know"—a uniquely North American concept, but not without its Cuban counterpart.

The broadcast media in pre-Castro Cuba did not take upon themselves the onerous burden of being social institutions defending important public rights. Instead, they portrayed themselves as primarily entertainment media. The suppression against the broadcast media, therefore, was not viewed so much as a violation of freedom of the press as just another violation against free enterprise.

In a classic treatise published almost 40 years ago on the role of the press in society, Siebert, Peterson and Schramm put forward the maxim that "the press always takes on the form and coloration of the social and political structures within which it operates."[3] This maxim held true for the broadcast media in pre-Castro Cuba. Radio and television in pre-Castro Cuba affected and were affected by the conditions of their time and the island's social, political and economic institutions.

Notes

FOREWORD

1. Andrew Zimbalist, "Dateline Cuba: Hanging on in Havana," *Foreign Policy* 92:151–167 (1993); Carmelo Meas-Lago, ed., *Cuba after the Cold War* (Pittsburgh: University of Pittsburgh Press, 1993); Gillian Gunn, *Cuba in Transition: Options for U.S. Policy* (Washington: Twentieth Century Fund Press, 1993).
2. Lawrence C. Soley and John S. Nichols, *Clandestine Radio Broadcasting* (New York: Praeger, 1987).
3. *Cuba and Fidel* (Churchill Films, 1975).
4. Frank Mankiewicz and Kirby Jones, *With Fidel: A Portrait of Castro and Cuba* (New York: Ballantine Books, 1975), 82.
5. Jonathan Kozol, "A New Look at the Literacy Campaign in Cuba," *Harvard Educational Review*, 48:343–349 (1978).
6. Kozol; Jesus Garcia Jimenez, *Television Educativa para America Latina* (Mexico: Editorial Porrua, 1970), 239; Jorge Werthein, "Education Television in Cuba," in George Gerbner, ed., *Mass Media Policies in Changing Cultures* (New York: John Wiley & Sons, 1977), 131.
7. Gerald Sussman, "Revolutionary Communications in Cuba: Ignoring New World Orders," *Critical Studies in Mass Communication*, 10:210 (1993); Martin Carnoy, "Educational Reform and Social Transformation in Cuba, 1959–1989," in Martin Carnoy and Joel Samoff, *Education and Social Transformation in the Third World* (Princeton, N.J.: Princeton University Press, 1990), 153–208; Marvin Leiner, "Cuba's Schools: 25 Years Later," in Philip Brenner, William M. LeoGrande, Donna Rich, and Daniel Siegel, eds., *Cuba Reader: The Making of a Revolutionary Society* (New York: Grove Press, 1989), 445–456.
8. Jorge I. Dominguez, *Cuba: Order and Revolution* (Cambridge: Harvard University Press, 1978), 167.

PREFACE

1. Herbert Matthews, *Revolution in Cuba: An Essay in Understanding* (New York: Charles Scribner's Sons, 1975), 126.
2. Kuo-jen Tsang, Yean Tsai, and Scott S.K. Liu, "Geographic Emphases of International News Studies," *Journalism Quarterly*, 65:191–196 (1988).
3. Jorge Dominguez, *Cuba: Order and Revolution* (Cambridge: Harvard University Press, 1978), 165; "TV Abroad: Starting to Boom," *Broadcasting*, June 1, 1959, 60; George A. Codding, Jr., *Broadcasting Without Barriers* (Paris: United Nations Educational, Scientific and Cultural Organization, 1959), 148; John A. Lent, *Mass Communications in the Caribbean* (Ames: Iowa State University Press, 1990), 344.
4. John Spicer Nichols, "Republic of Cuba," in George Thomas Kurian, ed., *World Press Encyclopedia* (London: Mansell Publishing Co., 1982), 257.

CHAPTER 1

1. "Quedo Oficialmente Inaugurada Ayer Radio Teleonico," *Diario de la Marina*, Oct. 11, 1922, 1, 6.
2. "Zayas Speaks to People of U.S. by Radio," *The Havana Post*, Oct. 11 1922, 1.
3. Francisco Mota, "La Radio Cubana se Inauguro el 10 de Octubre de 1922," *Bohemia*, March 4, 1966, 104–105.
4. John A. Lent, *Mass Communications in the Caribbean* (Ames: Iowa State University Press, 1990), 119.
5. Oscar Luis Lopez, *La Radio en Cuba: Estudio de su Desarrollo en la Sociedad Neocolonial* (Habana: Editorial Letras Cubanas, 1981), 10.
6. "Zayas' Speech Heard in Many Parts of the United States over Radio Telephone," *The Havana Post*, Oct. 12, 1922, 1.
7. Mota, "La Radio Cubana se Inauguro.
8. "Zayas Speaks to People."
9. Mota, "La Radio Cubana se Inauguro."
10. Luis Lopez, *La Radio en Cuba*, 81; Mota, "La Radio Cubana."
11. Mota, "La Radio Cubana se Inauguro."
12. "La Radio en Cuba," *Bohemia*, May 10, 1953, 106–113, 159–161.
13. Mota, "La Radio Cubana se Inauguro."
14. "La Radio en Cuba."
15. Luis Lopez, *La Radio en Cuba*, 52. The numbers of early Cuban stations cited in this chapter should be regarded as estimates. The author found sources with different, though generally similar, statistics.
16. Enrique C. Betancourt, *Apuntes para la Historia: Radio, Television y Farandula de la Cuba de Ayer* (San Juan, Puerto Rico, 1986), 46–47.
17. *Bohemia*, which was published as an independent publication until it was seized by the Castro government in 1960, was the largest circulation magazine in Latin America. It was widely read throughout Spanish-speaking nations.
18. "La Radio en Cuba," 108.
19. "La Radio en Cuba," 108. PWX programming was supported by a $1 tax on the sale of radio receivers.
20. Pablo Medina and Carolina Hospital, "The Golden Age of Radio: An Interview with Conchita Nogara," *Cuban Heritage*, 3(1):18–30 (1990).
21. Luis Lopez, *La Radio en Cuba*, 524.
22. Luis Lopez, *La Radio en Cuba*, 479.
23. "La Radio en Cuba," 106.
24. Alberto Giro, "Evolucion Historica de la Radio y la Television en Cuba," *Diario de la Marina*, Dec. 22, 1953, 92–93.
25. Luis Lopez, *La Radio en Cuba*, 524.
26. Mota, "La Radio Cubana se Inauguro."
27. Luis Lopez, *La Radio en Cuba*, 476–477.
28. Luis Lopez, *La Radio en Cuba*, 81.
29. Medina and Hospital, "The Golden Age."
30. "La Radio en Cuba," 108.
31. Luis Lopez, *La Radio en Cuba*, 531.
32. Betancourt, *Apuntes para la Historia*, 50; "A New List of Broadcasters," *The New York Times*, Feb. 10, 1929, X, 18.
33. Luis Lopez, *La Radio en Cuba*, 524.
34. Luis Lopez, *La Radio en Cuba*, 51.
35. "Nicolas Jovino Garcia. Radio Announcer in Cuba, Miami," *The Miami Herald*, June 12, 1993, 6B.
36. Medina and Hospital, "The Golden Age."
37. Medina and Hospital, "The Golden Age"; Luis Lopez, *La Radio en Cuba*, 470.
38. Medina and Hospital, "The Golden Age," 27; Luis Lopez, *La Radio en Cuba*, 471.

39. Luis Lopez, *La Radio en Cuba*, 470.
40. Medina and Hospital, "The Golden Age," 20.
41. Luis Lopez, *La Radio en Cuba*, 113.
42. Luis Lopez, *La Radio en Cuba*, 113–114.
43. Salvador Diaz-Verson, *One Man, One Battle* (New York: World Wide, 1980), 184.
44. Luis Lopez, *La Radio en Cuba*, 117.
45. Diaz-Verson, *One Man*, 184.
46. James Schwooch, *The American Radio Industry and Its Latin American Activities, 1900–1939* (Urbana: University of Illinois Press, 1990), 107–109.
47. "Cuban Law Creates New Department," *The New York Times*, July 3, 1925, 13; Luis Lopez, *La Radio en Cuba*, 339.
48. Jesus A. Chia Garzon, *El Monopolio del Jabon y el Perfume en Cuba* (Habana: Editorial de Ciencias Sociales, 1977), 77.
49. Roy W. Peet, "Soap Use Today," *Soap and Sanitary Chemicals*, August 1952, 46–49, 113.
50. Luis Lopez, *La Radio en Cuba*, 253–260.
51. Luis Lopez, *La Radio en Cuba*, 423–435.
52. "La Nueva Novena," *Bohemia*, May 22, 1949, 36–37; "El Ultimo 'Survey'," *Bohemia*, March 19, 1950, 58–59; "Survey Nacional," *Bohemia*, Nov. 13, 1948, 34.
53. Jose Manuel Viana, former vice president in charge of advertising at Sabates, personal interview, Miami, May 23, 1991.
54. Raul Gutierrez Serrano, "The Radio in Cuba," *International Journal of Opinion and Attitude Research*, 1:62–70 (June 1947); Richard Pack, "Report from Havana," *The New York Times*, April 28, 1946, II, 7.
55. Pack, "Report from Havana."
56. Pack, "Report from Havana."
57. Pack, "Report from Havana."
58. R. Hart Phillips, "Cuba: Soviet: Propaganda Center," *The American Mercury*, June 1945, 671–676.
59. Pack, "Report from Havana."
60. Gutierrez Serrano, "The Radio in Cuba."
61. Pack, "Report from Havana."
62. Phillips, "Cuba: Soviet Propaganda Center."
63. Para que Ahora Complicarse la Vida?" *Bohemia*, Jan. 12, 1950, 58.
64. Luis Lopez, *La Radio en Cuba*, 135.
65. "La Radio en Cuba," 113.
66. Betancourt, *Apuentes para la Historia*, 76.
67. Luis Lopez, *La Radio en Cuba*, 116–117.
68. "La Radio en Cuba," 113.
69. Luis Lopez, *La Radio en Cuba*, 139.
70. "Los Gavilanes," *Bohemia*, July 16, 1939, 28–30, 51; Luis Lopez, *La Radio en Cuba*, 137.
71. "La Radio en Cuba," 159. These were small "repeater" stations that retransmitted CMQ's signals from Havana. They were often operated by two or three people who monitored and maintained equipment.
72. "La Radio en Cuba," 113.
73. "La Radio en Cuba," 113.
74. Manolo Reyes, personal interview, Miami, April 4, 1991.
75. Viana, personal interview.
76. Reyes, personal interview.
77. Reyes, personal interview.
78. Luis Lopez, *La Radio en Cuba*, 167.
79. "La Radio en Cuba," 159.
80. "La Radio en Cuba," 159.
81. Luis Lopez, *La Radio en Cuba*, 167.

82. Luis Lopez, *La Radio en Cuba*, 167-168; "Funeral Rites Today for Amado Trinidad," *The Havana Post*, Aug. 12 1955, 1; Betancourt, *Apuentes para la Historia*, 70-75.
83. Luis Lopez, *La Radio en Cuba*, 168.
84. Viana, personal interview. Viana described Trinidad as extremely unsophisticated about radio operations and driven more by a desire for power than profits. This observation was confirmed by numerous other observers.
85. "La Radio en Cuba," 160.
86. Jack Alicoate, ed., *The 1941 Radio Annual* (New York: The Radio Daily, 1942), 1002-1004.
87. Ana E. Santiago, Minuca Villaverde and Cristina Vazquez, "Muere Pionero de TV Hispanoamericana," *El Nuevo Herald*, Nov. 28, 1991, 1B.
88. For an account of Goar Mestre's early career, see Octavio R. Costa, "Goar Mestre," *Bohemia*, July 12, 1953, 36-38, 97-100.
89. Costa, "Goar Mestre."
90. Goar Mestre, personal communication, Buenos Aires, Sept. 10, 1991.
91. Goar Mestre, personal interview, Key Biscayne, Fla. May 10, 1990.
92. Costa, "Goar Mestre."
93. Marvin Alisky, "Early Mexican Broadcasting," *Hispanic American Historical Review*, 34:516-519 (November 1954).
94. Goar Mestre, personal interview.
95. Abel Mestre, personal interview, Miami, April 14, 1991.
96. Luis Lopez, *La Radio en Cuba*, 136.

CHAPTER 2

1. Manolo Reyes, personal interview, Miami, April 4, 1991.
2. "Radiocentro Habana," *Newsweek*, March 22, 1948, 65.
3. Richard Pack, "Report from Havana," *The New York Times*, April 28, 1946, II, 7.
4. Goar Mestre, personal interview, Key Biscayne, Fla., May 10, 1990.
5. Goar Mestre, personal interview.
6. Goar Mestre, personal interview.
7. Goar Mestre, personal interview.
8. Jack Alicoate, ed., *The 1944 Radio Annual* (New York: The Radio Annual, 1945), 999.
9. "Commercial Series for Latin American Nations Viewed as Aid to Hemisphere Relations," *Broadcasting*, Oct. 15, 1940, 26; E. Roderick Deihl, "South of the Border: The NBC and CBS Radio Networks and the Latin American Venture, 1930-1942," *Communication Quarterly*, 25:2-12 (1977); Fred Fejes, *Imperialism, Media, and the Good Neighbor* (Norwood, N.J.: Ablex, 1986), 66; R. Hart Phillips, "The Future of American Propaganda in Latin America," *Public Opinion Quarterly*, 9:305-312 (1945); J.S. Wilson, "Short Wave War in Latin America," *Radio News* (September 1938), 10.
10. Alicoate, *The 1944 Radio Annual*, 999.
11. Fred Fejas, *Imperialism*, 115; Charles A.H. Thompson, *Overseas Information Service of the United States* (Washington, D.C.: The Brookings Institution, 1948), 130.
12. Goar Mestre, personal interview.
13. Charles Friedman, "Unrest in Cuban TV Studios," *The New York Times*, May 10, 1959, II, 14.
14. Goar Mestre, personal interview.
15. Goar Mestre, personal interview.
16. Goar Mestre, personal interview.
17. Goar Mestre, personal interview.
18. Oscar Luis Lopez, *La Radio en Cuba: Estudio de su Desarrollo en la Sociedad Neocolonial* (Habana: Editorial Letras Cubanas, 1981), 251.

NOTES

19. Goar Mestre, personal interview.
20. Goar Mestre, personal interview.
21. Enrique C. Betancourt, *Apuentes para la Historia: Radio, Television y Farandula de la Cuba de Ayer* (San Juan, Puerto Rico: Ramallo Bros., 1986), 62.
22. Raul Gutierrez Serrano, "The Radio in Cuba," *International Journal of Opinion and Attitude Research*, 1:62-70 (June 1947).
23. Gutierrez Serrano, "The Radio in Cuba."
24. Gutierrez Serrano, "The Radio in Cuba," 64-65.
25. Elihu Katz, M. Gurevitch and H. Haas, "On the Use of Mass Media for Important Things," *American Sociological Review*, 38:164-181 (1973).
26. Gutierrez Serrano, "The Radio in Cuba," 64.
27. Abel Mestre, personal interview, Miami, April 14, 1991.
28. "La Radio y las Elecciones," *Bohemia*, June 13, 1948, 33.
29. Goar Mestre, personal interview.
30. "La Radio y las Elecciones."
31. Luis Lopez, *La Radio en Cuba*, 76.
32. Luis Lopez, *La Radio en Cuba*, 76.
33. "La Radio en Cuba," *Bohemia*, May 10, 1953, 160.
34. Goar Mestre, personal interview.
35. Abel Mestre, personal interview.
36. Abel Mestre, personal interview.
37. "La Radio en Cuba," 161.
38. Gutierrez Serrano, "The Radio in Cuba," 67.
39. Luis Lopez, *La Radio en Cuba*, 181.
40. "Radiocentro Habana."
41. "Radiocentro Habana."
42. "Radiocentro Habana."
43. Que Acusacion mas Ridicula!" *Bohemia*, Aug. 22, 1948, 39-40.
44. Betancourt, *Apuentes para la Historia*, 76-77.
45. Betancourt, *Apuentes para la Historia*, 76-77.
46. Goar Mestre, personal interview.
47. Goar Mestre, personal interview.
48. Abel Mestre, personal interview; Goar Mestre, personal interview.
49. Goar Mestre, personal interview.
50. Abel Mestre, personal interview; Goar Mestre, personal interview.
51. Betancourt, *Apuentes para la Historia*, 76-77; Luis Lopez, *La Radio en Cuba*, 135-136; "Causa Honda Pena el Fallecimiento de Miguel Gabriel," *Diario de la Marina*, Dec. 11, 1945, 3.
52. Luis Lopez, *La Radio en Cuba*, 135-136.
53. Abel Mestre, personal interview; Goar Mestre, personal interview.
54. Ray Eldon Hiebert, Donald F. Ungurait and Thomas W. Bohn, *Mass Media VI* (New York: Longman, 1991), 252-253.
55. Hiebert, Ungurait and Bohn, *Mass Media VI*, 254.
56. "Para que Ahora Complicarse la Vida?" *Bohemia*, Jan. 12, 1950, 58.
57. Goar Mestre, personal interview.
58. "Para que Ahora Complicarse la Vida?"
59. Abel Mestre, personal interview.
60. "Para que Ahora Complicarse la Vida?"
61. Goar Mestre, personal interview.
62. Luis Lopez, *La Radio en Cuba*, 125-132.
63. Luis Lopez, *La Radio en Cuba*, 125-132.
64. Justo Carrillo Hernandez, personal interview, Miami, July 16, 1992.
65. Karl E. Meyer and Tad Szulc, *The Cuban Invasion: The Chronicle of a Disaster* (New York: Frederick A. Praeger, 1962), 80.
66. Carrillo, personal interview.

67. Carrillo, personal interview.
68. Carrillo, personal interview; Goar Mestre, personal interview.
69. Luis Lopez, *La Radio en Cuba,* 125-132.
70. Goar Mestre, personal interview.
71. "Radiocentro Habana."
72. "Radiocentro Habana."
73. Luis Lopez, *La Radio en Cuba,* 129.
74. Luis Lopez, *La Radio en Cuba,* 128-129.
75. Carlos Cabesas, personal interview, WQBA news announcer, Miami, June 15, 1990.
76. Pedro Sevcec, "Goar Mestre: 'Padre de TV Latinoamerica'." *El Nuevo Herald,* Dec. 4, 1989, 1, 6.
77. Carrillo, personal interview.
78. Luis Lopez, *La Radio en Cuba,* 132.
79. Goar Mestre, personal interview.
80. Goar Mestre, personal interview.
81. Goar Mestre, personal interview.
82. "Barraje a Traves de los Microfonos," *Bohemia,* March 12, 1950, 56-60, 90, 57.
83. Abel Mestre, personal interview; Goar Mestre, personal interview. Although the Mestre brothers did not directly respond to Pumarejo's accusations over CMQ microphones, Abel Mestre did refute the charges in interviews with the press. "Barraje a Traves de los Microfonos."
84. Manolo Cores, director of programming at CMQ, personal interview, Miami, July 11, 1990.
85. "Cuba," *Hispanic American Report,* March 1957, 125.
86. Luis Lopez, *La Radio en Cuba,* 342.
87. Goar Mestre, personal interview.
88. Luis Lopez, *La Radio en Cuba,* 342.
89. Luis Lopez, *La Radio en Cuba,* 342.
90. "Barraje a traves de los Microfonos," 58.
91. Declassified letter from Francis J. Donohue, the cultural affairs officer at the U.S. Embassy in Havana, to the U.S. Department of State, Sept. 4, 1958. Declassified documents are on microfilm and are indexed in Gregory Murphy, project coordinator; Blair D. Hydrick, compiler, *A Guide to Confidential U.S. Department Central Files: Cuba 1955-1959.* Decimal numbers 737, 837 and 937 and Foreign Affairs Decimal Numbers 637 and 611.37 (Frederick, Md.: University Publications of America, Inc., 1986).
92. Declassified letter.
93. Goar Mestre, personal interview.
94. Goar Mestre, personal interview.
95. Goar Mestre, personal interview.

CHAPTER 3

1. "Cuban Advertising at Peak," *The New York Times,* April 29, 1947, 40.
2. Alberto Giro, "Mr. Frank H. Jones Recibo en 1928 las Primeras Senales de 'TV' en Cuba," *Diario de la Marina,* Dec. 22, 1953, 92.
3. Irving Settel, *A Pictorial History of Television,* second edition (New York: Frederick Ungar Publishing Co., 1983), 30-31.
4. Alberto Giro, "Mr. Frank H. Jones."
5. Settel, *A Pictorial History of Television,* 30.
6. Settel, *A Pictorial History of Television,* 31.
7. Gabino Delgado, "Television en la Habana," *Carteles,* Oct. 8, 1950, 44-45; "Three Video Stations Racing for First, Union Slated to Win," *The Havana Post,* Sept. 10, 1950, 12.

8. "Three Video Stations."
9. Declassified letter from Raymond L. Harrell, attache in the U.S. Embassy in Cuba, to the U.S. State Department, Dec. 21, 1950. Declassified documents are on microfilm and are indexed in Michael C. Davis, editor; L. Lee Yanike, compiler, *A Guide to Confidential U.S. Department Central Files: Cuba 1950–1954*. Decimal numbers 737, 837 and 937 and Foreign Affairs Decimal Numbers 637 and 611.37 (Frederick, Md.: University Publications of America, Inc., 1986).
10. Mike Alonso, "On the Air" (column), *The Havana Post*, Nov. 24, 1953, 6.
11. Mike Alonso, "Radio and Air" (column), *The Havana Post*, Feb. 8, 1953, 6.
12. Declassified letter.
13. "Television en Cuba," *Bohemia*, Oct. 22, 1950, 52–53.
14. In 1951, Argentina became the fourth Latin American country to inaugurate a television station. It was followed by Venezuela in 1952, the Dominican Republic in 1953, Chile in 1954, Nicaragua in 1955, Uruguay in 1956, and Peru in 1958. Joseph Straubhaar, "Television," in Harold E. Hinds, Jr., and Charles M. Tatum, eds., *Handbook of Latin American Popular Culture* (Westport, Conn.: Greenwood Press, 1985), 111.
15. "Television in Set-Poor Mexico," *Business Week*, Jan. 10, 1953, 117–120.
16. Timothy Green, *The Universal Eye: The World Television* (New York: Stein and Day, 1972), 53.
17. Enrique C. Betancourt, *Apuntes para la Historia: Radio, Television y Farandula de la Cuba de Ayer* (San Juan, Puerto Rico: Ramallo Bros., 1986), 86–87.
18. "Television," *Bohemia*, April 9, 1950, 56–57.
19. "El Ultimo 'Survey,'" *Bohemia*, May 19, 1950, 58–59.
20. Carmelina Rey, *Adonde va la Television Cubana?* Havana, 1959 (based on the author's thesis at the University of Havana), 23.
21. Mike Alonso, "On the Air" (column), *The Havana Post*, April 23, 1953, 6.
22. *Television: A World Survey* (Paris: UNESCO, 1953), 49–50.
23. Clifford W. Slaybaugh, telephone interview, Princeton, N.J., Oct. 19, 1990.
24. Slaybaugh, telephone interview.
25. "Three Video Stations."
26. "Three Video Stations."
27. "Three Video Stations."
28. Alberto Vilar, personal interview, Miami, March 28, 1991; Martha Mestre Pumarejo, personal interview, Miami, April 18, 1991; Fermin Peraza Sarausa, *Personalidades Cubans (Cuba en el Exilo)* (Coral Gables, Fla.: Copyright by Fermin Peraza Sarausa and Elena Verez Peraza, 1968), 66–67; Information on Pumarejo's early years in radio can be found in Betancourt, *Apuntes para la Historia*, 81–83, 86–87.
29. "Cuba's First TV to be Tonight if Station is Ready," *The Havana Post*, Oct. 6, 1950, 1.
30. Declassified letter from Raymond L. Harrell, attache in the U.S. Embassy in Cuba, to the U.S. State Department, Aug. 25, 1950.
31. Mestre Pumarejo, personal interview.
32. "Cuba Held Hotbed of TV Smugglers," *The New York Times*, Dec. 26, 1952, 24.
33. Vilar, personal interview.
34. Alberto Giro, "Primer Programa 'TV'," *Diario de la Marina*, Oct. 19, 1950, 15; Alberto Vilar, personal interview.
35. Vilar, personal interview.
36. Vilar, personal interview.
37. Alberto Giro, "Por Fin, la Television," *Diario de la Marina*, Oct. 17, 1950, 15; Vilar, personal interview.
38. "TV on Air Today as Union Radio Continues Test," *The Havana Post*, Oct. 17, 1950, 2.
39. Vilar, personal interview.
40. "Video Pasado por Agua," *Bohemia*, Nov. 12, 1950, 60.
41. Vilar, personal interview.

42. Vilar, personal interview.
43. Alberto Giro, "Desde Hoy se Ofreceran Todas las Noches Programas de Television," *Diario de la Marina,* Oct. 25, 1950, 15; Alberto Giro, "Televisara Union Radio Desde el Martes Los Juegos de Pelota," *Diario de la Marina,* Oct. 26, 1950, 15; "Television in Havana," *The New York Times,* Oct. 25, 1950, 51.
44. "El Video Sigue su Marcha," *Bohemia,* Oct. 22, 1950, 54.
45. Mestre Pumarejo, personal interview.
46. Hugh Thomas, *Cuba: The Pursuit of Freedom* (New York: Harper & Row, 1971), 755.
47. *Television: A World Survey,* 50.
48. "Cuba Held Hotbed."
49. "Cuba Held Hotbed."
50. Jose Pardo Llada, personal interview, Miami, Feb. 24, 1992.
51. Pardo Llada, personal interview.
52. Pardo Llada, personal interview.
53. Pardo Llada, personal interview.
54. Vilar, personal interview.
55. Pardo Llada, personal interview.
56. Vilar, personal interview.
57. Vilar, personal interview.
58. "Three Video Stations."
59. "La Television es el Tema," *Bohemia,* Sept. 10, 1950, 63–64.
60. Vilar, personal interview.
61. Declassified letter from R.M. Connell, First Secretary at the U.S. Embassy in Havana, to the U.S. Department of State, May 15, 1951.
62. Declassified letter, May 15, 1951.
63. Vilar, personal interview.
64. Vilar, personal interview.
65. Vilar, personal interview.
66. Anthony Slide, *The International Film Industry: A Historical Dictionary* (New York: Greenwood Press, 1989), 98; "Otra Emisora de Television," *Bohemia,* May 19, 1950, 60–61.
67. "Otra Emisora."
68. Vilar, personal interview.
69. Goar Mestre, personal communication, Buenos Aires, Sept. 10, 1991.
70. "Barraje a Traves de los Microfonos," *Bohemia,* March 12, 1950, 56–60, 90.
71. "Les Presento al Nuevo Presidente de Union Radio," *Bohemia,* Aug. 5, 1951, 54–55. Pelleya contended that the estimated $1.4 to $1.6 million debt reported in the popular press was too high. While he did not recall the exact figure, he said that it exceeded $1 million. Jose Luis Pelleya, personal interview, Miami, Aug. 3, 1992.
72. "Les Presento"; Pelleya, personal interview.
73. "Les Presento."
74. "Les Presento."
75. "Les Presento," 55.
76. Rodolfo Rodriguez Zaldivar, "Reto a Pardo Llada a que Demuestrestre que el Dinero de UR-TV es de los Prios," *Bohemia,* Aug. 21, 1951, 52–53.
77. Rodriguez Zaldivar, "Reto a Pardo Llada," 52.
78. Pelleya, personal interview.
79. Pardo Llada, personal interview.
80. Manolo Alonso, personal communication, New York, Sept. 13, 1991.
81. Vilar, personal interview.
82. "La Union de los Canales," *Bohemia,* April 20, 1952, 42–43.
83. Alonso maintained that there was no coercion on him to sell Union Radio. Alonso, personal interview; Co-owner Pelleya also said there was no government pressure to sell the station. Pelleya, personal interview.

NOTES 179

84. Pelleya, personal interview.
85. Pelleya, personal interview.
86. "La Union."
87. "La Union."
88. Luis J. Botifoll, personal interview, Miami, December 10, 1990; Pelleya, personal interview.

CHAPTER 4

1. CMQ-TV was "officially" inaugurated during a gala celebration on March 11, 1951. "American Visitors Leave after TV Inauguration," *The Havana Post,* March 13, 1951, 1.
2. Mirta Ojito, "What Turns 400 Million Viewers Worldwide On," *The Miami Herald,* May 26, 1992, 1E, 3E; Oscar Luis Lopez, *La Radio en Cuba: Estudio de su Desarrollo en la Sociedad Neocolonial* (Habana: Editorial Letras Cubanas, 1981), 211–213.
3. "Cuba," *Hispanic American Report,* July 1951, 24.
4. Luis Lopez, *La Radio en Cuba,* 291.
5. "Lo que Sea, ya se Vera," *Bohemia,* Feb. 24, 1957, 61.
6. "Preparando la Ofensiva," *Bohemia,* May 11, 1952, 44–45.
7. Declassified memorandum from Raymond L. Harrell, attache at the U.S. Embassy in Havana, addressed to the Department of State, May 7, 1952. Declassified documents are on microfilm and are indexed in Michael C. Davis, editor; L. Lee Yanike, compiler, *A Guide to Confidential U.S. Department Central Files: Cuba 1950–1954.* Decimal numbers 737, 837 and 937 and Foreign Affairs Decimal Numbers 637 and 611.37 (Frederick, Md.: University Publications of America, Inc., 1986).
8. "Comentarios a una Publicidad," *Bohemia,* April 6, 1952, 42; "Philco Signs Accords to Install TV Networks in Cuba," *The Havana Post,* May 2, 1952, 10.
9. "Comentarios." While Barletta was part of Television Nacional, the station often referred to itself using *El Mundo*'s name. The newspaper, however, was a separate legal entity from Television Nacional.
10. Mike Alonso, "On the Air" (column), *The Havana Post,* Feb. 18, 1953.
11. Alberto Vilar, personal interview, Miami, March 28, 1991.
12. These companies never carried out their plans for television.
13. Declassified memorandum.
14. Alberto Vilar, telephone interview, Miami, Dec. 7, 1990; Declassified letter from the U.S. Embassy in Havana to The Department of State, "Cuban Radio and Television Broadcasting Stations," Feb. 2, 1955, 7. Declassified documents are on microfilm and are indexed in Gregory Murphy, project coordinator; Blair D. Hydrick, compiler, *A Guide to Confidential U.S. Department Central Files: Cuba 1955–1959.* Decimal numbers 737, 837 and 937 and Foreign Affairs Decimal Numbers 637 and 611.37 (Frederick, Md.: University Publications of America, Inc., 1986).
15. "TV Crisis in Cuba," *Business Week,* May 8, 1954, 176–177.
16. Charles Friedman, "Si! Aqui TV en Ingles," *The New York Times,* Sept. 11, 1955, II, 13.
17. Mike Alonso, "On the Air" (column), *The Havana Post,* April 7, 1953, 6.
18. Mike Alonso, "On the Air" (column), *The Havana Post,* June 2, 1953, 6.
19. Goar Mestre, personal interview, Key Biscayne, Fla., May 10, 1990.
20. Declassified memorandum, May 7, 1952.
21. Daniel James, *Cuba: The First Soviet Satellite in the Americas* (New York: Avon, 1961), 212–213.
22. C. Wright Mills, *Listen Yankee* (New York: McGraw-Hill, 1960), 139–140.
23. "El Senor Barletta No Esta!" *Bohemia,* Aug. 14, 1955, 41.
24. Abel Mestre, personal interview, Miami, March 7, 1990.
25. Raoul Alfonso Gonse and Jorge L. Marti, *En Defensa de El Mundo* (Habana: Tipografia Ponciano, S.A., 1956).

26. "Dominicans Free Italian Ex-Consul," *The New York Times,* May 22, 1935, 11; "Italy Threatens Santo Domingo," *The New York Times,* May 16, 1935, 12; Alfonso Gonse and Marti, *En Defensa,* 31–41.
27. "Italian's License Canceled," *The New York Times,* Aug. 10, 1941, 20.
28. Alfonso Gonse and Marti, *En Defensa,* 41; "Italian's License."
29. Luis J. Botifoll, personal interview, Miami, Dec. 10, 1990. Botifoll was Barletta's attorney in Cuba, the editor-in-chief of *El Mundo,* and part of the group that purchased *El Mundo* in 1949 with Barletta. Also see Hermino Portell Vila, *Medio Siglo de 'El Mundo': Historia de un Gran Periodico* (Habana: Editorial Lex, 1951), 158.
30. Portell Vila, *Medio Siglo,* 158.
31. "Truce Prevails in *El Mundo*'s Internal Feud," *Editor & Publisher,* Jan. 16, 1954, 50.
32. Portell Vila, *Medio Siglo,* 147.
33. Goar Mestre, personal interview.
34. Botifoll, personal interview.
35. Goar Mestre, personal interview.
36. Observation of the author from scanning the entertainment sections of *El Mundo.*
37. John A. Lent, *Bibliography of Cuban Mass Communications* (Westport, Conn.: Greenwood Press, 1992), 3.
38. "Truce Prevails."
39. Botifoll, personal interview.
40. "Truce Prevails."
41. "Truce Prevails."
42. "Expone Botifoll lo Ocurrido en el Diario *El Mundo,*" *Diario de la Marina,* Jan. 3, 1954, 1.
43. Botifoll, personal interview.
44. All of Goar Mestre's Cuban business ventures were in collaboration with his brothers, Abel and Luis Augusto.
45. Goar Mestre, personal interview.
46. "Declaraciones de Goar Mestre Sobre la Nueva Empresa de Video CMBF, Cadena Nacional, S.A.," *Radiomania & Television,* April 5, 1957, 7; Wilson P. Dizard, *Television: A World View* (Syracuse, N.Y., 1966), 45–50.
47. "Contracto," *Bohemia,* May 4, 1952, 36.
48. "'Survey' de Television," *Bohemia,* April 12, 1953, 40–41.
49. Mike Alonso "On the Air" (column), *The Havana Post,* June 30, 1953, 6.
50. Mike Alonso, "On the Air" (column), *The Havana Post,* Jan. 18, 1957, 6.
51. Luis Lopez, *La Radio en Cuba,* 293.
52. Goar Mestre, personal interview.
53. Mike Alonso, "On the Air" (column), *The Havana Post,* Jan. 7, 1958, 6.
54. Alonso, "On the Air," Jan. 7, 1958, 6.
55. Mike Alonso, "On the Air" (column), *The Havana Post,* June 14, 1957, 6.
56. Goar Mestre, personal interview; Alberto Vilar, personal interview, Miami, March 28, 1991.
57. Goar Mestre, personal interview.
58. Mike Alonso, "On the Air" (column), *The Havana Post,* March 29, 1957, 6.
59. "Baraunda," *Bohemia,* Nov. 14, 1954, 44.
60. Vilar, personal interview.
61. Mike Alonso, "On the Air" (column), *The Havana Post,* Nov. 15, 1953, 6; "Cuba's 5th TV Station Opens," *The New York Times,* Nov. 12, 1953, 43.
62. Mike Alonso, "On the Air" (column), *The Havana Post,* July 23, 1953, 6.
63. Mike Alonso, "On the Air" (column), *The Havana Post,* Oct. 22, 1953, 6.
64. Mike Alonso, "On the Air" (column), *The Havana Post,* March 20, 1954, 6.
65. Declassified letter from Victor M. Fernandez, film director at Television del Caribe, to the U.S. Department of State, July 23, 1953.
66. Mike Alonso, "On the Air" (column), *The Havana Post,* Nov. 20, 1953, 6.

67. Alonso, "On the Air," March 20, 1953.
68. "TV Crisis in Cuba."
69. Declassified letter from David S. Green, commercial attache at the U.S. Embassy in Havana, to the Department of State, April 30, 1954.
70. Mike Alonso, "On the Air" (column), *The Havana Post,* Aug. 4, 1954, 6.
71. Declassified letter, April 30, 1954.
72. Friedman, "Si! Aqui."
73. "5th TV Station Slated for December 1," *The Havana Post,* Nov. 15, 1956, 1.
74. "5th TV Station."
75. Joe Cohen, "Cuba's New Ch. 10 Just as Yanks Like It—Flock to U.S. Pix; Mould's Slated to Grab Mestre's NBC Label," *Variety,* Aug. 6, 1958, 1.
76. Cohen, "Cuba's New Ch. 10."
77. Cohen, "Cuba's New Ch. 10."
78. Mike Alonso, "On the Air" (column), *The Havana Post,* Feb. 5, 1959, 6.
79. "Barletta Loses All to Govt.," *The Havana Post,* March 10, 1960, 1.
80. Mike Alonso, "On the Air" (column), *The Havana Post,* Aug. 16, 1953, 6.
81. Mike Alonso, "On the Air" (column), *The Havana Post,* Aug. 23, 1953, 6.
82. Alonso, "On the Air," Aug. 16, 1953, 6.
83. "Detras de la Pelota," *Bohemia,* Aug. 19, 1956, 46–47.
84. "La Serie Mundial por TV," *Bohemia,* Oct. 11, 1953, 40–41.
85. Mike Alonso, "On the Air" (column), *The Havana Post,* Sept. 24, 1954, 6. In addition, during the 1920s there were experimental television broadcasts between the United States and Europe. Irving Settel, *A Pictorial History of Television,* second edition (New York: Frederick Ungar Publishing Company, 1983, 31.
86. "Yo Veo esto Desde mi Casa! *Bohemia,* Oct. 4, 1954, 48.
87. Mike Alonso, "On the Air" (column), *The Havana Post,* Oct. 3, 1954, 6.; "'Yankee Stadium' al Aleance de la Mano," *Bohemia,* Oct. 3, 1954, 40–41.
88. Mike Alonso, "On the Air" (column), *The Havana Post,* Oct. 1, 1954, 6.
89. Abel Mestre, personal interview, Miami, March 7, 1990.
90. Manolo Cores, director of programming at CMQ, personal interview, Miami, July 11, 1990.
91. Mike Alonso, "On the Air" (column), *The Havana Post,* Oct. 6, 1954, 6.
92. "By Plane from Havana," *TV Guide,* Dec. 31, 1955, 20–21; J.P. Shanley, "Cuban TV: Big Business in the Rhumba Beat," *The New York Times,* Nov. 20, 1955, II, 11.
93. Roger A. Valdes, "U.S.–Cuba Radio Hook-Up Assures Increased Service," *The Havana Post,* May 5, 1957, 1; "FCC Grants Permit for Cuba–U.S. TV," *The Havana Post,* June 1, 1957, 1.
94. Valdes, "U.S.–Cuba Radio Hook."
95. "Base Ball!" *Bohemia,* Oct. 23, 1960, 30, 90.
96. Joe O'Connell, spokesman, Voice of America, telephone interview, Washington, D.C., Feb. 7, 1991.
97. Lydia Martin, "Panel Recommends Halting TV Marti," *The Miami Herald,* March 19, 1993, 6A.
98. Henry Goethals, "Hours of Preparation Precede Steve Allen's TV Program," *The Times of Havana,* Jan. 16, 1958, 2; "Cuba Goes Over the Horizon to U.S.," *The Times of Havana,* Jan. 20, 1958, 1.

CHAPTER 5

1. Hilda Perera Soto, "Un 'Tanto Gusto' a la Television," *Bohemia,* Sept. 10, 1950, 38–39, 112–113, 112.
2. Susan Schroeder, *Cuba: A Handbook of Historical Statistics* (Boston: G.K. Hall & Co., 1982), 333.
3. "Roosevelt, de la Fe Discuss American Investment in Cuba," *The Havana Post,*

April 27, 1952, 1.
4. Mike Alonso, "On the Air," (column), *The Havana Post,* June 13, 1953, 6.
5. Alonso, "On the Air," June 13, 1953.
6. Mike Alonso, "On the Air," (column), *The Havana Post,* April 9, 1953, 6.
7. Goar Mestre, personal interview, Key Biscayne, Fla., May 10, 1991; Manolo Reyes, personal interview, Miami, April 4, 1991.
8. Jesus A. Chia Garzon, *El Monopolio del Jabon y el Perfume en Cuba* (Habana: Editorial de Ciencias, 1977), 202.
9. Reyes, personal interview.
10. Armando Garcia Sifredo, personal interview, Miami, April 16, 1991; Max Lesnick, personal interview, Miami, Feb. 19, 1991; Jose Pardo Llada, personal interview, Miami, Feb. 24, 1992.
11. Pardo Llada, personal interview.
12. "Righteous Wrath," *Time,* Dec. 12, 1955, 34.
13. Pardo Llada, personal interview.
14. Garcia Sifredo, personal interview; Pardo Llada, personal interview.
15. Garcia Sifredo, personal interview.
16. Garcia Sifredo, personal interview.
17. Pardo Llada, personal interview.
18. Mike Alonso, "On the Air" (column), *The Havana Post,* July 19, 1956, 6.
19. "Nueva Cadena Nacional," *Bohemia,* June 27, 1954, 42–43.
20. "Dos Personajes en Busca de Interpretes," *Bohemia,* Aug. 15, 1954, 42–44.
21. "Al Aire," *Bohemia,* Aug. 1, 1954, 44.
22. Oscar Luis Lopez, *La Radio en Cuba: Estudio de su Desarrollo en la Sociedad Neocolonial* (Habana: Editorial Letras Cubanas, 1981), 200–201; "Es la Television . . . o la Falta de Mejores Programas?" *Bohemia,* March 29, 1953, 44–46.
23. Mike Alonso, "On the Air" (column), *The Havana Post,* June 15, 1956, 6.
24. Luis Lopez, *La Radio en Cuba,* 451.
25. Luis Lopez, *La Radio en Cuba,* 201.
26. Luis Lopez, *La Radio en Cuba,* 202.
27. Lydia Martin, "Israel Pimentel Molina, Radio Host of Cuban Music," *The Miami Herald,* March 4, 1993, 4B.
28. Luis Lopez, *La Radio en Cuba,* 202.
29. Goar Mestre, personal interview.
30. Jose Luis Pelleya, personal interview, Miami, Aug. 3, 1992.
31. Jorge Losada, "Batista: Master of the Coup D'etat," *United Nations World,* April 1953, 31–35.
32. Goar Mestre, personal interview.
33. Richard Pack, "Report from Havana," *The New York Times,* April 28, 1946, II, 7.
34. Goar Mestre, personal interview.
35. Hugh Thomas, *Cuba: The Pursuit of Freedom* (New York: Harper & Row, 1971), 767; Jaime Suchlicki, *Historical Dictionary of Cuba* (Metuchen, N.J.: The Scarecrow Press Inc., 1988), 209.
36. William S. Stokes, "The 'Cuban Revolution' and the Presidential Elections of 1948," *Hispanic American Historical Review,* 1951, 31:37–79, 60.
37. "Self-made Martyr," *Time,* Aug. 13, 1951, 47.
38. Suchlicki, *Historical Dictionary,* 209.
39. "Cuba," *Hispanic American Report,* August 1959, 16.
40. Goar Mestre, personal interview.
41. Goar Mestre, personal interview.
42. Thomas, *Cuba,* 751.
43. "Cuban Broadcasters Protest New Decree," *The New York Times,* Aug. 17, 1950, 12.
44. "Batista Raps Radio Reply; Seizure of Hoy," *The Havana Post,* Sept. 10, 1950, 2.
45. Abel Mestre, personal interview, Miami, March 7, 1990.

46. "Diez Estaciones de Radio de La Habana Apoyan el Decreto 2273," *Diario de la Marina,* Aug. 22, 1950, 1.
47. Goar Mestre, personal interview.
48. Octavio Jordon, "Cuba's Right-to-Reply Law in Radio Broadcasting," *Journalism Quarterly,* 28:358–363, 369 (1951).
49. "Cuba," *Hispanic American Report,* Feb. 1951, 14.
50. "Chibas Calls Henchmen to Havana," *The Havana Post,* Feb. 18, 1951, 1, 2.
51. "Varona Urges Curb on Chibas Following Bloody Sunday Riot," *The Havana Post,* Feb. 19, 1951, 1.
52. Thomas, *Cuba,* 767.
53. Luis Conte Aguero, *Eduardo Chibas: el Adalid de Cuba* (Mexico City: Editorial Jus, 1955), 772.
54. "Dr. Chibas, Cuban Senator, Dies of Wounds Self-inflicted as He Ended Radio Broadcast," *The New York Times,* Aug. 17, 1951, 1.
55. Emilio Ochoa, former president of the Ortodoxo Party, personal interview, Miami, Oct. 16, 1991.
56. Suchlicki, *Historical Dictionary,* 131.
57. Thomas, *Cuba,* 770.
58. Goar Mestre, personal interview.
59. "Chibas Funeral Held," *The New York Times,* Aug. 18, 1951, 3.
60. Conte Aguero, *Eduardo Chibas.*
61. Tad Szulc, *Fidel: A Critical Portrait* (New York: Avon Books, 1986), p. 211.
62. Pardo Llada, personal interview.
63. Lee Lockwood, *Castro's Cuba, Cuba's Fidel* (New York: Random House, 1969), 157.

CHAPTER 6

1. Cuba ranked sixth in the world in number of stations, behind such advanced nations as the United States, Italy, West Germany, the Soviet Union and Great Britain. See "TV Girdles the Globe," *Television Age,* May 20, 1957, 33–37, 73.
2. Alberto Vilar, personal interview, Miami, Dec. 7, 1990; Declassified letter from the U.S. Embassy in Havana to The Department of State, "Cuban Radio and Television Broadcasting Stations," Feb. 2, 1955, 7. Declassified documents are on microfilm and are indexed in Gregory Murphy, project coordinator; Blair D. Hydrick, compiler, *A Guide to Confidential U.S. Department Central Files: Cuba 1955–1959.* Decimal numbers 737, 837 and 937 and Foreign Affairs Decimal Numbers 637 and 611.37 (Frederick, Md.: University Publications of America, Inc., 1986).
3. Vilar, personal interview.
4. Vilar, personal interview.
5. Vilar, personal interview.
6. Vilar, personal interview.
7. "Otra Vez el 'Survey'," *Bohemia,* March 24, 1957, 56–60.
8. Vilar, personal interview.
9. Vilar, personal interview.
10. Martha Mestre Pumarejo, personal interview, Miami, April 18, 1991.
11. Mestre Pumarejo, personal interview.
12. "La Radio en Cuba," *Bohemia,* May 10, 1953, 106–113, 159–161.
13. "Cuban Radio Chain Sold," *The New York Times,* April 30, 1952, 3. Although at least one Cuban entrepreneur was part of the group, this was probably to adhere to Cuban law restricting foreign ownership of Cuban broadcast media. In reality, the purchase was likely a U.S. venture.
14. *Television: A World Survey* (Paris: UNESCO, 1953), 49.
15. "El Ultimo 'Survey,'" *Bohemia,* March 23, 1952, 44.

16. "La Radio en Cuba," 161.
17. "Cuba's Highest Honor Won By Heads of CBS," *The New York Times,* June 10, 1943, 12.
18. "Todovia No Sabemos lo que Vamos a Hacer," *Bohemia,* May 4, 1952, 36–38; Oscar Luis Lopez, *La Radio en Cuba: Estudio de su Desarrollo en la Sociedad Neocolonial* (Habana: Editorial Letras Cubanas), 193; "Batista Honors Writers," *The New York Times,* Aug. 30, 1944, 13.
19. Edmund A. Chester, *A Sergeant Named Batista* (New York: Holt Rinehart, 1954).
20. "Roosevelt, de la Fe Discuss American Investment in Cuba," *The Havana Post,* April 27, 1952, 1.; "La Venta Estaba al Producirse," *Bohemia,* April 27, 1952, 40.
21. Mike Alonso, "On the Air" (column), *The Havana Post,* April 16, 1953, 6; "Radio Chain in Cuba Sold," *The New York Times,* May 20, 1953, 39.
22. Mike Alonso, "On the Air" (column), *The Havana Post,* April 24, 1953, 6.
23. "'Survey' Radial," *Bohemia,* July 19, 1953, 46.
24. "Escuela de Television: Extraordinario Acontecimiento," *Bohemia,* May 17, 1953, 45–46.
25. Mike Alonso, "On the Air" (column), *The Havana Post,* April 12, 1953, 6.
26. Mike Alonso, "On the Air" (column), *The Havana Post,* Nov. 3, 1953, 6.
27. Mike Alonso, "On the Air" (column), *The Havana Post,* April 30, 1953, 6.
28. Mike Alonso, "On the Air" (column), *The Havana Post,* Feb. 9, 1954, 6.
29. Mike Alonso, "On the Air" (column), *The Havana Post,* March 6, 1954, 6.
30. Mike Alonso, "On the Air" (column), *The Havana Post,* Sept. 7, 1955, 6.
31. "Amado Trinidad ha Vuelto a Trabajar la Tierra," *Bohemia,* Dec. 13, 62, 64, 85.
32. "Guajiro Siempre," *Bohemia,* Aug. 21, 1955, 42–43; "Funeral Rites Today for Amado Trinidad," *The Havana Post,* Aug. 12, 1955, 1.
33. "Escuela de Television."
34. Mike Alonso, "On the Air" (column), *The Havana Post,* March 18, 1955, 6. Also see "'Lolita' es Insustituible," *Bohemia,* Feb. 6, 1955, 44–45.
35. "Pumarejo al Canal 2," *Bohemia,* July 17, 1955, 42–43.
36. Pedro Pablo Chavez, editor, *Anuario Cinematografico y Radio Cubano* (Havana, 1956, Vol. 16), 136.
37. "Cambios en la Programacion," *Bohemia,* July 28, 1957, 56, 96.
38. Mestre Pumarejo, personal interview.
39. "Mr. TV, Cuban Style," *Television Age,* Sept. 8, 1958, 42, 90.
40. "Dinero, Dinero, Dinero!" *Bohemia,* June 15, 1958, 76.
41. "Control Remoto," *Bohemia,* July 27, 1958, 58–60.
42. "Survey de TV," *Bohemia,* Sept. 22, 1957, 61.
43. "Survey de TV," *Bohemia,* Jan. 5, 1958, 54.
44. Minuca Villaverde, "Vivo y en Directo," *El Nuevo Herald,* June 25, 1990, 1C.
45. Mike Alonso, "On the Air" (column), *The Havana Post,* Feb. 9, 1956, 6.
46. "Cuban Television Star Gaspar Pumarejo at 61," *The Miami Herald,* March 26, 1975, 4B.
47. "Detras del Suceso," *Bohemia,* March 10, 1957, 44–45.
48. Villaverde, "En Vivo"; Mike Alonso, "On the Air" (column), *The Havana Post,* June 20, 1957, 6.
49. "Cuba," *Hispanic American Report,* May 1957, 247.
50. Mike Alonso, "On the Air" (column), *The Havana Post,* Sept. 11, 1954, 6.
51. "Atracciones Internacionales," *Bohemia,* July 15, 1956, 52–53.
52. "Mr. TV," 42; Charlie Seiglie, "Liberace," *El Mundo,* Aug. 19, 1956, D4.
53. "El 'Show' de la Baker," *Bohemia,* Feb. 22, 1953, 42–46; Villaverde, "En Vivo"; Manolo Cores, director of programming at CMQ, personal interview, Key Biscayne, Fla., July 11, 1990.
54. "Otra Acontecimiento: Liberace," *Bohemia,* June 3, 1956, 40–41.
55. "Liberace Pays Call on Batista," *The Havana Post,* Aug. 23, 1956, 1.
56. Mary Louise Wilkinson, "A Date with Liberace—Almost," *The Havana Post,* Aug.

26, 1956, 3.
57. "Mr. TV."
58. "'Sarita' Habia Firmado," *Bohemia,* June 22, 1958, 22.
59. "Anecdotario de 'Sarita'," *Bohemia,* Oct. 12, 1958, 58–59, 112.
60. Vilar, personal interview.
61. "Mr. TV," 42, original parentheses. As *Television Age* suggested, and as Pumarejo's widow confirmed, the $400,000 figure was a vast exaggeration. Mestre Pumarejo, personal interview.
62. "Cuban Group to Be Checked," *The New York Times,* Oct. 31, 1946, 33; Jose Manuel Viana, personal interview, Miami, May 23, 1991.
63. Juan Jose Tarajano, *Etica en Radio y Television: Un Sistema Ejemplar de Autocritica en Cuba Republicana* (Published by the author, Miami, 1989); Jose Manuel Viana, personal interview, Miami, May 23, 1991.
64. H. Espinet Borges, "La Comision de Etica Radial," *Carteles,* July 31, 1949, 54–56.
65. Goar Mestre, personal interview.
66. Espinet Borges, "La Comision de Etica Radial."
67. Espinet Borges, "La Comision de Etica Radial.
68. Tarajano, *Etica en Radio;* H. Espinet Borges, "La Comision de Etica Radial," *Carteles,* July 31, 1949, 54–56.
69. "Los Politicos y la Etica Radial," *Bohemia,* March 5, 1950, 60; Tarajano, *Etica en Radio;* Tarajano, personal interview.
70. "Los Politicos; Tarajano, personal interview.
71. Tarajano, personal interview.
72. "Asi lo Acordo la Com. de Etica Radial por Infringir Normas," *Diario de la Marina,* Aug. 18, 1950, 15; Tarajano, personal interview.
73. Ernesto Montaner, "Sigue la Farsa," *Bohemia,* Oct. 3, 1954, 46–47; Hugh Thomas, *Cuba: The Pursuit of Freedom* (New York: Harper & Row, 1971), 798; Tarajano, *Etica en Radio.*
74. "La Tempestad en el Vaso de Agua," *Bohemia,* Aug. 10, 1952, 44–45.
75. Jose Luis Pelleya, personal interview, Miami, Aug. 3, 1992.
76. "Cuban Radio Station Punished," *The New York Times,* Aug. 5, 1952, 3. This incident illustrated how the Batista government used the rulings of a nongovernment, self-regulatory agency to impose censorship. Ironically, part of the reason for the creation of the Ethics Commission was to avoid government censorship.
77. "Cuba," *Hispanic American Report,* August 1952, 16.
78. Tarajano, *Etica en Radio;* Tarajano, personal interview.
79. Pelleya, personal interview.
80. "Coreografia Censurada," *Bohemia,* Aug. 9, 1953, 42.
81. Tarajano, *Etica en Radio,* 34.
82. "Pumarejo Vs. Tarajano," *Bohemia,* June 17, 1956, 40–44.
83. "La Comision y el Ministerio," *Bohemia,* April 29, 1956, 36–37; "Resolucion Inesperada," *Bohemia,* April 22, 1956, 46–47.
84. "Resolucion Inesperada."
85. "Pumarejo Vs. Tarajano."
86. "Pumarejo Vs. Tarajano," 42.
87. "Pumarejo Vs. Tarajano," 43.
88. "Pumarejo Vs. Tarajano," 43.
89. "El Ultimo 'Rollo'," *Bohemia,* June 24, 1956, 39.
90. "Rock 'n Roll Banned from TV Here," *The Havana Post,* Feb. 14, 1957, 1.
91. "Rock 'n Roll Banned."
92. "Rock 'n Roll Banned."
93. "Cuba Restores Rock 'n' Roll," *The New York Times,* Feb. 16, 1957, 14.
94. "Rock 'n Roll U.S. Style on TV Today, Ban Lifted," *The Havana Post,* Feb. 16, 1957, 6.

CHAPTER 7

1. Tad Szulc, *Fidel: A Critical Portrait* (New York: Avon, 1986), 213.
2. Mary Brigid Gallagher, *The Public Addresses of Fidel Castro Ruz: Charismatic Leader of a Modern Revolution*. Ph.D. Dissertation, University of Pittsburgh, 1970, 45.
3. Szulc, *Fidel,* 213–214.
4. Szulc, *Fidel,* 214–216.
5. Szulc, *Fidel,* 210.
6. "Cuba," *Hispanic American Report,* January 1957, 16. As a formality, the Congress had to ratify the president's request to suspend civil liberties.
7. "Broadcasters Summoned by Propaganda Minister," *The Havana Post,* March 12, 1952, 1.
8. "Minister Denies News Restriction," *The Havana Post,* March 21, 1952, 1.
9. Fulgencio Batista, *The Growth and Decline of the Cuban Republic* (New York: The Devin-Adair Press, 1964), 90–91.
10. Clarence W. Moore, personal interview, Miami, March 26, 1991.
11. Declassified letter from Richard G. Cushing, information officer at the U.S. Embassy in Havana, to the U.S. Department of State ["Suspension of Cuban Radio Station and Two Commentators"], Washington, D.C., Dec. 18, 1952. Declassified documents are on microfilm and are indexed in Michael C. Davis, editor; L. Lee Yanike, compiler, *A Guide to Confidential U.S. Department Central Files: Cuba 1950–1954*. Decimal numbers 737, 837 and 937 and Foreign Affairs Decimal Numbers 637 and 611.37 (Frederick, Md.: University Publications of America, Inc., 1986).
12. Declassified letter.
13. Declassified letter from Richard G. Cushing, information officer at the U.S. Embassy in Cuba, to the U.S. Department of State, Washington, D.C., March 13, 1953.
14. "The Cardinal's Forehead," *Time,* Sept. 7, 1953, 38.
15. Santiago Rey, personal interview, Miami, Oct. 15, 1991.
16. "Meet Backs Cuban Radio Freedom," *The Havana Post,* March 23, 1952, 1.
17. Goar Mestre, personal interview, Key Biscayne, Fla., May 10, 1990.
18. Ana E. Santiago, Minuca Villaverde and Cristina Vazquez, "Muere Pionero de TV Hispanamericana," *El Nuevo Herald,* Nov. 28, 1991, 1B.
19. Abel Mestre, personal interview, Miami, Dec. 5, 1990.
20. "Broadcasters Summoned by Propaganda Minister," *The Havana Post,* March 12, 1952, 1.
21. Abel Mestre, personal interview.
22. Abel Mestre, personal interview.
23. Jay Mallin, "Cuba's Stormy Journalist Apes Our Joe," *Editor & Publisher,* July 31, 1954, 35.
24. Mallin, "Cuba's Stormy Journalist."
25. Goar Mestre, personal interview.
26. Jose Pardo Llada, personal interview, Miami, Feb. 24, 1992.
27. Luis Gutierrez Delgado, "Jorge Manach: Cuban Man of Letters," *Americas,* November 1961, 26–28.
28. Goar Mestre, personal interview.
29. Oscar Luis Lopez, *La Radio en Cuba: Estudio de su Desarrollo en la Sociedad Neocolonial* (Habana: Editorial Letras Cubanas, 1981), 336.
30. Gutierrez Delgado, "Jorge Manach," 26–28; Andres Valdespino, *Jorge Manach y su Generacion en las Cubanas* (Miami: Ediciones Universal, 1976).
31. Madeline Sternlicht, *Man or Myth: Jose Marti in the Biographies of Jorge Manach, Alberto Baeza Flores, and Ezequiel Martinez Estrada*. Ph.D. Dissertation, Columbia University, 1976, 107–108.
32. Sternlicht, *Man or Myth,* 107–108.
33. Sternlicht, *Man or Myth,* 112.
34. "Cuban TV Network Cancels Press Show," *The New York Times,* June 4, 1953, 43.

35. Abel Mestre, personal interview; Goar Mestre, personal interview.
36. "Army Chief Names Officer to Probe Disorders at CMQ," *The Havana Post,* May 6, 1952, 1.
37. "Cuban TV Network."
38. "Ministers Barred from Appearing on TV Program," *The Havana Post,* May 29, 1953, 1.
39. "Ministers Barred."
40. Cuban TV Network"; "Ministers Barred."
41. While Matthews sympathized with Castro's position, the accusation that he was an apologist was false or an exaggeration. Jerry W. Knudson, *Herbert L. Matthews and the Cuban Story, Journalism Monographs* No. 54 (Lexington, KY: Association for Education in Journalism, 1978).
42. Herbert L. Matthews, "Batista Promises Presidential Vote," *The New York Times,* Oct. 17, 1953, 5.
43. Matthews, "Batista Promises."
44. "Cuban Censorship Lifted by Batista," *The New York Times,* Oct. 25, 1953, 31; "Batista Moves Forward," *The New York Times,* Oct. 28, 1953, 28.
45. "Pearson in Bongoland," *Time,* Oct. 10, 1955, 54–55. The father, Amadeo Barletta, owned the daily newspaper *El Mundo,* the Telemundo television network and numerous other businesses.
46. "On the Havana Merry-Go-Round," *The Havana Post,* Sept. 27, 1955, 1.
47. "Pearson in Bongoland."
48. "Pearson in Bongoland."
49. "Pearson in Bongoland."
50. Don Grierson, "Herbert Matthews and Castro's Revolution: A Lapse in Discretion at *The New York Times,*" *World Communication,* 1991, 20:3–10); Jerry W. Knudson, *Herbert L. Matthews.*
51. Szulc, *Fidel,* 271.
52. "Cuban Censorship Lifted by Batista," *The New York Times,* Oct. 25, 1953, 31.
53. "End of Hope," *Time,* March 28, 1958, 41.
54. Agustin Alles Soberon, "Amenazada le Libertad de Expresion," *Bohemia,* Nov. 13, 1955, 64–65, 91.
55. "Interview in the Night," *Time,* Nov. 2, 1953, 36, 38; "Por la Formacion del Frente Unico Revolucionario," *Diario la Marina,* Jan. 7, 1959, 6B.
56. Knudson, *Herbert L. Matthews.*
57. Knudson, *Herbert L. Matthews,* 9.
58. Marvin Alisky, "Censorship Replaces Bribery," *Nieman Reports,* April 1957, 17–18.
59. Ray Brennan, *Castro, Cuba and Justice* (New York: Doubleday, 1959), 162.
60. Brennan, *Castro, Cuba,* 166. Another Venezuelan station, Radio Rumbos, was also used by the July 26th Movement to broadcast to Cuba. See "Cuba," *Hispanic American Report,* July 1958, 377.
61. Brennan, *Castro, Cuba,* 166.
62. Brennan, *Castro, Cuba,* 166.
63. Mike Alonso, "On the Air" (column), *The Havana Post,* March 18, 1959, 6.
64. "Meruelo Gets 30-Year Term," *The Havana Post,* Jan. 12, 1959, 1.
65. Declassified letter from V. Chapin, minister-counselor in the U.S. Embassy in Havana, to the U.S. Department of State, Washington, D.C., Aug. 8, 1957. Declassified documents are on microfilm and are indexed in Gregory Murphy, project coordinator; Blair D. Hydrick, compiler, *A Guide to Confidential U.S. Department Central Files: Cuba 1955–1959.* Decimal numbers 737, 837 and 937 and Foreign Affairs Decimal Numbers 637 and 611.37 (Frederick, Md.: University Publications of America, Inc., 1986).
66. Declassified letter, Aug. 8, 1957.
67. Batista's control of the networks was subtle. In many cases, even the owners did not know that Batista was taking control of their companies. Batista was reputed to have gained control of Circuito Nacional Cubano, Cadena Oriental de Radio, and Union Radio

by having his associates purchase shares in the networks. See "Cuba," *Hispanic American Report,* October 1957, 530.
68. Luis Lopez, *La Radio en Cuba,* 443–445.
69. Henry Goethals, "'Bohemia' is a Friday Tradition in Cuban Homes," *The Times of Havana,* Nov. 4, 1957, 13.
70. Henry Goethals, "'Zig Zag' Magazine Reflects National Sense of Humor," *The Times of Havana,* April 3, 1958, 2.
71. Jerry Redding, "'Castro-ating' the Media," *Educational Broadcast Review,* June 1971, 35–42.
72. Grierson, "Herbert Matthews."
73. "Fidel Castro 'Stars' on Television Program," *The Times of Havana,* May 20, 1957, 3.
74. "Cuban Newsmen Protest Lack of Facilities," *The Havana Post,* June 9, 1957, 1.
75. "Newsman Reports Visit of Castro Messenger," *The Havana Post,* Feb. 27, 1958, 1.
76. "Claims Castro Wants Cuban Newspapermen to Visit Sierra," *The Havana Post,* March 5, 1958, 1.
77. John A. Lent, *Mass Communications in the Caribbean* (Ames: Iowa State University Press, 1990), 121
78. "Los Primeros Periodistas Cubanos en la Sierra Maestra," *Bohemia,* Feb. 11, 1959, 121–122.
79. Jose Pardo Llada, *Memorias de la Sierra Maestra* (Habana: Instituto del Libro, 1960).
80. Pardo Llada, personal interview.
81. Terence Cannon, *Revolutionary Cuba* (New York: Thomas Y. Crowell, 1981), 87.
82. Carlos Franqui, telephone interview, San Juan, P.R., July 11, 1992.
83. Enrique Nunez Rodriguez, "La Radio y la Television en el Movimiento Revolucionario," *Carteles,* Jan. 18, 1959. 84–85, 109.
84. "Violeta Casals: Voice of Castro's Radio," *The Miami Herald,* Oct. 30, 1992, A14.
85. Don Galaor, "Violeta Casals: La Voz Femenina de Radio Rebelde," *Bohemia,* Jan. 18, 1959, 16–18, 142.
86. "Will Arrest All Censors," *The Havana Post,* Feb. 1, 1959, 1.

CHAPTER 8

1. "Censorship Slapped on All Newspapers, Radio Stations," *The Havana Post,* Jan. 16 1957, 1. In the past, the Congress went through the formality of ratifying the president's decree to suspend civil liberties. This time, however, Congress failed to gather a quorum, and normal legal procedures were bypassed. "Cuba," *Hispanic American Report,* January 1957, 16.
2. Carl Spielvogel, "Advertising, Double Trouble in Cuba," *The New York Times,* Oct. 17, 1957, 48.
3. Clarence Moore, personal interview, Miami, March 26, 1991; "New Paper is 10 Cents Monday, 5 Cents Thurs.," *Editor & Publisher,* Feb. 23, 1957, 34. In October 1958, the paper published thrice-weekly, with never-realized plans for becoming a daily. "Toward a Daily," *Editor & Publisher,* Oct. 18, 1958, 64.
4. Despite the political turmoil, Cuba was in sound financial condition. For economic statistics, see "Cuba," *Hispanic American Report,* January 1957, 18.
5. "Cuba," *Hispanic American Report,* May 1957, 247.
6. "Atracciones Internacionales," *Bohemia,* July 15, 1956, 52–53.
7. Val Adams, "Actor Insurance for Cuba Sought," *The New York Times,* Jan. 17, 1958, 47.
8. Gustavo Adolfo Otero, *La Cultura y el Periodismo en America* (Quito, Ecuador: Casa Editora Liebmann, 1980).

9. "Baraunda," *Bohemia,* May 31, 1958, 58, 101.
10. Rafael Lechuga Otero, *La Informacion en Television* (Santiago de Cuba: Editora Liebmann), 295–310.
11. Antonio Milla Espinosa, telephone interview, Miami, FL., May 11, 1992; "Television Camaguey," *Bohemia,* July 6, 1958, 62.
12. "En Camaguey," *Bohemia,* Sept. 20, 1959, 54.
13. "En Camaguey."
14. "Baraunda."
15. Milla, telephone interview.
16. Milla, telephone interview.
17. "El Canal 12," *Bohemia,* April 8, 1956, 37; Humberto Hedman, "Tres Vivas," *Radiomania,* January 1975, 43.
18. Roger A. Valdes, "Cuba to Have First Color TV Station in Latin America," *The Havana Post,* Feb. 21, 1958, 1.
19. Fermin Peraza Sarausa, *Personalidades Cubans (Cuba en el Exilo)* (Coral Gables, Fla.: Copyright by Fermin Peraza Sarausa and Elena Verez Peraza, 1968), 66–67.
20. Mike Alonso "On the Air" (column), *The Havana Post,* Aug. 26, 1954, 8.
21. Goar Mestre, personal interview; "Videotape en Cuba," *Bohemia,* Sept. 6, 1959, 54–55.
22. Valdes, "Cuba to Have First."
23. "Bright Future Predicted for Cuban Color TV," *The Times of Havana,* Sept. 23, 1957, 13.
24. "Bright Future"; "TV en Colores," *Bohemia,* March 30, 1958, 57–58.
25. "Bright Future."
26. Ray Eldon Hiebert, Donald F. Ungurait and Thomas W. Bohn, *Mass Media VI* (New York: Longman, 1991), 254–255.
27. Abel Mestre, personal interview, Miami, March 7, 1990.
28. Abel Mestre, personal interview.
29. Clifford W. Slaybaugh, telephone interview, Princeton, N.J., Nov. 9, 1990.
30. Many of these problems might have been due to the high-frequency signal of Channel 12, rather than anything inherent in the color technology.
31. "Nueva Programacion," *Bohemia,* Aug. 10, 1958, 58.
32. Agustin Tamargo, Channel 12's news director, personal interview, Miami, Dec. 19, 1990.
33. Mike Alonso, "On the Air" (column), *The Havana Post,* April 8, 1958, 6.
34. Jose Suarez Nunez, *El Gran Culpable* (Caracas, copyright by the author, 1963), 34.
35. "A la Opinion Publica" (advertisement), *Bohemia,* Nov. 10, 1959, 53.
36. Mike Alonso, "On the Air" (column), *The Havana Post,* June 5, 1958, 6.
37. Carlos Castaneda, personal interview, Miami, April 14, 1991.
38. "CMQ Stations Putting Out Peaceful Signal," *Broadcasting,* Feb. 2, 1959, 68.
39. Ramona Bechtos, "Goar Mestre Spurs TV in Argentina After Castro Confiscates Property," *Advertising Age,* April 16, 1962, 79–80; George Rosen, "The Best of Gaucho," *Variety,* Oct. 10, 1962, 20; Pedro Sevcec, "Goar Mestre: 'Padre de TV Latinoamerica,' " *El Nuevo Herald,* Dec. 4, 1989, 1, 6.
40. Goar Mestre, personal interview, Key Biscayne, Fla., May 10, 1990.
41. Goar Mestre, personal interview.
42. For example, see Alfred L. Padula, *The Fall of the Bourgeoisie: Cuba, 1959–1961.* Ph.D. Dissertation, The University of New Mexico, 1974.
43. Goar Mestre, personal interview.
44. George Rosen, "Mestre Rides Again," *Variety,* Jan. 13, 1965, 8.
45. Miguel A. Santin, "Television in Puerto Rico," *The New York Times,* Jan. 12, 1958, II, 13.
46. Mike Alonso, "On the Air" (column), *The Havana Post,* Dec. 5, 1956, 6.
47. Abel Mestre, personal interview.

48. "Films South of the Border: Mestre Explains New Organization's Aims," *Broadcasting*, Feb. 9, 1959, 146.
49. Goar Mestre, personal interview.
50. Goar Mestre, personal interview.
51. Abel Mestre, personal interview.
52. Elizabeth de Cardona, "Multinational Television," *Journal of Communication*, 25(2):122–127 (1974).
53. de Cardona, "Multinational Television."
54. "Films South of the Border."
55. Elizabeth Fox and Patricia Anzola, "Politics and Regional Television in Colombia," in Elizabeth Fox, ed., *Media and Politics in Latin America* (Newbury Park, Calif.: Sage, 1988), 82–92.
56. "Films South of the Border," 146.
57. "Films South of the Border," 146.
58. de Cardona, "Multinational Television," 124.
59. Goar Mestre, personal interview.
60. Goar Mestre, personal interview.
61. P. Sirven, *Quien te ha Visto y Quien TV* (Buenos Aires: Ediciones de la Flor, 1988).
62. Timothy Green, *The Universal Eye: The World Television* (New York: Stein and Day, 1972), 52.
63. Ramona Bechtos, "Ex-Cuba Mestre Shop Builds in Argentina," *Advertising Age*, Aug. 26, 1968, 226, 228, 230.
64. "Goar Mestre Spurs TV in Argentina After Castro Confiscates Property," *Advertising Age*, April 16, 1962, 79–80.
65. Bechtos, "Ex-Cuba Mestre Shop."
66. Bechtos, "Ex-Cuba Mestre Shop."
67. "Argentine Radio Hit Anew," *The New York Times*, July 24, 1948, 2; "Argentina's Radio Said to be Gagged," *The New York Times*, July 12, 1948, 32; "Argentina Loses in Vote on Radio," *The New York Times*, July 11, 1948, 23.
68. Goar Mestre, personal interview; Marvin Alisky, "Government-Press Relations in Peru," *Journalism Quarterly*, 53:661–665 (1976).
69. Carlos Malpica, *Los Duenos del Peru* (Lima: Ediciones Ensayos Sociales, 1968).
70. Malpica, *Los Duenos*.
71. Green, *The Universal Eye*, 50.
72. Goar Mestre, personal interview.
73. Goar Mestre, personal interview.
74. Goar Mestre, personal interview.
75. Green, *The Universal Eye*, 57.
76. Green, *The Universal Eye*, 57.
77. Green, *The Universal Eye*, 57.
78. Green, *The Universal Eye*, 57.
79. David Manning White, "Television in Argentina: An Interview with Sr. Goar Mestre," *Television Quarterly*, Summer 1969, 23–34, quote on 30–31.
80. Goar Mestre, personal interview.
81. Goar Mestre, personal interview.

CHAPTER 9

1. Alfred A. Padula, *The Fall of the Bourgeoisie: Cuba, 1959–1961*. Ph.D. Dissertation, The University of New Mexico, 249.
2. Charles Friedman, "Unrest in Cuban TV Studios," *The New York Times*, May 10, 1959, II, 14.
3. "CMQ Stations Putting Out Peaceful Signal," *Broadcasting*, Feb. 2, 1959, 68.
4. "CMQ Stations."

NOTES

5. "CMQ Stations."
6. Goar Mestre, personal interview, Key Biscayne, Fla., May 10, 1990.
7. John Dorschner and Roberto Fabricio, *The Winds of December* (New York: Coward, McCann & Geoghegan, 1980), 333–334.
8. Jules Dubois, *Rebel-Liberator or Dictator?* (Indianapolis: The New Bobbs-Merrill Company, 1959), 348.
9. Dorschner and Fabricio, *The Winds*, 396.
10. Dorschner and Fabricio, *The Winds*, 396.
11. Dorschner and Fabricio, *The Winds*, 421.
12. "Rebelde en el Eter," *Bohemia*, Feb. 8, 1959, 60, 62, 64, 116.
13. Carlos Castaneda, personal interview, Miami, April 14, 1991.
14. Dubois, *Fidel Castro*, 345.
15. "Rebeldia en el Eter."
16. Dubois, *Fidel Castro*, 345.
17. Oscar Luis Lopez, *La Radio en Cuba: Estudio de su Desarrollo en la Sociedad Neocolonial* (Habana: Editorial Letras Cubanas, 1981), 447.
18. Abel Mestre, personal interview, Miami, Dec. 5, 1990.
19. Guillermo Villaronda, "Esto lo que Ocurrio en Columbia Despues de la Caida del Regimen," *Bohemia*, Jan. 11, 1959, 130–136.
20. Abel Mestre, personal interview.
21. Mario Llerena, *The Unsuspected Revolution: The Birth and Rise of Castro* (Ithaca: Cornell University Press, 1978), 102–103; Dubois, *Fidel Castro*, 13.
22. Emilio Guede, telephone Interview, San Juan, P.R., Nov. 8, 1990.
23. Herbert L. Matthews, "Casinos Wrecked," *The New York Times*, Jan. 3, 1959, 1; Dubois, *Fidel Castro*, 348.
24. Gene Strul, "Television Reports a Revolution," *The Quill*, May 1959, 18.
25. Guede, telephone interview.
26. Goar Mestre, personal communication, Buenos Aires, June 20, 1990.
27. Guede, telephone interview.
28. Guede, telephone interview.
29. Dorschner and Fabricio, *The Winds*, 426.
30. Guede, telephone interview.
31. Guede, telephone interview.
32. Daniel James, *Cuba: The First Soviet Satellite in the Americas* (New York: Avon, 1961), 203.
33. *Editor & Publisher Year Book 1958* (New York: Editor & Publisher, 1959), 393–394.
34. Luis Lopez, *La Radio en Cuba*, 451; Jerry Redding, "'Castro-ating' the Media," *Educational Broadcasting Review*, June 1971, 35–42.
35. Paul D. Bethel, *The Losers* (New Rochelle, N.Y.: Arlington House, 1969), 158; Guillermo Martinez Marques, "Cuba's Free Press: A Target of Coercion," *The Miami Herald*, May 15, 1960, 16B; Hugh Thomas, *Cuba: The Pursuit of Freedom* (New York: Harper & Row, 1971), 1136.
36. "Will Arrest All Censors," *The Havana Post*, Feb. 1, 1959, 1.
37. "'I Was Batista's Enemy'; de la Fe," *The Havana Post*, Jan. 21, 1959, 1.
38. Carlos Todd, "Communist Destruction of the Free Press in Cuba," in *Communist Penetration and Exploitation of the Free Press*. 87th Congress, second session, Washington, D.C.: U.S. Government Printing Office, 1962, 30.
39. Lee Hall and Wilson Hall, "Cuba's Unsponsored TV Star," *TV Guide*, June 25, 1960, 6–7.
40. "Defense Minister Raps 'Foreign News Agents'," *The Havana Post*, Jan. 15, 1959, 1.
41. Strul, "Television Reports a Revolution."
42. Hall and Hall, "Cuba's Unsponsored TV Star."
43. "Cuba," *Hispanic American Report*, January 1960, 26.

44. Jerry Redding, "'Castro-ating' the Media," *Educational Broadcasting Review,* June 1971, 35–42, 40.
45. Herbert Matthews, "Journalism and its Responsibilities," *The Times of Havana,* March 2, 1959, 15.
46. "Dos Periodistas a Quienes el Pueblo de Cuba, Rinde Emocionado Tributo," *Bohemia,* Jan. 11, 1959, 74.
47. Don Grierson, "Herbert Matthews and Castro's Revolution: A Lapse in Discretion at *The New York Times," World Communication,* 20(3):3–10 (1991).
48. John Spicer Nichols, "Cuba," in George T. Kurian, ed., *World Press Encyclopedia* (New York: Facts on File, 1982), 258.
49. Marvin Alisky, *Latin American Media: Guidance and Censorship* (Ames: Iowa State University Press, 1981), 157.
50. Declassified letter from Daniel M. Braddock, charge d'affaires in the U.S. Embassy in Havana, to the Department of State, Washington, D.C., Feb. 9, 1959. Declassified documents are on microfilm and are indexed in Gregory Murphy, project coordinator; Blair D. Hydrick, compiler, *A Guide to Confidential U.S. Department Central Files: Cuba 1955–1959.* Decimal numbers 737, 837 and 937 and Foreign Affairs Decimal Numbers 637 and 611.37 (Frederick, Md.: University Publications of America, Inc., 1986).
51. Declassified letter.
52. Declassified letter.
53. John A. Lent, "Five Historical Stages of Cuban Mass Media, 1723–1983," *Studies in Latin American Popular Culture,* 8:253–270 (1989), 257.
54. Robert M. Hallett, "Bribes to Press Keep Cuba in Vise," *The Christian Science Monitor,* April 1, 1955, 5; Bertram B. Johansson, "Anxiety Cloaks Press in Cuba," *The Christian Science Monitor,* May 8, 1959, 8.
55. Carlos Todd, "Let's Look at Today" (column) *The Times of Havana,* June 8, 1959, 8.
56. Padula, *The Fall of the Bourgeoisie,* 136.
57. Padula, *The Fall of the Bourgeoisie,* 136.
58. Samuel Faber, *Revolution and Social Structure in Cuba, 1933–1959.* Ph.D. Dissertation, University of California, Berkeley, 1969, 475.
59. "New Cuban Daily Will Build Plant," *Editor & Publisher,* Sept. 19, 1959, 44.
60. Jorge L. Marti, "The Press in Cuba: Its 'Rebirth' Since 1939," *Journalism Quarterly,* 22(2):124–129 (1944), 125.
61. Marti, "The Press in Cuba."
62. *Editor & Publisher Year Book 1935* (New York: Editor & Publisher, 1936), 228; During the mid to late 1800s, about 125,000 Chinese laborers (derogatorily known as "coolies") were brought to Cuba to work on plantations for low wages. Franklin W. Knight, *Slave Society in Cuba During the Nineteenth Century* (Madison, Wis.: The University of Wisconsin Press, 1970), 116–119.
63. Jeffrey A. Kahn, *The History of the Jewish Colony in Cuba* (Rabbinic thesis, Hebrew Union College, Jewish Institute of Religion, Cincinnati, Ohio, 1981), 73–76.
64. Kahn, *The History of the Jewish Colony,* 73–76.
65. Alisky, *Latin American Media,* 157; Marti, "The Press in Cuba."
66. Hallett, "Bribes to Press."
67. *Editor & Publisher Year Book 1958,* 393–394.
68. *Editor & Publisher Year Book 1958,* 393.
69. Clarence Moore, personal interview, Miami, March 26, 1991.
70. Alisky, *Latin American Media,* 157.
71. For a summary of this Voltairian perspective as it relates to journalism, see J. Herbert Altschull, *From Milton to McLuhan: The Ideas Behind American Journalism* (New York: Longman, 1990), 77–84.
72. Edward C. Stein, *Cuba, Castro and Communism* (New York: Macfadden, 1962), 99.
73. Angel Fernandez Varela, personal interview, Miami, March 7, 1991.

74. Dorschner and Fabricio, *The Winds,* 98–99.
75. Lawrence C. Soley and John S. Nichols, *Clandestine Radio Broadcasting* (New York: Praeger, 1987); Tad Szulc, "Cuban Television's One-Man Show," in Robert Lewis Shayon, ed., *The Eighth Art* (New York: Rinehart and Winston Inc., 1962), 198.
76. Timothy Green, *The Universal Eye: The World of Television* (New York: Stein and Day, 1972), 54.
77. "Cuba Won't Take Over Radio–TV, Says New Communications Chief," *Broadcasting,* June 1, 1959, 79.
78. Cuba Won't Take Over."
79. Friedman, "Unrest in Cuban TV."
80. "Bola Desintegrada," *Bohemia,* Feb. 25, 1959, 64.
81. "Guild Raps Manager of TV Station," *The Havana Post,* March 2, 1960, 1.
82. "Despues de la Tempestad," *Bohemia,* Feb. 22, 1959, 60–61.
83. "Piden Intervengan el Canal 12 de TV," *Revolucion,* March 9, 1959, 1; "Y sin Embargo, se Hundia . . .," *Bohemia,* March 16, 1959, 70.
84. "Intervencion y Planes," *Bohemia,* March 29, 1959, 53–54.
85. "Colour Transmissions in Cuba," *COMBROAD,* April–June 1977, 58.
86. Carlos Todd, "Let's Look at Today" (column), *The Times of Havana,* May 28, 1959, 8.
87. Todd, "Let's Look at Today," May 28, 1959.
88. Todd, "Let's Look at Today," May 28, 1959.
89. "Superproduccion en Colores," *Bohemia,* June 21, 1959, 54, 98.
90. Todd, "Let's Look at Today," 28, May 1959.
91. Todd, "Let's Look at Today," May 28, 1959.
92. "Well-known TV Star Arrested as Swindler," *The Havana Post,* April 11, 1959, 1; "Alegato por TV," *Bohemia,* April 26, 1959, 54–58, 100.
93. "Well-known TV Star."
94. "El Experimento de Otto," *Bohemia,* Aug. 30, 1959, 56.
95. "Survey de TV y Radio," *Bohemia,* July 5, 1959, 51.
96. "El Caso Pumarejo," *Bohemia,* June 14, 1959, 112.
97. "Superprodccion en colores."
98. "Pumarejo en Borinquen," *Bohemia,* Jan. 10, 1960, 44, 46.
99. "Cuban Television Star Gaspar Pumarejo, at 61," *The Miami Herald,* March 26, 1975, 4B.
100. "Cansado y Decepcionado del Peru Gaspar Pumarejo Deja el Canal 4," *La Prensa* (Lima, Peru), Sept. 20, 1963, 6; "'Surveys' Destan Guerra en T.V.," *La Prensa* (Lima, Peru), Sept. 20, 1963, 1. Although Pumarejo accused Mestre of driving Trinidad to suicide, more likely it was some undisclosed illness which drove Trinidad to take his life. In a rare interview with Trinidad in December 1953, a *Bohemia* reporter wrote that the illness "had left its signals." "Amado Trinidad ha Vuelto a Trabajar la Tierra," *Bohemia,* Dec. 13, 1953, 62, 64, 85.

CHAPTER 10

1. P. D. Eldred, "There is Freedom of Expression," *The Havana Post,* Oct. 8, 1959, 1.
2. Bertram B. Johannson, "Anxiety Cloaks Press in Cuba," *Christian Science Monitor,* May 8, 1959, 3; Carlos Todd, "Let's Look at Today" (column), *The Times of Havana,* April 16, 1959, 8.
3. R. Hart Phillips, "Society-News Tax? Cuban Editors Shocked," *The New York Times,* June 2, 1959, 16.
4. Alfred L. Padula, *The Fall of the Bourgeoisie: Cuba, 1959–1961.* Ph.D. Dissertation, The University of New Mexico, 1974, 16.
5. Phillips, "Society-News Tax?"

6. Phillips, "Society-News Tax?"
7. Padula, *The Fall of the Bourgeoisie*, 275.
8. Padula, *The Fall of the Bourgeoisie*, 219–226; "Cuba," *Hispanic American Report*, June 1959, 320.
9. Abel Mestre, personal interview, Miami, Dec. 14, 1990.
10. Abel Mestre, personal interview.
11. Abel Mestre, personal interview.
12. Ramona Bechtos, "Ex-Cuba Mestre Shop Builds in Argentina," *Advertising Age*, April 16, 1962, 226, 228, 230, quote on 226.
13. Samuel Faber, *Revolution and Social Structure in Cuba, 1933–1959*. Ph.D. Dissertation, University of California, Berkeley, 1969, 456–461.
14. Paul D. Bethel, *The Losers* (New Rochelle, N.Y.: Arlington House, 1969), 164.
15. Kevin B. Tierney, *American-Cuban Relations*. Ph. D. Dissertation, Syracuse University, 1977, 70.
16. Manuel Urrutia Lleo, *Fidel Castro & Company, Inc.* (New York: Frederick A. Praeger, 1964), 46–47.
17. Urrutia, *Fidel Castro & Company*, 160.
18. Urrutia, *Fidel Castro & Company*, 35–44.
19. Urrutia, *Fidel Castro & Company*, 49–50.
20. Urrutia, *Fidel Castro & Company*, 50–51.
21. Urrutia, *Fidel Castro & Company*, 51.
22. Abel Mestre, personal interview.
23. Abel Mestre, personal interview.
24. "Dorticos is New President," *The Havana Post*, July 18, 1959, 1; Ray Brennan, *Castro, Cuba and Justice* (Garden City, N.Y.: Doubleday and Company, 1959), 281.
25. "Dorticos is New President."
26. "'Urrutia's House' Comes Tumbling Down," *The Times of Havana*, July 18 1959, 1; "Urrutia Plans Legal Action Against Todd," *The Times of Havana*, July 18, 1959, 1.
27. "Dorticos is New President."
28. Tad Szulc, "Cuban Television's One-Man Show," in Robert Lewis Shayon, ed., *The Eighth Art* (New York: Holt, Rinehart and Winston, 1962), 176–206.
29. Bethel, *The Losers*, 167.
30. Bethel, *The Losers*, 167.
31. Bethel, *The Losers*, 161.
32. Bethel, *The Losers*, 161–162.
33. Abel Mestre, personal interview.
34. Bethel, *The Losers*, 168.
35. Bethel, *The Losers*, 169.
36. Carlos Franqui, telephone interview, San Juan, Puerto Rico, July 11, 1992.
37. Carlos Todd, "Let's Look at Today" (column), *The Times of Havana*, Oct. 22, 1959, 6.
38. "Illegal Deals During Batista Regime to Backfire in Property Seizure," *The Times of Havana*, July 9, 1959, 2.
39. Michael B. Salwen and Bruce Garrison, *Latin American Journalism* (Hillsdale, N.J.: Lawrence Erlbaum Associates, 1991), 30–33.
40. P.D. Eldred, "IAPA Clears Cuban Newspapers of Charges," *The Havana Post*, Oct. 6, 1959, 1.
41. Eldred, "IAPA Clears"; "Shop Talk at Thirty," *Editor & Publisher*, Oct. 10, 1959, 78.
42. Eldred, "There is Freedom."
43. P.D. Eldred, "Cuban Editor in Heated IAPA Assembly Discussion," *The Havana Post*, Oct. 9, 1959, 1.
44. Padula, *The Fall of the Bourgeoisie*, 288.
45. John A. Lent, *Mass Communications in the Caribbean* (Ames: Iowa State University Press, 1990).
46. "Castro Methods Hurt Cuba Press," *The New York Times*, Aug, 24, 1959, 8.

NOTES

47. Hermino Portell Vila, *Nueva Historia de la Republica de Cuba* (Miami, Fla.: La Moderna Poesia, Inc., 1986), 750–754.
48. Portell Vila, *Nueva Historia*, 750–754.
49. "Cuban Papers Lose Editorial Freedom," *Editor & Publisher*, Jan. 23, 1960, 12; Henry Goethals, "Editors Protest Forced Use of Cable Footnotes," *The Times of Havana*, Jan. 18, 1960, 1, 16.
50. Goethals, "Editors Protest."
51. "Workers, Newsmen Publish 'Avance," *The Havana Post*, Jan. 19, 1960, 1.
52. "Castro Rips Into Zayas and Avance," *The Times of Havana*, Jan. 21, 1960, 16.
53. "'Avance', other Zayas Property Intervened," *The Havana Post*, Jan. 23, 1960, 1.
54. "Photo Ban Ordered at Avance," *The Miami Herald*, Jan. 25, 1960, 1.
55. "Cuban Paper Plans Edition in Exile," *Editor & Publisher*, July 23, 1960, 42.
56. Henry Goethals, "Matthews Gets Pat on the Back, Zayas Back of the Hand by Revolucion," *The Times of Havana*, Jan. 25, 1960, 17.
57. Jorge Zayas, "Is Castro a Red? Definitely, Says Former Editor," *The Miami Herald*, Jan. 26, 1960, 1; "Violent Downfall Ahead for Castro, Says Editor Zayas," *The Miami Herald*, Jan. 28, 1960, 1; "Why Doesn't U.S. Tag Castro a Red?—Zayas," *The Miami Herald*, Jan. 30, 1960, 1.
58. Agustin Tamargo, personal interview, Miami, Dec. 19, 1990.
59. "'Objection Notes' are Added in Cuba Press After Ike's Talk," *The Miami Herald*, Jan. 28, 1960, 9.
60. "Guild Calls IAPA Remarks Slander," *The Havana Post*, March 24, 1960, 1.
61. "Cuba," *Hispanic American Report*, February 1960, 99.
62. David Kraslow, "Fidel Indicted as Dictator by his Words?" *The Miami Herald*, April 5, 1960, 18.
63. Angel Fernandez Varela, personal interview, Miami, March 7, 1991; "Cuba," *Hispanic American Report*, May 1960, 309.
64. Irving Peter Pflaum, *Tragic Island: How Communism Came to Cuba* (Englewood Cliffs, N.J.: Prentice Hall, 1961), 62.
65. "Castro Union Seizes Last Free Papers," *Editor & Publisher*, May 21, 1960, 14.
66. "'Get Out, U.S.,' Screams Cuban Student Mob," *The Miami Herald*, May 14, 1960, 13.
67. "Castro Union"; "Cuba," *Hispanic American Report*, May 1960, 309.
68. Faber, *Revolution and Social Structure*, 440–445.
69. Boris Goldenberg, *The Cuban Revolution and Latin America* (New York: Praeger Press, 1966), 203.
70. "U.S. Protest on Seizure of U.S. Newsmen," *Editor & Publisher*, July 23, 1960, 10.
71. Carlos Franqui, *Diary of the Cuban Revolution* (New York: Viking Press, 1984), 80.
72. "El Crisol Folds," *Editor & Publisher*, June 18, 1960, 10.
73. Moore, personal interviews.
74. "Cuba," *Hispanic American Report*, November 1960, 791.
75. "Cuban Press Shackled," *Editor & Publisher*, Jan. 21, 1961, 6.
76. Fernandez Varela, personal interview.
77. "Limitadas a 16 las Paginas de los Diarios," *Informacion*, Oct. 4, 1960, 1.
78. Fernandez Varela, personal interview.
79. Fernandez Varela, personal interview.
80. "Cuban Press Shackled"; Wyatt MacGaffey and Clifford R. Barnett, *Twentieth-Century Cuba: The Background of the Castro Revolution* (Garden City, N.J.: Anchor Books, 1962), 333.
81. John A. Lent, *Mass Communications in the Caribbean* (Ames: Iowa State University Press, 1990), 129.
82. Goar Mestre, personal interview, Key Biscayne, Fla., May 10, 1990.
83. "Responsibilities of Cuban Government for Increased International Tensions in the Hemisphere," *The Department of State Bulletin*, No. 1105, Aug. 29, 1960.
84. "Responsibilities of Cuban Government"; Carlos Todd, "Let's Look at Today"

(column), *The Times of Havana,* March 14, 1960, 8.
85. "Buchanan Flying Home After P. del Rio Trial," *The Havana Post,* Dec. 23, 1959, 1.
86. Jay Mallin, "Castro Soon Forgets, Chastises U.S. Press," *Editor & Publisher,* Aug. 22, 1959, 59; "2 AP Men Released by Castro Agents," *Editor & Publisher,* May 14, 1960, 92.
87. "Fidel's Kind of Freedom," *Time,* Jan. 11, 1960, 45; "Castro Press Raps Dubois," *Editor & Publisher,* Aug. 15, 1959, 52.
88. "Matthews Proposed as U.S. Ambassador," *The Havana Post,* Jan. 13, 1960, 1.
89. "Cuba Press Freedom Eroded," *Christian Science Monitor,* Oct. 7, 1959, 10; "Dictators Intensify 'Smear', Dubois Says," *Editor & Publisher,* Oct. 10, 1959, 62A.
90. "Dictators Intensify."
91. "Dubois Replaced in Havana," *The New York Times,* Oct. 29, 1959, 17.

CHAPTER 11

1. Charles Friedman, "Unrest in Cuban Studios," *The New York Times,* May 10, 1959, II, 14.
2. Samuel Faber, *Revolution and Social Structure in Cuba, 1933–1959.* Ph.D. Dissertation, University of California, 1969, Berkeley, 335.
3. Max Lesnick, telephone interview, Miami, June 20, 1990; Jose Pardo Llada, personal interview, Miami, Feb. 24, 1992.
4. "U.S. Still Target of Radio Cuba," *The Miami Herald,* Jan. 31, 1960, 2.
5. Luis Conte Aguero, personal interview, Miami, March 9, 1990.
6. Emilio Ochoa, personal interview, Miami, October 15, 1991.
7. Alfred L. Padula, *The Fall of the Bourgeoisie: Cuba, 1959–1961.* Ph.D., The University of New Mexico, 1974, 308.
8. Abel Mestre, personal interview, Miami, Dec. 14, 1990; Goar Mestre, personal interview, Key Biscayne, Fla., May 10, 1990.
9. Abel Mestre, personal interview.
10. Abel Mestre, personal interview.
11. Tad Szulc, *Fidel: A Critical Portrait* (New York: Avon, 1986), 568–571.
12. "Nebraskan Held Briefly in Cuba," *The New York Times,* March 8, 1960, 18.
13. Jose Pardo Llada, *El "Maine" y "La Coubre," 1898–1960* (Habana: Patronato del Libre Popular, 1960).
14. Carlos Todd, "Let's Look at Today" (column), March 17, 1960, 8.
15. Todd, "Let's Look at Today," March 17, 1960.
16. Kevin B. Tierney, *American-Cuban Relations.* Ph.D. Dissertation, Syracuse University, 1977, 92–95.
17. "Many Friendly Cubans Turn Against U.S. After Castro Tirade Over Ship Explosion," *Wall Street Journal,* March 7, 1960, 2.
18. Conte Aguero, personal interview.
19. Conte Aguero, personal interview.
20. Conte Aguero, personal interview.
21. Henry Goethals, "Communists Trying to Take Over Cuban Revolution," *The Times of Havana,* March 24, 1960, 1.
22. Conte Aguero, personal interview.
23. "Ex-Castro Friend Gets U.S. Asylum, *The New York Times,* April 7, 1960. 3.
24. Conte Aguero, personal interview.
25. "Refuta Pardo Llada a Luis Conte Aguero," *Revolucion,* March 24, 1960, 1.
26. "Refuta Pardo Llada."
27. "Emplazamiento a Luis Conte Aguero," *Revolucion,* March 25, 1960, 1, 2 [Text of Pardo Llada's speech over Cadena Oriental de Radio on March 24, 1960].
28. Max Lesnick, personal interview, Miami, Feb. 19, 1991.

NOTES

29. Henry Goethals, "Controversy Swirls Around Conte Aguero," March 31, 1960, 1.
30. "Responsibilities of Cuban Government for Increased International Tensions in the Hemisphere," *The Department of State Bulletin*, No. 1105, Aug. 29, 1960.
31. Ruby Hart Phillips, *The Cuban Dilemma* (New York: Ivan Obolensky, Inc., 1962), 182.
32. "Near Riot Erupts in Front of CMQ," *The Havana Post*, March 26, 1960, 1.
33. Conte Aguero, personal interview.
34. Goar Mestre, personal interview.
35. Goar Mestre, personal interview.
36. Goar Mestre, personal interview.
37. Castro's TV Chain Adds Another Link," *The Miami Herald*, March 27, 1960, 2.
38. "El Programa Hablado Mas Destacado del Mes," *Bohemia*, Jan. 27, 1957, 52–56, 57; "Declaraciones de Goar Mestre Sobre la Nueva Empresa de Video CMBF, Cadena Nacional, S.A.," *Radiomania & Television*, April 5, 1957, 7.
39. Carlos Todd, "Let's Look at Today" (column), *The Times of Havana*, April 4, 1960, 8.
40. Alberto Vilar, personal interview, Miami, April 9, 1991.
41. Goar Mestre, personal interview.
42. Alberto Vilar, personal interview; also see John A. Lent, *Mass Communications in the Caribbean* (Ames: Iowa State University Press, 1990), 129.
43. "Castro Accuses Conte of 'Divisionist' Plan," *The Havana Post*, March 29, 1960, 1; "Castro Uses TV to Blast Old Friend," *The Miami Herald*, March 29, 1960, 1.
45. Goethals, "Controversy Swirls."
46. Abel Mestre's speech over CMQ-TV's "Meet the Press," March 31, 1960, mimeograph.
47. Abel Mestre's speech.
48. "Ex-Castro Friend."
49. "Castro Pro-Red Prisoner, Says Exiled Newsman," *The Miami Herald*, April 17, 1960, 9.
50. Tad Szulc, "Brazilian to Shorten Cuba Visit over 'Misquotation' about U.S.," *The New York Times*, April 1, 1960, 12; Hugh Thomas, *Cuba: The Pursuit of Freedom* (New York: Harper & Row, 1971), 1262.
51. Abel Mestre, personal interview, Miami, March 7, 1990.
52. Nicolas Rivero, *Castro's Cuba: An American Dilemma* (Washington, D.C.: Luce, 1962), 153.
53. "Radio Station Is Intervened," *The Havana Post*, July 5, 1960, 1, 6.
54. Conte Aguero, personal interview; Abel Mestre, personal interview, March 7, 1990; Goar Mestre, personal interview.
55. Tad Szulc, "Cuban Television's One-Man Show," in Robert Lewis Shayon, ed., *The Eighth Art* (New York: Holt, Rinehart and Winston), 203.
56. Abel Mestre, personal interview, March 7, 1990.
57. Abel Mestre, personal interview, March 7, 1990.
58. Paul P. Kennedy, "Cuban Defector Decries Red Line," *The New York Times*, March 23, 1961, 88.
59. R. Hart Phillips, "Castro Sees Help of All Americas," *The New York Times*, March 26, 1961, 31.
60. "Condenacion y Asco Provoca la Traicion de Pardo Llada," *Revolucion*, March 27, 1960, 1.
61. "Condenacion y Asco Provoca."
62. Thomas, *Cuba*, 1343.
63. "Leaving the Ship," *Time*, April 7, 1961, 36.
64. Lesnick, personal interview.
65. Lesnick, personal interview.
66. Lesnick, telephone interview.
67. Pardo Llada, personal interview.

68. Pardo Llada, personal interview.
69. Boris Goldenberg, *The Cuban Revolution and Latin America* (New York: Praeger, 1966), 203–204; Marvin Alisky, *Latin American Media: Guidance and Censorship* (Ames: Iowa State University Press, 1981), 154; Faber, *Revolution and Social Structure*, 446.
70. Jose Pardo Llada, "Yo que fui Fidelista," *Bohemia Libre*, May 1961, 34–37, 58–59.
71. "Cuba Has No Comment," *The New York Times*, October 2, 1960, 27; "Pardo Llada Escapes Life Attempt in Vedado," *The Havana Post*, July 10, 1960, 1.
72. Pardo Llada, "Yo que fui Fidelista," 36.
73. Pardo Llada, "Yo que fui Fidelista," 37.
74. Juan Carlos Coto, "Periodista se Vuelve Voz del Exilo ante Castro," *El Nuevo Herald*, July 19, 1991, 4A.
75. Pardo Llada, personal interview.
76. Conte Aguero, personal interview.
77. Pardo Llada, personal interview.
78. Conte Aguero, personal interview.
79. Tad Szulc, telephone interview, Washington, D.C., April 17, 1990.
80. Phillips, *The Cuban Dilemma*, 173–174; "Cuba," *Hispanic American Report*, February 1960, 100.
81. "Barletta Loses All to Govt.," *The Havana Post*, March 10, 1960, 1.
82. Phillips, *The Cuban Dilemma*, 173–174.
83. "*El Mundo* Puts Out Final Edition," *The Christian Science Monitor*, Feb. 3, 1962, 5.
84. Goar Mestre, personal interview.
85. "Responsibilities of Cuban Government."
86. "Responsibilities of Cuban Government"; "Dispuso Trabajo la Intervencion de CMQ," *Revolucion*, Sept. 13, 1960, 1 [Text of the official Cuban government explanation for the confiscation of CMQ].
87. "Base Ball!" *Bohemia*, October 23, 1960, 30, 90.
88. Itiel Perez, "Television in Cuba," *Radio and Television OIRT Information*, April 1961, 51–54, 52.
89. "Los Mestre, CMQ y Radio Swan," *Revolucion*, Sept. 14, 1960, 2 [Text of Pardo Llada's speech].
90. "Los Mestre."
91. Pardo Llada, personal interview.
92. Carlos Todd, "Let's Look at Today" (column), *The Times of Havana*, Sept. 8, 1960, 9.
93. David Kraslow, "Fidel Indicted as Dictator By His Words?" *The Miami Herald*, April 5, 1960, 18; Thomas, *Cuba*, 1274; "FIEL: Frente Independiente de Emisoras Libres," *Verde Olivio*, April 24, 1960, 18–19.
94. Ruby Hart Phillips, "Cuban TV: The Fidel Show," *The New York Times*, July 23, 1961, 8.
95. "FIEL."
96. Pardo Llada, personal interview.
97. "Los Mestre."
98. Abel Mestre, personal interview, March 7, 1990.
99. Abel Mestre, personal interview, March 7, 1990.
100. Abel Mestre, personal interview, March 7, 1990.
101. "American Radio in the Caribbean Counters Red Campaign in Cuba," *The New York Times*, Sept. 9, 1960, 1.
102. Abel Mestre, personal interview, March 7, 1990.

CHAPTER 12

1. Michael Salwen, "Three Pioneers of Cuban Television," *World Communication*,

20(1):11-22 (1992).
   2. Sydney W. Head, *World Broadcasting Systems: A Comparative Analysis* (Belmont, Calif.: Wadsworth, 1985), 27.
   3. Fred S. Siebert, Theodore Peterson, and Wilbur Schramm, *Four Theories of the Press* (Urbana, Ill.: University of Illinois Press, 1956).

Index

Abbott and Costello, 61
ABC (American Broadcasting Co.),
  112, 117, 118, 120
ABC (Audit Bureau of Circulation), 132
Actors, 11, 13–14, 34, 40, 47, 51,
  56–57, 81, 85
Adan, Juvenil, 110
Admiral (company), 16
Advertising, 5, 7, 8–9, 14, 20–23, 34,
  51–52, 64, 86–91, 108, 145
  competition for, 51–52
  Cuban Advertising Association and,
    9, 55
  Ethics Commission and, 86–91
  expenditures on, 20, 34
  extortion methods in, 87
  Goar Mestre and, 20–21
  methods of, 7, 8–9
  postwar boom in, 34
  quantity on radio, 23, 134
  rates for, 20, 51
  rotative advertising, 20–23
  soap manufacturers and, 8–9, 14,
    22–23, 64, 145
  spot advertising, 20
  on television, 34
Advertising Age, 140
Agramonte, Roberto, 93
Agrarian reform, 139
"Alegrias de Hatuey," 69
Alerta, 126, 131
  Ramon Vasconcelos and, 126
Alexanderson, E. F. W., 35
"Alfred Hitchcock Presents," 55
Alicoate, Jack, 15
Alisky, Marvin, 128, 132
Allen, Steve, 61, 109
Alles Soberon, Agustin, 106

Alonso, Manuel (Manolo), xvi, 36, 37,
  44–47, 69, 79
  background of, 36, 44
  Amadeo Barletta and, 47
  color film company of, 47
  Pedro Cue and, 54
  films of, 44
  Julian Lastra and, 38, 47, 49
  Miguel Humara and, 47
  motion picture industry, 36, 44
  Jose Pardo Llada and, 45–46
  Jose Luis Pelleya and, 44–45, 69
  Carlos Prio and, 45
  Gaspar Pumarejo and, 44–45
  Union Radio and, 44–47, 69
  Alberto Vilar and, 79
Alonso, Mike, 58, 60
Alvarez Ferrera, Alberto, 15
Amador, Carlos, 82
Ambar Motors, 51, 57, 77
American Broadcasting Co., 112, 117,
  118, 120
American (U.S.) colony (in Cuba), 58,
  149
American Federation of Radio and
  Television Artists, 109
American Home Products, 16
Ampex Corp., 111
"Ante la Prensa." *See* "Meet the
  Press"
Anti-Communism, 7, 138, 140–143,
  146, 154, 156
Antonio Alonso, Jose, 11
AP (Associated Press), 78
Aragon Dulzaides, Luis, 6, 13, 88
Argentina, 15, 37, 53, 70, 117–118,
  120–121, 144, 153, 159, 165
Armstrong, Louis, xiv

201

Arnaz, Desi, 55
Artalejo Fernandez, Arturo,
  15, 150
Associated Press, 78
Ataja, 126, 131
  Alberto Salas Amaro and, 126
Audit Bureau of Circulation (ABC), 132
Autentico Party (Partido
  Revolucionario Cubano), 46, 64,
  67-68
  corruption in, 71-72, 94, 167
  Eduardo Chibas denounces, 72
  Ramon Grau San Martin and, 71, 94
  Ortodoxo Party and, 64, 72, 93
  presidential election of 1944, 71
  presidential election of 1952, 12, 93
  Carlos Prio and, 46
  radio programs of, 64, 67-68
Autran, Manuel, 56
Avance, 131, 142, 146-147
  Fidel Castro denounces, 146
  confiscation of, 146
  Manuel Urrutia and, 142
  Bernardo Viera and, 142
  Jorge Zayas and, 146-147
Azcarraga, Emilio, 6-7, 26-27, 37,
  115, 116

Baez, Vicente, 124-125
Baker, Josephine, xiv
Ball, Lucille, 55
Baralt, Luis, 99
Barletta, Amadeo, xvi, 47-48, 49,
  52-53, 57, 59, 77-79, 82-83,
  101, 163
  Manolo Alonso and, 47
  in Argentina, 53
  asylum in Italian Embassy, 163
  automobile business, 51, 57, 77
  background of, 52-54
  Amadeo Barletta, Jr., and, 53, 101
  Fulgencio Batista and, 54, 163, 164
  Luis J. Botifoll and, 47, 54
  businesses confiscated, 59, 163
  Angel Cambo and, 48-49
  competition with CMQ, xvi, 51-52,
    163-164
  Pedro Cue and, 54
  in the Dominican Republic, 52-53,
    163
  Fascist sympathies of, 53
  flees Cuba, 163
  Ramon Grau San Martin and, 54
  Eliseo Guzman Alvarez and, 54
  under house arrest, 163
  Miguel Humara and, 47, 49
  Julian Lastra and, 47, 49
  Abel Mestre and, 52-53, 77, 163
  Goar Mestre and, 51-52, 54, 58, 77
  in Miami, 163
  Jose Ignacio de Montaner and, 29,
    49
  Benito Mussolini and, 52-53
  Jose Pelleya and, 47
  plans to expand Telemundo tele-
    vision and Union Radio
    television into networks, 49
  Carlos Prio Socarras and, 54
  publishes *El Mundo* in exile, 163
  Gaspar Pumarejo and, 82-83
  purchases *El Mundo,* 53-54, 77
  purchases Television del Caribe, 57
  Telemundo and, xvi, 49, 51, 79,
    163-164
  Rafael Trujillo and, 52-53
  Union Radio
    purchase of, 48
    selling of, 79
  Alberto Vilar and, 49, 79
Barletta, Jr., Amadeo, 53, 101
Barrall, Mario, 48
Barranco, Angel, 56
Barreiro, Manuel, 109
Baseball, xiv, 38, 40, 43, 59-61, 164
  Cuban Winter League, 38, 40, 59
  Gaspar Pumarejo's broadcasts of,
    38, 40
  television coverage of, 40
  World Series (U.S.) on Cuban
    television, xiv, 59-61, 164
  World Series (U.S.) taken off
    television by Castro
    government, 164
Batista y Zaldivar, Fulgencio, vii, xii,
  xvi, 12, 24, 32, 46-48, 58,
  70-81, 89, 92-108, 114,
  122-124, 126-129, 133-134,
  139, 143-144, 152, 157,
  163-164, 167-169
  attempted assassination of, 32
  Amadeo Barletta and, 54, 163, 164
  Luis J. Botifoll and, 47, 54

in Camp Columbia, 122
Fidel Castro and, viii, xiii, 93–95, 102–103, 114, 133, 152
censorship under, xvi, 12, 89, 92, 94, 95–98, 100–107, 108, 128, 152, 168, 169
Edmund Chester and, 81, 103
Eduardo Chibas and, 93–94
Communist Party and, 143
Luis Conte Aguero and, 94
coup by (March 10, 1952), xvi, 24, 32, 46–47, 48, 80, 93–94, 95, 98, 168, 169
denounced by Ortodoxo Party members, 93
Ernesto de la Fe and, 98
flees Cuba, 122, 123–124, 134, 152
Ramon Grau San Martin and, 71
Inter-American Association of broadcasters (IAAB) and, 97, 114
Inter American Press Association (IAPA) and, 100–101, 103, 114
Gerardo Machado and, 101, 139
Herbert Matthews and, 100–101
Abel Mestre and, 97–98, 114
Goar Mestre and, 96–97, 114, 123
Emilio Ochoa and, 99–100
opinion about journalism, 95
Jose Pardo Llada and, 67, 94, 152–156, 160–162
Drew Pearson on, 101
presidential election of 1944, 12
presidential election of 1958, 161
press subsidies and, xvii, 128–129, 144
Carlos Prio and, 94
right-to-reply law and, 73
Elliott Roosevelt and, 81
secretly purchases radio stations, 70, 126, 167
secretly purchases television stations, 157, 167
Battisti, Amletto, 15
Bay of Pigs invasion, 144
Beer industry, 51, 145
Benitez, Jose, 7
Bergen, Edgar (and Charlie McCarthy), 61

Berrio, Lolita, 81, 82
Bestov Products, S.A., 16
Betancourt, Enrique, 23
Bethel, Paul, 140, 143–144
Bianchi, Armando, 48
Blanco, Antonio, 39
Bohemia (magazine), xv, 13, 25, 29, 45–46, 63, 82, 90, 101–102, 105–106, 124, 128, 161–162
censorship of, 101–102, 105, 106
Pardo Llada writes in, 161–162
published in exile (as *Bohemia Libre*), 161–162
Miguel Angel Quevado and, 46, 161
refuses to accept press subsidies, 128
story on Amado Trinidad, 82
suspends publication of "Seccion en Cuba," 105
Bohemia Libre, 161–162
"La Bolsa del Saber" ("The Sack of Wisdom"), 6
Bonsal, Philip W., 143
Botifoll, Luis J., 47, 54, 66, 69–70
Amadeo Barletta and, 47, 54
Fulgencio Batista and, 54
Confederacion de Trabajadores de Cuba (CTC) and, 69–70
El Mundo and, 47, 54
Jose Luis Pelleya and, 47, 69–70
purchases Union Radio, 47, 69–70
Boxing, xiv, 4–5, 56
Bravo, Nicholas, 143
Brazil, 36, 70, 160
Brentanos bookstore, 21
Broadcasting. *See* Radio; Television
Buchanan, James, 150
Buendia, Miguel, 10–11
Burnett, Meade, 37
Business Week, 51

Caballero, Eduardo, 86, 114, 134, 136
"Cabaret Regalias" ("Royal Cabaret"), 48, 89
Cable News Network (CNN), xi
Cadena Azul. *See* RHC–Cadena Azul
La Cadena de las Americas, 21
Cadena Nacional, 55, 61
Cadena Nacional Telefonica, 8
Cadena Oriental de Radio, 35, 50, 64, 66–68, 95–96, 153, 160, 165

Ricardo Miranda Cortez and, 64, 67–68
Jose Pardo Llada and, 64, 67, 96, 153, 160, 165
plans to expand into television, 35, 50, 68
political commentators on, 64, 67–68
programming on, 64, 67–68
stations in the network, 66
Cadena Panamerican, 21
Cadena Rojo, 15
Cadena Venezolana de la Television (CVTV), 118
Cal, Mimi, 115
Calloway, Cab, xiv
Cambo & Gabriel, S.A., 10, 17
Cambo Ruiz, Angel, 10, 17, 22–29, 32, 48–49, 55, 56
Amadeo Barletta and, 48–49
CMQ
departure from, 32
purchase of, 17
Miguel Gabriel and, 10, 22–28, 32, 49
Abel Mestre and, 17
Goar Mestre and, 17, 22–24, 28–29, 32, 49
Luis Augusto Mestre and, 28
opinion about television in Cuba and the United States, 28–29
purchases Union Radio, 49
Television Nacional and, 49, 56
Camp Columbia, 100, 122, 124
Cantillo, Eulogio, 124
Carbo, Sergio, 8, 124, 148
Prensa Libre and, 124, 148
Carrillo, Justo, 29–31
Carteles, xv, 7, 87
Casals, Violeta, 107
Casanova, Gabriel (Salum Nasser), 135–136
Casas Rodriguez, Luis, 5
Casas Romero, Luis, 4, 15
"Casino de Alegria" ("Casino of Joy"), 48
Castaneda, Carlos, 113–114
Castellanos, Nicholas, 58
Castrillon, Juan B., 109
Castro, Herbert, 90
Castro, Orlando, 67
"Castroika," x

Castro Ruz, Fidel, vii-x, xi, xvi, 29, 51, 76, 93, 100, 102–103, 106–108, 114–115, 117, 126–127, 133, 136, 138, 140–141, 143–147, 151, 153–154, 156, 158–160, 162, 165
Avance denounced by, 146
Fulgencio Batista and, viii, xiii, 93–95, 102–103, 114, 133, 152
Justo Carrillo and, 29
Raul Castro and, 140
Eduardo Chibas and, 76, 93
CMQ and, 142, 153–154
Communist Party and, 153
Luis Conte Aguero and, 102, 106, 153–154, 156, 158, 159
La Coubre incident, 154–155
critical press reports of, 126–127
denounced by, 126–127, 138, 144–145, 150–151
criticizes foreign press coverage, 127, 150–151
cultivates good will with Cuban and foreign press, 106
Jules Dubois and, 127, 150–151
financial support from Cuban businesspeople, 114–115
forms July 26th Movement, 102
Carlos Franqui and, 29
freedom of the press defended by, xvii, 106, 126, 138, 145, 162
Ernesto "Che" Gueverra and, 140
Hoy defended by, 140
marches into Havana, 122, 147
Marxism and, 162
Herbert Matthews and, xiii, 100, 103, 106, 127
Abel Mestre and, 154
Goar Mestre and, 114–115, 117, 133
in Mexico, 29, 102
Moncada uprising, 102
opinion about Eduardo Chibas, 76
Ortodoxo Party member, 76, 93
Bernadette Pardo and, 162
Jose Pardo Llada and, 106–107, 144, 160, 165
pardoned from prison, 102
position on Communism, 140, 153
Carlos Prio and, 76, 93
promises free elections, 122

INDEX

Gaspar Pumarejo and, 136
Radio Rebelde and, 133
radio used by, viii, xiii, 93, 133
resigns as prime minister, 141
in the Sierra Maestra, 103, 106, 126, 133
Robert Taber and, 106
on television, 133, 140
testifies at Batistiano trials, 127
Carlos Todd and, 149
in the United States, 140
Manuel Urrutia and, 122, 140–143
Jorge Zayas and, 146–147
Zig Zag denounced by, 126–127
Castro Ruz, Raul, 140–142
Fidel Castro and, 140
Ernesto ("Che") Gueverra and, 140
Abel Mestre and, 141–142
Catholicism, 150
CBS, 80, 106, 112, 117–118, 119–120
Censorship, xvi, 10–12, 89, 92, 94–95, 100–108, 114, 126, 128, 130, 148–149, 152, 168, 169
advertising, 108
Fulgencio Batista's methods of, viii, xiii, 12, 89, 92, 94–98, 102–107, 108, 128, 152, 168–169
of *Bohemia*, 101–102, 104, 106
Fidel Castro's methods of, 148–149
of CMQ, 10–11, 114
Ernesto de la Fe institutes, 94
intellectual views of, 101, 130
Gerardo Machado and, 10–11
Herbert Matthews' views of, 100
Drew Pearson's views of, 101
rock and roll music, 92
Ramon Vasconcelos and, 92
of *Zig Zag*, 104–105
Central Intelligence Agency, 166
Chateaubriand, Francisco de Assis, 36
"Che." *See* Guevarra, Ernesto
Chequeos, 9, 51, 55, 87
Chester, Edmund A., 80–81, 103
Fulgencio Batista and, 81, 103
CBS and, 81
Heriberto Hernandez and, 81
Gerardo Machado and, 81
Gaspar Pumarejo and, 81
and RHC–Cadena Azul, 81

Elliott Roosevelt and, 81
Amado Trinidad and, 80
Chibas, Eduardo ("Eddie") Rene, xvi, 19–20, 46, 71–76, 93, 152, 158
assassination attempt against, 72
Autentico Party denounced by, 72
Fulgencio Batista and, 93–94
Fidel Castro and, 76
CMQ and, 19–20, 71–76, 93, 158
Luis Conte Aguero and, 76, 152
Ramon Grau San Martin and, 71
honesty of, 72
Rolando Masferrer and, 74
Abel Mestre and, 158
Goar Mestre and, 19–20, 71–76
Ortodoxo Party and, 72, 152
Jose Pardo Llada and, 76, 93, 152
personality of, 72–73
political situation after the death of, 76, 93
presidential election of 1952, 72, 93
Carlos Prio and, 73
radio programs of, xvi, 19–20, 71–76
radio style of, xvi, 20, 71–76, 152
Aureliano Sanchez Arango and, 75–76
suicide of, xvi, 46, 71, 75–76, 93
Chibas, Raul, 76
Chicago Tribune, 124, 127, 150–151
Children's programming, 51
Chinese-language newspapers, 130, 147
Chopin, Frederic, 32
Circuito CMQ, S.A. *See* CMQ
Circuito Nacional Cubano (CNC), 64, 67–68, 105, 126
allegations of Batista ties with, 68, 105, 126
anti-Batista radionovela on, 105
confiscation of, 126
creation of, 68
Jose Luis Piedra and, 67, 68, 126
programming for the countryside, 68
RHC–Cadena Azul and, 68
Alberto Sotolongo and, 68
stations in the network, 67
"Cisco Kid," 55
Civic Resistance Movement (CRM), 124–125
Clandestine radio, viii, xiii, 133

Clavelito (Miguel Alfonso Pozo),
    88–89, 92
CMBF (radio), 29–32
CMBF-TV, 55, 157
CMC, 6
CMCB, 10, 64
CMK, 41
CMQ (Circuito CMQ, S.A.), xvi, 9–14,
    17–20, 22–29, 32, 35–36, 48,
    51–52, 56, 58–61, 63–65, 67,
    69, 71–77, 79, 81, 83–84,
    98–100, 103–104, 109–111,
    115, 124–125, 139–140,
    143–144, 150, 153–159,
    164–166
  advertising on, 64
  Amadeo Barletta and, xvi, 51–52,
    163–164
  baseball on, 59–61
  beginnings of, 10–12
  Angel Cambo and, 10, 17, 22–29
  Fidel Castro and, 142, 153–154
  censorship of, 10–11, 114
  Eduardo Chibas and, 19–20,
    71–76, 93, 158
  confiscation of, 61, 115, 159, 164
  Luis Conte Aguero and, 154–159
  Manolo Cores and, 111
  Ethics Commission and, 89
  expansion into television, 35–36
  Miguel Gabriel
    departure from, 24–28
    role in, 10–11, 13, 17, 22–24
  Manolo Iglesias and, 103–104
  investment in videotape technology,
    111
  labor-management disputes at,
    139–140, 164
  Rolando Masferrer and, 74
  Abel Mestre and, 17–18, 158–159,
    166
  Goar Mestre and, 14–19, 73–74,
    114–115, 123, 157–159
  "Meet the Press" program, 98–100,
    143, 158–159
  musical programming on, 32
  news on, 10–11, 98–100,
    103–104
  occupation of Civic Resistance
    Movement (rebels), 124–125
  Jose Pardo Llada denounces,
    164–165
  plans for color television, 111
  presidential campaign coverage on,
    24, 71
  programming on, 11, 28, 32, 48, 164
  Radiocentro Building and, 26–27,
    30, 43, 59, 74, 100, 111, 125,
    155, 157
  radionovelas on, 19
  Radio Progreso and, 69, 158
  Radio Swan and, 166
  ratings of, 9, 26, 36, 56, 63, 79, 81,
    83–84, 137
  research at, 23, 79
  Manolo Reyes and, 19
  RHC–Cadena Azul and, 9–10,
    12–14, 19, 35, 77
  soap manufacturers and, 9
  stations in the radio network, 65
  Telemundo and, xvi, 51–52, 79
  television in Puerto Rico and, 115
  television network, 48
  Union Radio and, 35–37, 48
  United States Information Service
    and, 144
  Alberto Vilar and, 64, 79
  World Series television broadcasts,
    59–61, 164
"CMQ News" ("Noticiero CMQ"), 10,
    98, 103–104
CMX, 10, 26
CMZ, 8, 88
CNC. *See* Circuito Nacional Cubano
COCO, 35–36, 42, 96
COCQ, 22
Codding, George A., Jr., 70
Coincidentals, 9, 51, 55, 87
Coletillas, 146–147, 150
Colgate-Palmolive, 8, 14, 22
Collegium of Journalists, 106
Colombia, xiv, 116–117
Color films, 47, 113
Color television, xvii, 47, 110–114,
    135
  CMQ's plans for, 111
  programming on, 113
  Gaspar Pumarejo and, xvii,
    110–114, 124, 134–136
  David Sarnoff's plans for, 112
  taken off the air by Castro
    government, 135
  in the United States, 111–112
Commercial, 131

El Commercio, 131
Commission on Radio and Television Ethics, 86–92
 advertisers and, 87–88
 Luis Aragon Dulzaides and, 88
 Luis J. Botifoll and, 88
 Clavelito (Miguel Alfonso Pozo) and, 88–89
 creation of, 87–88
 Manolo Fernandez and, 88
 Goar Mestre and, 87–88
 Jose Luis Pelleya and, 88
 RHC–Cadena Azul and, 88
 rules of, 88
 Juan Jose Tarajano and, 87–92
 Amado Trinidad and, 88
 Ramon Vasconcelos and, 90–92
 Jose Manuel Viana and, 88
Committee of Lisa, 114
Communication theory and research, 23
Communism, viii, xvii, 7, 10, 33, 95, 138, 140–143, 146, 153–159, 167
 anti-Communism, 7, 138, 140–143, 146, 154, 156
 becomes a major political issue, 140
 Fidel Castro's position on, 140, 153
 fear of, 140
 Ernesto de la Fe's attacks against, 98
 U.S. Senate subcommittee investigation of, 142
Communist Party, xvii, 33, 71, 140–143, 155–160
 Fulgencio Batista and, 143
 Fidel Castro defends, 140
 Luis Conte Aguero's accusations against, 153, 155–159
 Jose Pardo Llada and, 160
 President Manuel Urretia denounces, 140–143
Communist radio station, 10, 26, 168
Compania Argentina de Television, 117
La Competidora Gaditana, 40
Conde, Cuco, 59
Confederacion de Trabajadores de Cuba (CTC), 69–70
"Con la Manga al Codo," 150

Conte Aguero, Luis, xvii, 64, 76, 93–94, 101–102, 106, 141, 152–159, 162–163
 asylum in Argentine Embassy, 153, 158–159
 background of, 163
 Fulgencio Batista and, 94
 campaign against Communism, 153, 155–159
 Fidel Castro and, 102, 106, 156, 158, 159
 Eduardo Chibas and, 76, 152
 CMQ television program of, 141, 154, 156
 La Coubre incident and, 154–155
 dispute with Jose Pardo Llada, 154–155, 156
 flees Cuba, xvii, 158
 Max Lesnick and, 156
 Abel Mestre and, 154, 157–159
 Goar Mestre and, 157, 159
 in Miami, 159
 Ricardo Miranda Cortez and, 64
 Ortodoxo Party member, 64, 93
 Jose Pardo Llada and, xvii, 94, 152–156, 162
 Drew Pearson criticized by, 101
 radio program of, 156
 Radio Progreso and, 102, 153, 156, 158–159
 speaking style of, 163
 threatened by mobs, 156–157
 Manuel Urretia and, 141, 154
Cores, Manolo, 111
"La Corte de la Felicidad" ("The Court of Happiness"), 110
"La Corte Suprema del Arte" ("The Supreme Court of Art"), 11, 28
Costello, Lou, 61
Cothron, William C., 39
La Coubre incident, 154–155
Crain, Thomas, 33
El Crisol, 131, 147, 149
Cristal (company), 39
Cristobal Diaz Gonzalez, Ingeniero, 8, 13, 16–17, 25
Cronicas, 8, 138–139
Cronistas, 138–139
Cronkite, Walter, 119
Crusellas Touzet, Ramon F., 22–23

Crusellas y Compania, 8, 14, 22
Cruz, Celia, 69
Cuban Advertising Association, 9, 55, 63, 87
Cuban Association of Radio and TV Critics (CARTV), 83, 104, 114
Cuban Federation of Radio and Television Broadcasters, 94, 102, 124
Cuban Newspaper Guild, 134
Cuban Petroleum News Digest, 108
Cuban Press Bloc, 124
Cuban Telephone Co., 3, 5, 8
Cuban Winter League Baseball, 38, 40, 59
Cue Abreu, Pedro, 54
Cuervo Navarro, Pelayo, 100

Delgado, Gabino, 60
Delgado Parker, Genaro, 115
Dempsey, Jack, 4–5
Denny, Clarence R., 29
Diario de la Marina, xv, 5, 6, 33, 34, 36, 49–50, 53, 125–126, 130–131, 138–139, 147–149, 156, 165
  circulation of, 131
  coletillas in, 147–149
  confiscated by Castro government, 148, 165
  conservative policies of, 53, 125, 148
  Luis Conte Aguero and, 156
  Francisco Franco and, 149
  Carlos Franqui denounces, 148–149
  labor-management disputes, 148
  mobs march on, 125–126, 148
  El Mundo and, 53
  Jose Pardo Llada denounces, 165
  plans to expand into television, 36, 49–50
  Prensa Libre and, 147–149
  press subsidies and, 130
  radio and television news section of, 6
  Jose Ignacio Rivero and, 33, 148, 165
Diario Espanol, 131
Diario Finanzas, 131
Diario Nacional, 101, 131, 145
Diaz Lanz, Luis, 142

Diaz Verson, Salvador, 7–8
"El Dictador del Valle Azul" ("The Dictator of the Blue Valley), 105
Directorio Revolucionario, 125
La Discussion, 131
D'Mant, Carlos, 58
Domingo y Castillo, Andres, 135
Dominguez, Jorge, I., x
Dominican Republic, 52–53, 163
Dominican Tobacco Co., 53
Donohue, Francis, J., 33
"Doorways to Heaven," 113
Dorschner, John, 123
Drogueria Mestre y Espinosa (company), 14
Dubois, Jules, 124, 127, 150–151
  Fidel Castro and, 127, 150–151
  leaves Cuba, 151
  Herbert Matthews and, 127, 150–151
  viewed (wrongly) as a Castro supporter, 127

Editor & Publisher, 131
Educational radio, 8, 15, 88
Educational television, 37, 99, 116
Enriquez, Jorge, 107
Escalante, Anibal, 98
Escrin, Adela, 48
"Escuela de Television." *See* "School of Television"
"Espectaculos de Otto Sirgo, S.A.," 136
Espinosa, Vicente, 15
Esso, 111
Estrada, Carlos, 65
Ethics Commission. *See* Commission on Radio and Television Ethics
Ethical issues pertaining to radio and television. *See* Commission on Radio and Television Ethics
Evening News (Havana), 131
Excelsior, 131
Executions of Batistianos, 127
Exile Cuban newspapers, 163

Fabricio, Roberto, 123
Falcon, Raul, 4
"La Familia Pilon," 11–12
Fascism, 7
Fe, Ernesto de la, 94, 98, 100, 126
  attacks against Communism, 98

Fulgencio Batista and, 98
boycotts CMQ's "Meet the Press," 100
censorship decree of, 94
Anibal Escalante and, 98
jailed by Castro government, 126
Jorge Manach and, 100
Rolando Masferrer and, 98
Abel Mestre and, 94, 98
radio program of, 98
Federal Communications Commission (FCC) (U.S.), 29, 60, 112, 115, 133-134
Fernandez, Delfin, 56
Fernandez, Leopoldo, 115
Fernandez, Tony, 165
Fernandez, Victor, 57
Fernandez Cruz, Domingo, 69
Fernandez Cruz, Manuel (Manolo), 15, 35, 65, 68-69, 82, 88, 124, 159
  in Camp Columbia, 124
  Eulogio Cantillo and, 124
  Ethics Commission and, 88
  Ovidio Fernandez and, 65, 69, 159
  flees Cuba, 159
  in Miami, 159
  plans for television, 35
  Radio Progreso and, 68-69, 159
  RHC–Cadena Azul and, 82
Fernandez Cruz, Ovidio, 65, 69, 159
Fernandez Duran, Juan, 15
Fernandez Varela, Angel, 132-133, 148-149
FIEL (radio network), 165
"Fifty Years of Cuban Television," 84
Finanzas, 131
Firpo, Luis Angel, 4-5
Foreign press, 127, 150-151
Fraga Iribarne, Manuel, 119-120
Franco, Francisco, 119-120, 149
Franqui, Carlos, 107, 129-130, 144, 148-149
  Fidel Castro and, 144
  defection of, 148-149
  Diario de la Marina denounced by, 148-149
  newspapers denounced by, 148-149
  Jose Pardo Llada and, 107, 144
  Prensa Libre and, 148-149
  Radio Rebelde and, 107

Revolucion and, 129-130, 144, 149
  visits the *New York Times,* 129-130
Freedom of speech, 138
Freedom of the press, xvii, 96, 106, 126, 132-133, 138, 147, 162, 169
Freud, Sigmund, 89
Friedman, Charles, 122, 152

Gabriel, Miguel, 10-11, 13, 22-28, 32, 49
  Jose Antonio Alonso and, 11
  Angel Cambo and, 10, 22-28, 32, 49
  death of, 28
  and CMQ, 27-28
  Abel Mestre and, 27
  Goar Mestre and, 16-17, 19, 22-25, 27-28, 32
  RHC–Cadena Azul, 19, 27-28
  role in early Cuban radio, 10-11
  "The Supreme Court of Art" and, 11, 28
  Amado Trinidad and, 13, 27-28
Gaby, Fofo and Miliki, 40
Gainza Paz, Alberto, 144-145
Galileo, Galilei, 75
Gandero Alberto, 40
Garcia Inclan, Guido, 35-36, 96
Garcia Serra, Jorge, 15
Garcia Sifredo, Armando, 67, 68, 96
Gardner, Arthur, 33
Gatica, Lucho, 85
General Electric (GE), 34-35
General Foods, 16
General Motors, 16, 47, 52, 53
Gibraltar Steamship Co., 166
Gil, Adolfo, 15, 67
Giquel, Humberto, 4
Giro, Alberto, 6, 34-35
Goar Mestre and Associates, 117
Godoy, Augusto, 16
Gogol, Nikolai, 6
Goebbels, Josef, 160-161
Gomez Kemp, Ramiro, 38
Gomez Wanguemert, Luis, 165
Grau San Martin, Ramon, 68, 71-72, 94, 121, 130, 167
  Amadeo Barletta and, 54
  Fulgencio Batista and, 71

Fidel Castro's denunciations of, 93
Eduardo Chibas' denunciations of, 71
corruption of, 71–72, 94, 167
Gerardo Machado and, 71
Ricardo Miranda Cortez and, 68
Jose Pardo Llada and, 67
presidential election of, 12, 71
Carlos Prio and, 94, 167
press subsidies of, 130
"La Guajira Guantanamera," 12
Guede, Emilio, 124–125
  Vicente Baez and, 124–125
  Civic Resistance Movement and, 124–125
  Diario de la Marina and, 125–126
  Mestre brothers (Abel and Goar) and, 125
  role in the takeover of CMQ studios, 124–125
Gueverra, Ernesto ("Che"), 140, 165
  Fidel Castro and, 140
  Raul Castro and, 140
  FIEL network and, 165
  Jose Pardo Llada and, 165
  Peronism and, 165
  Radio Rebelde and, 165
Gutierrez, Mike, 56
Gutierrez, Oscar, 15
Gutierrez Serrano, Raul, 23–24, 26
Guzman Alvarez, Eliseo, 54

"Hablar con Conte Aguero," 153
Harrell, Raymond L., 50
The *Havana Post*, xv, 38, 58, 63, 108
Havana Reporters Association, 147
Havana Sports Palace, 127
Havaner Leben–Vida Habanera, 130
Henriques, Guillermo, 66
Heraldo de Commercial, 131
Heraldo de Cuba, 6, 131
Hermida, Ramon, 100
Hernandez, Aurelio, 15
Hernandez, Celimo, 39
Hernandez, Heriberto, 81
Hevia, Carlos, 93
Hill Olivera, Ernesto, 85
Hitchcock, Alfred, 55
Hitler, Adolph, 42, 160
"Home Club" ("Hogar Club"), 84–86, 113–114, 134–135
  confiscated by the Castro government, 135
  creation of, 84
  Sarita Montiel on, 86
  Gaspar Pumarejo and, 84–86, 113–114, 134–135
"Hogar Club." *See* "Home Club"
Hoi Men Kong Po, 131
"Hopalong Cassidy," 55
"Hora Multiple," 13
"The House of Stockings," 10
Hoy. See *Noticias de Hoy*
Hull, Cordell, 53
Humara, Miguel, 29, 38, 47, 49
  Manolo Alonso and, 47
  Amado Barletta and, 47, 49
  Julian Lastra and, 38, 47, 49
  Jose Ignacio de Montaner and, 29, 49
  Gaspar Pumarejo and, 38, 47
  purchases Television Nacional, 49
  purchases Union Radio, 49
Humara y Lastra, 38, 47, 49
Humor magazines, 105–106, 126–127

"I Love Lucy," 55
"I Was a Fidelista" (by Jose Pardo Llada), 161–162
IAAB (Inter-American Association of Broadcasters), 97, 114, 118
  Goar Mestre and, 97, 114, 118
  Juan Domingo Peron and, 118
IAPA (Inter American Press Association), 100, 103, 144–145
  Fulgencio Batista and, 100–101, 103
  clashes with Castro government, 144–145
  defends Cuban newspapers, 144–145
  fails to condemn Batista government press censorship, 103
  investigates charges of press bribery, 144–145
  Jose Ignacio Rivero and, 148
  Jorge Zayas and, 147
Ibero-American Summit Conference, 162
Ichaso, Francisco, 99
Iglesias, Manolo, 103–104

INDEX

Illiteracy, in Cuba, ix-x
El Imperial, 131
India, 165
Industria y Comercio, 131
Informacion, 49, 128, 130, 131, 132, 146, 148, 149-150
Inter-American Association of Broadcasters. *See* IAAB
Inter American Press Association. *See* IAPA
"International Day," 113
International Telephone & Telegraph, 3, 61
Italy, xi, 32, 46, 52-53

Jewish newspapers, 130
Jones, Frank H., 5, 34-35
Jones, Merle, 119-120
Journalism, 7-8, 41, 95, 99, 128-132, 167
  Fulgencio Batista's opinion of, 95
  corruption in, 128-132, 167
  Jorge Manach's opinion of, 99
  Jose Pardo Llada's opinion of, 41
  radio journalism, 7-8
Journalists, 7-8, 46, 105, 106, 140
Journalists' Day, 40, 101
Jovina Garcia, Nicholas, 6

Kauppe, Eric, 39
Kinescope recordings, 59, 111
Knotts, Don, 61
Kolynos toothpaste, 16
Kresto soft drink, 16
Kuomintang Nationalist Party, 131

Labor unions, 139, 150-151
Lastra, Julian, 29, 38, 47, 49
  Manolo Alonso and, 38, 47, 49
  Amadeo Barletta and, 47, 49
  Miguel Humara and, 47, 49
  Jose Ignacio de Montaner and, 29, 49
  Gaspar Pumarejo and, 38, 47
  purchases Television Nacional, 49
  purchases Union Radio, 49
Lavin Gomez, Francisco, 15
Law of Public Order (No. 997), 101
Lawrence, Steve, 61
Lechuga Hevia, Carlos, 78-79, 123
Leninism, viii
Lent, John, 54

Lesnick, Max, 67, 153, 156, 161, 165
  Luis Conte Aguero and, 156
  on FIEL radio network, 165
  Jose Pardo Llada and, 153, 156, 161
  radio program of, 67
Leyva, Rolando, 105
Liberace, xiv, 85-86
  Gaspar Pumarejo and, 85-86
Libertad, 133
Libertarian press theory, 132
"Life of Riley," 59
Literacy campaign, ix
Llanes, Miguel, 165
Llera, Evangelina de la, 125
Llerandi, Manuel, 86, 114
Lobo, Julio, 129
Lopez, Jesus, 7
Lopez Fresquet, Rufo, 139
Lopez Guiral, Raul, 65
Lopez Toca, Ramon, 22
Lopez Vilaboy, Jose, 126
Losada, Jess, 60
Luis Lopez, Oscar, 25
Luis Martin, Juan, 138
Luis Maso, Jose, 66
Luz, 131

Machado y Morales, Gerardo, 8, 10-11, 29, 99, 123, 139
Mafiosco, 52
Magazines, xv, 3, 6, 7, 13, 25, 29, 34, 45-46, 46, 63, 82, 87, 90, 99, 101-102, 105-106, 124, 128, 144, 156, 161-162, 169. *Also see* Names of magazines
Man Sen Yat Po, 131
Manach Robato, Jorge, 99, 100
  Ernesto de la Fe and, 100
  Gerardo Machado and, 99
  "University of the Air," 99
Manana, 126, 131
  Jose Lopez Vilaboy and, 126
Mann, Anthony, 86
Manuel Gonzalez, Jose, 15
Marti, Jose, 156
Martin, Eddy, 165
Martinez, Andres, 15
Martinez, Ricardo, 107
Marx, Karl, 155-156
Marxist theory, 10, 156, 162

Masferrer, Rolando, 74, 98, 104–105, 125, 133
  atrocities of, 125
  Eduardo Chibas and, 74
  CMQ and, 74
  criticized by U.S. Embassy, 104–105
  escapes from Cuba, 125
  Ernesto de la Fe and, 98
  newspapers published by, 125, 133
  private army of, 133
  reputation of, 104–105, 133
  Carlos Prio and, 74
  right-to-reply law and, 74
  El Tiempo and, 98, 104–105, 125, 133
Mas Martin, Luis, 107
Matthews, Herbert, xiii, 100–101, 103, 127, 150–151
  Fulgencio Batista praised by, 100–101
  Fidel Castro and, xiii, 100, 103
  criticizes U.S. press coverage of Castro, 127
  Jules Dubois and, 127, 150–151
  lionized by Castro government, 127
  in the Sierra Maestra, 103
  viewed (wrongly) as a Castro supporter, 100
  views on Cuban television, xiii
McCann Erikson (U.S. advertising agency), 117
McCarthy, Joseph, 98
McLuhan, Marshall, 42
Mederas, Agustin, 66
"Meet the Press" (Cuban program "Ante la Prensa"), 70, 98–100, 143, 153, 158–159
  Luis Baralt and, 99
  Nicholas Bravo and, 143
  Fidel Castro and, 153
  censorship of, 99–100, 153
  Pelayo Cuervo Nevarro and, 100
  Francisco Ichaso and, 99
  Jorge Manach and, 99–100
  Abel Mestre and, 99, 143, 158–159
  Goar Mestre and, 98–99
  Emilio Ochoa and, 99–100
  Francisco Tabernilla and, 100
"Meet the Press" (U.S. program), 70, 98, 140

Menendez, Fernandito, 60
Menendez, Manolo, 29–31
Mercado, Survey y Publicidad, 68
"Merry-Go-Round" (newspaper column), 101
Meruelo, Otto, 104
Mestre, Alberto, 39
Mestre, Nico, 39
Mestre Espinosa, Abel, 10–11, 14, 17–19, 23, 25–29, 60–61, 65, 73, 77, 100, 102, 109, 112, 114–116, 124, 139–142, 143–144, 154, 157–159, 164, 166
  Amadeo Barletta and, 52–53, 77, 163
  Fulgencio Batista and, 97–98, 114
  Paul Bethel and, 143–144
  Philip W. Bonsal and, 143
  Angel Cambo and, 42
  in Camp Columbia, 124
  Eulogio Cantillo and, 124
  Fidel Castro and, 154
  Raul Castro and, 141–142
  Eduardo Chibas and, 158
  CIA and, 166
  CMQ and, 17–18, 158–159, 166
  confiscation of properties, 115, 164
  Luis Conte Aguero and, 154, 157–159
  criticizes Batista government censorship, 102
  Pedro Cue and, 54
  Ernesto de la Fe and, 94, 98
  financial assets frozen, 159
  flees Cuba, 116
  Miguel Gabriel and, 27
  "Meet the Press" and, 99, 143, 158–159
  Goar Mestre and, 10–11, 25–26, 97, 102, 115, 158, 159, 166
  Luis Augusto Mestre and, 28–29
  in Miami, 166
  negotiates for purchase of El Mundo, 54
  negotiates labor contract, 139–140
  opinion about color television, 112
  opinion about dealing with dictatorships, 97–98, 102
  opinion about foreign ownership of broadcast media, 116

INDEX

Jose Pardo Llada and, 164
plans to broadcast U.S. government
  position in Cuba, 143–144
Radio Swan and, 166
right-to-reply law, 73
television in Puerto Rico, 115
Manuel Urretia and, 141–142
World Series television broadcast,
  60–61
Mestre Espinosa, Goar, xv, 10–11,
  14–22, 25–26, 28–32, 36, 45,
  48–49, 51–52, 54–56, 58,
  60–62, 64–65, 69, 71–77,
  88–90, 96–98, 102, 109,
  111–121, 123, 125, 133–134,
  137, 140, 143, 150, 157, 159, 164,
  166
advertising innovations of, 20–21
in Argentina, 117–118, 120–121
Emilio Azcarraga and, 16–17, 115
background of, 14–18
Amadeo Barletta and, 51–52, 54,
  58, 77
Fulgencio Batista and, 96–97, 114,
  123
Paul Bethel and, 143
Cadena Nacional, 55–56, 157
Angel Cambo and, 17, 22–24,
  28–29, 32, 49
Justo Carrillo and, 29–31
Fidel Castro and, 114–115, 117,
  133
CBS and, 117–118, 119–120
Eduardo Chibas and, 19–20,
  71–76
Civic Resistance Movement (CRM)
  and, 125
CMBF radio and, 29–32
CMBF-TV and, 55
CMQ and, 14–19, 73–74,
  114–115, 123, 157–159
color television and, 111–113
confiscations of properties, 115, 121
Luis Conte Aguero and, 157, 159
Ingeniero Cristobal Diaz and,
  16–17, 25
Pedro Cue and, 54
Genaro Delgado Parker and, 115
diverts money out of Cuba, 109, 115
Ethics Commission and, 88–89
expands into television, 28–29
expands into television network, 48

film production companies of,
  117–118, 119, 121
financial assets frozen, 159
flees Cuba, 157–159
Manuel Fraga Iribarne, 119–120
Francisco Franco and, 119–120
funnels money to Fidel Castro,
  114–115
Miguel Gabriel and, 16–17, 19,
  22–25, 32
Inter-American Association of
  Broadcasters (IAAB), 97, 114,
  118
invests in broadcasting companies
  overseas, 114–121
"Meet the Press" and, 98, 99
Merle Jones and, 119–120
Abel Mestre and, 10–11, 97, 102,
  115, 159, 166
Luis Augusto Mestre and, 28–29
Alicia Mestre Martin and, 118
NBC and, 21, 55, 118
negotiates for purchase of *El
  Mundo*, 54
Enrique Oltuski and, 134
opinion about Cuban radio owners,
  20
opinion about dealing with
  dictatorships, 97–98, 102
opinion about free enterprise
  systems, 120–121
opinion about the future of radio and
  television in Cuba, 62
opinion about local cultural
  programming in Latin America,
  120
William S. Paley and, 119
Jose Pardo Llada and, 164
Juan Peron and, 117
personality of, 25
William Phelps and, 115
plans to start third network, 16
programming innovations of, 19–20
Producciones Argentinas de
  Television (Proartel) and, 118,
  119
protests Batista government
  censorship, 96, 109, 123
Gaspar Pumarejo and, 31, 32, 45,
  48, 69, 90, 111–112, 137
Radio Reloj, 29–32
Radiocentro building and, 26, 157

radionovelas and, 19
reorganizes Cadena Nacional, 56
Manolo Reyes and, 19, 64
RHC–Cadena Azul and, 18, 19
right-to-reply law and, 73–74
John Royal and, 21
in self-imposed exile, 114
speaking style of, 69
Teleproducciones Independientes, S.A. (Teleinde) and, 121
television in Argentina, 117–118, 120–121
television in Colombia, 116–117
Television Interamericana, S.A., and, 115–116
Television Nacional and, 55–56, 59
television in Peru, 117–118
television in Puerto Rico, 115
television in Spain, 119–120
television in Venezuela, 118
Time-Life Corp. and, 117
Amado Trinidad and, xv, 25, 137
Jose Manuel Viana and, 88
Alberto Vilar and, 56, 79, 157
David Manning White interviews, 120
World Series broadcasts, 60–61
Mestre Espinosa, Luis Augusto, 14, 19, 27, 28–29, 65, 116
Mestre Martin, Alicia, 118
Mestre Pumarejo, Martha, 39, 80
Mestre y Godoy, 16
Metropolitan Radio of Havana, 15
Mexico, xi, 16, 26, 36, 39, 70, 101, 102, 104, 115, 160
Mexico City, 26, 36, 101, 113, 160, 161
Miami, xiv, 30, 39, 41, 46, 61, 113, 117, 125, 137, 146–147, 159, 162, 166
Miami Herald, xv, 147, 150
Mier Zurbano, Casto, 35
Mil Diez (CMX), 10
Milanes, Cainas, 139
Military coup (led by Fulgencio Batista on March 10, 1952) xvi, 24, 32, 46–47, 48, 80, 93–94, 95, 98, 168, 169
Military Intelligence Service (SIM), 100, 135
Milla Espinosa, Antonio, 109–110
Milla y Cebrian, 109

Mills, C. Wright, 52
Ministry of Commerce, 149
Ministry of Communications, 29, 50, 73, 74, 89, 92, 95–96, 110
Ministry of Education, 15, 18, 132
Ministry of Foreign Relations, 159
Ministry of Labor, 139
Ministry of Recovery of Stolen Property, 52, 136, 144
Ministry of the Treasury, 139, 157
Miranda Cortez, Ricardo, 35, 64, 66, 67–68
Moncada military assault, 102
Montaner, Jose Ignacio de, 29, 49
Montecristi organization, 29
Montejo, Consuela de, 116–117
Montiel, Fauto, 15
Montiel, Sarita, 86
Moore, Carl, 95
Moore, Clarence, 95, 108, 149
Morin, Vincente, 13–14
Moulds, Reuben, 58
"Multiple Hour" ("Hora Multiple"), 6–7, 13
El Mundo, xv, 47, 52–54, 77, 130, 131–132, 138, 160, 163
Amado Barletta and, 47, 52–54, 77, 163
Audit Bureau of Circulation (ABC), 131–132
Luis J. Botifoll and, 47, 54
circulation of, 131–132
confiscation of, 163
Pedro Cue and, 54
Diario de la Marina and, 53
editorial quality of, 54
Eliseo Guzman Alvarez and, 54
Juan Luis Martin and, 138
Mestre brothers (Abel and Goar) negotiate to purchase, 54
Jose Pardo Llada and, 160
press subsidies and, 130
published in exile, 163
purchased by Amado Barletta, 53–54
television section of, 54
"El Mundo en Television" ("El Mundo on Television"), 78
Mussolini, Benito, 53

Nasser, Gamal Abdal, 162
National Association of Cattlemen, 139

INDEX

National Association of Industrialists, 97
National Broadcasting Co. See NBC
National Commission on Tourism, 4
Nationalist Revolutionary Party, 161
NBC (National Broadcasting Co.), 16, 21, 28, 58–59, 60–61, 112, 118, 120
Nehru, Jawaharlai, 162
Network of the Americas, 81
"The New Adventures of Charlie Chan," 55
Newspapers, xvii, 6, 46, 95, 108, 126, 128–133, 138–139, 144–145, 147–150, 156, 169. Also see names of newspapers
  burnings of, 144
  Chinese-language newspapers, 130, 147
  confiscations of, xvii, 126, 132–133, 144, 146–150
  criticized by Fidel Castro, 144–145
  English-language newspapers, 95, 108, 128, 148, 149
  exaggerated circulations of, 132
  freedom of the press and, 132–133, 169
  Inter American Press Association (IAPA) and, 144
  Jewish (Yiddish-language) newspapers, 130
  labor-management relations, xvii, 146, 148, 150
  Libertarian press theory and, 132
  newsprint restrictions, 149
  objectivity, 132, 148
  Jose Pardo Llada criticizes, 144
  photographs in, 128, 139
  proposed tax on, 138–139
  radio programming information in, 6
  social pages of, 138–139
  sports newspapers, 147
  statistics on, 130, 131, 147
  subsidies to, xvii, 46, 126, 128–132, 144
  subsidies withdrawn by Castro government, 126, 145
  in the United States, 132
Newsprint restrictions, 149
News programming, xiv–xv, 7–8, 70–71, 78, 98–100, 103–104, 110, 134
Newsreels, xvi, 36, 37
Newsweek, xv
New York City, xiv, 4–5, 46, 78–79, 112, 113
New York Journal American, 132
The New York Times, xv, 10, 53, 76, 100, 103, 122, 127, 134, 152, 156, 159, 163
Nichols, John S., vii–xi, xiv, 128
Night clubs, 48, 86
Nixon, Richard, 150
Nogara, Conchita, 7
Nogueras, Pedro, 5
Norwich Pharmaceutical, 16
Noticias de Hoy, 96, 98, 129, 131, 133, 140–141, 144, 147, 149
  Fidel Castro defends, 140
  circulation of, 131
  criticized by Carlos Todd, 129
  newspapers denounced by, 144, 147
  protests press censorship, 96
  Carlos Rafael Rodriguez and, 141
  President Manuel Urretia denounces, 140–141
"Noticiero CMQ" ("CMQ News"), 10, 98, 103–104
"Noticiero Guajiro," 68
Noticiero Mercantil, 131
Noticiero Nacional, 36, 37
Noticolor, 47
Nye, Louis, 61

Ochoa, Emilio, 99–100, 153
O'Farrill, Romulo, 36, 39
Oltuski, Enrique, 133–134
Onda Hispano Cubano, 96
Operation Truth, 127
Ortega, Gregorio, 164
Ortodoxo Party (Partido del Pueblo Cubano), 46, 64, 67–68, 72, 93–94, 99, 102, 152, 153
  Autentico Party and, 64, 72, 93
  beginnings of, 72, 152
  Fidel Castro's membership in, 76, 93
  Luis Conte Aguero and, 64, 93, 102
  formed by Eduardo Chibas, 72, 152
  members of, 93
  Emilio Ochoa and, 153
  Jose Pardo Llada and, 93
  political commentators of, 152

presidential election of 1952, 93-94
radio program of, 64, 67-68
Otero, Lisandro, 113
"Over-the-horizon" television, 61

Paar, Jack, 58, 86, 109
El Pais, 131
Palace of Radio (RHC-Cadena Azul), 26
Paley, William S., 119
Panama, 70, 97, 117
Pan American broadcasting, 21
"Panel de Prensa," 110
Pantel (Peru), 118
Pardo, Bernadette, 162
Pardo Llada, Jose, xvii, 41-42,
  45-46, 64, 67, 93-96, 101,
  106-107, 110, 113, 136, 144,
  147, 152-156, 160-166
  Roberto Agramonte and, 93
  Manolo Alonso and, 45-46
  anti-Communists and, 156, 162
  apologia of, 160-161
  assassination attempt on, 161-162
  background of, 41-42, 163
  Fulgencio Batista and, 67, 94,
    152-156, 160-162
  Cadena Oriental de Cuba and,
    64-67, 96, 153, 160, 165
  Fidel Castro and, xvii, 106-107,
    144, 165
  Eduardo Chibas and, 76, 93, 152
  CMQ employees denounced by,
    164, 166
  Luis Conte Aguero and, xvii, 94,
    152-156, 162
  La Coubre incident, 154-155
  Cuban exile community and, 162
  defection of, 160-163
  Diario de la Marina denounced by, 165
  disagreements with Communists,
    160, 162, 165
  FIEL network and, 165
  Carlos Franqui and, 107, 144
  Ramon Grau and, 67
  "Che" Gueverra and, 165
  Adolph Hitler's radio style discussed
    by, 42
  Max Lesnick and, 153, 156, 161
  Abel Mestre and, 164
  Goar Mestre and, 164

in Mexico, 160
Ricardo Miranda Cortez and, 64, 67
newspapers criticized by, 144, 147
non-aligned movement and, 162
opinion of journalism, 67
opinion of Marshall McLuhan's
  communication theory, 42
Drew Pearson and, 101
Peronism and, 165
presidential election of, 161
Carlos Prio and, 45-46, 67, 93
protests the closure of Radio
  Mambi, 96
Gaspar Pumarejo and, 41-42, 136
Miguel Angel Quevado and, 46
radio programs of, 152-153
Radio Rebelde and, 107
Revolucion and, 160, 161
Rivero family and, 165
in the Sierra Maestra, 106-107,
  152-153, 161
in Spain, 161
speaking style of, 152, 160, 163
on Television Camaguey, 110
television personality of, 42
television programs of, 41-42, 110,
  113
Union Radio announcer, 41-42,
  45-46
Alberto Vilar and, 42
Partido del Pueblo Cubano. See
  Ortodoxo Party
Pearson, Drew, 101
Pelleya, Jose Luis, 44-45, 47, 66,
  69-70, 88-89
  Manolo Alonso and, 44-46, 69
  Amadeo Barletta and, 47
  Luis J. Botifoll and, 47, 69-70
  Confederacion de Trabajadores de
    Cuba (CTC), 69-70
  Ethics Commission and, 89
  Carlos Prio Soccaras and, 47
  Gaspar Pumarejo and, 44-45, 47
  and Union Radio, 44-45, 47,
    69-70
"Pepe Cortes" (radio program), 13-14
Peterson, Theodore, 169
Perez, Faustino, 137
Perez Garcia, Luis, 15
Perez, Guillermo, 107
Perez, Itiel, 164
Perez y Chisolm, S.A., 15

Peron, Isabel, 121
Peron, Juan Domingo, 117, 165
Peronism, 165
"Perry Mason," 119
Peru, 115, 118, 137, 148
Philco Corp., 49
Phelps, William, 115, 116
Philharmonic Orchestra of Havana, 7
Piedra, Jose Luis, 67, 68, 126
Pilon (company), 11
"The Pilon Family," 11–12
Pimentel Molina, Israel, 69
Pirula, 90
"Play Ball," 58
Political commentators, xiv, 19–20, 64, 67–68, 94–95, 105, 127, 152–153, 167
   on Cadena Oriental de Radio, 64, 67–68, 153
   after Fidel Castro came to power, 152–153
   censorship under Batista government, 94–95, 152
   Eduardo Chibas as a model, 93, 152
   defenders of Cuban culture, 67
   and the Ortodoxo Party, 152
   Jose Pardo Llada's description of, 67
   style of, 19–20, 152
Political corruption, 71–72, 94, 167
Ponce de Leon Broadcasting Co. (Puerto Rico), 115
"The Poor People of Guantanamo," 12
Pope Pius XII, 60
Portell Vila, Hermino, 113, 136
Posten, Tom, 61
Prensa Libre, 124, 128, 131, 138–139, 143, 147–149, 156
   Fulgencio Batista and, 143
   Sergio Carbo and, 124, 148
   circulation of, 131
   coletillas and, 147–149
   confiscation of, 148
   criticized proposed tax on newspapers, 138–139
   Diario de la Marina and, 147–149
   editorials in, 148
   Carlos Franqui and, 107
   liberal policy of, 148
   refused to accept press subsidies, 128, 148
   reports Luis Conte Aguero's attacks on Communism, 156
Press subsidies, xvii, 126, 128–132, 144
Press theory, 132
Prio Socarras, Antonio, 45
Prio Socarras, Carlos, 40, 41, 45–46, 73–74, 93–94, 130, 167
   asylum in the Mexican Embassy, 94
   Autentico Party and, 46
   Amadeo Barletta and, 54
   Fulgencio Batista and, 94
   Fidel Castro and, 76, 93
   Eduardo Chibas and, 73
   corruption in the administration of, 94, 167
   Ramon Grau San Martin and, 94, 167
   inaugurates first television station, 40
   Rolando Masferrer and, 74
   Ortodoxo Party's denunciations of, 93
   Jose Pardo Llada and, 41, 45–46
   press subsidies of, 130
   Gaspar Pumarejo and, 40
   right-to-reply law, 73
   secretly purchases Union Radio, 45–47
Prio Socarras, Paco, 45
Privatization of broadcasting in Argentina, 117
Procter and Gamble, 8, 14, 88
Producciones Argentinas de Television (Proartel), 118, 119
Provental, 118
Publicidad Godoy, 16
Publicidad Mestre & Co., 26
Pueblo, 126, 131
   F. Valdes Gomez and, 126
Puerto Rico, xiv, 70, 137
"Pumarejo's Birthday Party," 84
Pumarejo y Sunc, Gaspar, xvi, xvii, 12, 31–32, 38–46, 48, 59, 69, 77–86, 89–92, 109–114, 124, 134–137, 164
   alleged political aspirations of, 113–114
   Manolo Alonso and, 44–45
   background of, 44, 82
   Amadeo Barletta and, 82–83
   Lolita Berrio and, 81

brings television to the countryside, 44
businesses confiscated by Castro government, 135
Eduardo Caballero and, 86, 114, 134, 136
Justo Carrillo and, 31
Gabriel (Salum Nasser) Casanova, 135-136
Carlos Castaneda and, 113-114
Fidel Castro and, 136
Edmund Chester and, 81
color television enterprise of, xvii, 110-114, 124, 134-136
Cuban Newspaper Guild and, 134
death of, 137
denounced as Batista supporter, 134, 135-136, 164
Andres Domingo y Castillo, 135
endorses products, 81-82
excoriated on television program, 135-136
flees Cuba, 135
Lucho Gataica and, 85, 135
"Hogar Club" ("Home Club") and, 84-86, 113-114, 134-135
Miguel Humara and, 38, 47
joins RHC—Cadena Azul, 81
Julian Lastra and, 38, 47
Liberace and, 85-86, 135
Manuel Llerandi and, 86, 114
Goar Mestre and, 31, 32, 45, 48, 69, 90, 111-112, 137
Sarita Montiel and, 86, 135
NBC and, 112
negotiates to broadcast Cuban Winter League Baseball, 59
opinion about broadcasting research, 79
Jack Paar and, 86
Jose Pardo Llada and, 41-42, 136
Jose Luis Pelleya and, 44-45, 47
plans to construct a television network, 43-44
Hermino Portell Vila and, 113, 136
Carlos Prio and, 40
Radio Reloj, 31
rumors of Batista connections, 89, 109, 113, 134
David Sarnoff advises, 112
"School of Television" and, 81-82, 135

Otto Sirgo and, 135-136
in Spain, 136
speaking style of, 41-42, 69
starts first Cuban television station, xvi, 38, 48
Juan Jose Tarajano and, 89-91
on television outside Cuba, 137
television programs of, 40, 78, 81-82
Television del Caribe and, 59
Carlos Todd and, 135
Amado Trinidad and, 44, 80, 137
Union Radio and, xvi, 31, 38-46, 48, 69, 79, 112
Ramon Vasconcelos and, 91-92
Alberto Vilar and, 39, 42, 45, 79, 86
"Pumarejo y sus Amigos," 83
PWX, 3-6

"Queen for a Day," 83
Quevado, Miguel Angel, 46, 124, 161-162
Jose Pardo Llada and, 46
publishes *Bohemia* in exile, 161-162
La Quincena, 150
Quiz programs, 10, 84-85

Racial issues, 139
Radiario Nacional, 7-8
Radio, xiii, xiv-xvii, 3-10, 14, 19-20, 23, 29, 36, 47, 62-64, 70-76, 79, 94-95, 98, 109, 134, 138, 144-145, 167. *Also see* names of radio stations and networks
actors on, 5
advertising on, 23, 134
Fulgencio Batista's flight from Cuba reported on, 123-124
beginnings of, xv, 3-10
Fidel Castro on, viii, xiii, 93, 133
censorship of, 94, 95
Eduardo Chibas on, 19-20, 71-76
clandestine, viii, xiii, 133
Communist Party station, 10
confiscations of, xvii, 138
escapist programming, 167
ethical aspects of. *See* Commission on Radio and Television Ethics
Ernesto de la Fe on, 98
first radio stations and programs, 3-10

influence of television on, xvi,
  62–64
intellectuals' views of, 4
listening trends, xvi, 62–64
quality of, 5–6, 10, 63–64
raffles and quiz programs on, 10,
  109
regulation of, 8
research on, 79
right-to-reply law, 73
soap manufacturers and, 8–9, 145
sports on, xiv, 4–5, 29, 47
statistics on, xiv, 3, 4, 5, 9, 14, 23,
  36, 62–63, 70
subsidies to stations, xvii
United States influence on, xv, 3–4,
  8, 9
uses and gratifications (theory) of,
  23
Radio Annual, 14–15
Radio Atwater-Kent, 10, 15
Radio Belgrano-TV (Argentina), 117
Radio Cadena Habana, 95
Radio Capital Artalejo, 15, 150
Radio Caracas-TV (Venezuela), 115,
  118
Radiocentro (CMQ) Building, 26–27,
  30, 43, 59, 74, 100, 111, 125, 155,
  157
Radio Continental, 96
Radio Continente, 104
Radio Corporation of America (RCA),
  22, 36–38, 47, 48, 112
Radio Garcia Serra, 15
Radio Grafico, 6
Radio Havana Cuba–Cadena Azul.
  See RHC–Cadena Azul
Radio Mambi, 95–96, 126
Radio-newspapers, 7–8
Radionovelas, xiv, 11–12, 19, 64, 105
  as political protest, 11–12, 105
Radio Popular, 15
Radio Progreso, 15, 26, 35–36,
  63–64, 68–69, 81, 102, 124,
  125, 153, 158–159
  Civic Resistance Movement (CRM)
    and, 125
  CMQ and, 69, 158
  confiscation of, 159
  Luis Conte Aguero's program on,
    102, 153, 156, 158–159
  creation of, 68–69

Fernandez Cruz family and, 68–69,
  159
labor-management disputes, 159
plans to expand into television, 35,
  69
programming on, 69
ratings of, 26, 36, 63, 81
stations in the radio network, 65
Radio Rebelde, 107
Radio Reloj, 29–32, 64
  Fulgencio Batista's March 10, 1952,
    coup and, 31–32
  beginnings of, 29–30
  Justo Carrillo and, 29–31
  format of, 30–31
  Manolo Menendez and, 29–31
  Goar Mestre and, 29–32
  Gaspar Pumarejo and, 31
  Alberto Vilar and, 64
Radio research, 79
Radio Salas, 15, 42, 124
Radio Screenwriters Association, 87
Radio Suaritos, 15, 42
Radio Swan, 166
Radio Telefonica Comercial of
  Havana, 15
Radio Television El Mundo. *See*
  Telemundo
Radio Ten-ten (1010), 126
Ramon Quinones, Jose, 115
Ramos, Angel, 115, 116
Ratings, 9, 51, 55, 87
Ravel, Maurice, 7
RCA, 22, 36–38, 47, 48, 112
Religious programming, 158
Revolucion, xv, 117, 122, 128–130,
  144, 147, 156, 160, 164
  advertisers and, 122
  Luis Conte Aguero denounced by,
    156
  discloses list of journalists and
    newspapers that accepted
    subsidies, 128
  Carlos Franqui and, 129–130, 144,
    149
  newspapers criticized by, 144, 147
  Jose Pardo Llada and, 160, 161
  takes over facilities of *Alerta,* 129
  Carlos Todd criticizes, 129
Revolution (of 1933), 8, 122–123,
  130, 139, 148, 149
Rey, Santiago, 97

Reyes, Carmela, 85
Reyes, Manuel (Manolo), 11–12, 19, 64
RHC–Cadena Azul, 8–9, 12–14, 19, 21, 24–25, 27–28, 35, 49–50, 62–63, 64, 67, 68–69, 73, 77, 80–82, 88–91, 137
   CBS and, 21
   Edmund S. Chester and, 80–81
   Circuito Nacional Cubano (CNC) and, 68
   closing of, 82
   CMQ and, 9–10, 12–14, 19, 35, 77
   creation of, 8, 12–14
   Ingeniero Cristobal Diaz Gonzalez and, 8, 12–13
   decline of, 62–63
   Ethics Commission and, 88
   Manolo Fernandez and, 82
   financial troubles of, 80
   Miguel Gabriel and, 19, 27–28
   Goar Mestre and, 18, 19
   plans to expand into television, 35, 49–50
   presidential election coverage on, 24
   programming on, 13–14
   Gaspar Pumarejo and, 81, 137
   ratings of, 9, 25, 81
   regulation of, 8
   right-to-reply (radio) law, 73
   Elliott Roosevelt and, 81
   soap manufacturers and, 9, 14
   sold to U.S. buyers, 81
   stations in, 14
   Juan Jose Tarajano and, 88, 91
   Amado Trinidad and, 12–14, 25, 27–28, 44, 63, 73, 77, 80–82, 137
Rio de Plata-TV (Argentina), 118
Rivadulla, Mario, 67
Rivero, Jose Ignacio, 33, 148
"Rock and Roll Club," 92
Rodriguez, Carlos Rafael, 107, 144
Rodriguez, Primitivo, 67, 96
Rodriguez, Rafael, 15
Rodriguez Diaz, Jose, 10–12
Rojas Pinilla, Gustavo, 116
Romeu, Ruben, 68
Roosevelt, Elliott, 81
Roosevelt, Franklin D., 81
Rossini, Gioacchino, 4

Rotative advertising, 20–23
Royal, John, 21

Salwen, Michael B., vii–viii, xi
Sabates, 8, 14
Saladrigas y Zayas, Ernesto, 71
Salas, Guillermo, 4–5, 15, 124
Salas, Manuel, 4–5, 15
Salar Amaro, Alberto, 126
Sanchez Arango, Aureliano, 75–76, 103
   Eduardo Chibas and, 75–76
   clandestine radio station of, 103
"School of Television" ("Escuela de Television"), 81–84, 110, 114, 135–136
   Amado Barletta and, 82–83
   beginnings of, 81–82
   Lolita Berrio and, 81
   confiscated by the Castro government, 135
   goes off the air, 136
   programming on, 81, 83–84
   Gaspar Pumarejo and, 81–82, 135
   ratings of, 83–84
   on Telemundo, 82–83
Schools for radio and television, ix
Schramm, Wilbur, 169
"Senderos de Amor" ("Paths of Love"), 48
"La Serpienta Roja" ("The Red Serpent"), 44
Serrano, Manolo, 10–12
Shropshire, Albert W., 56
Siebert, Fred S., 169
Sierra Maestra, 103, 106–107, 126, 133, 152–153, 161
SIM (Military Intelligence Service), 100, 135
Sirgo, Otto, 135–136
"The $64,000 Question," 83
Slaybaugh, Clifford W., 37, 112–113
"The Sleepless Hour," 10
Soap manufacturers, 8–9, 14, 22, 64, 145
Soap operas. See Radionovelas; Telenovelas
"Social Life," 113
Sotolongo, Alberto, 67, 68
Sousa, John Philip, 42
Soviet Union, vii, x, 10, 141

INDEX

Spain, 4, 38, 46, 113, 119–120, 136–137, 148, 161
"Speak with Conte Aguero" ("Hablar con Conte Aguero"), 153
"The Spectacular Programs of Otto Sirgo, Inc.," 136
"Sports Life," 113
Spanish Civil War, 101
"The Spirit," 51
Spot advertising, 20
Stein, Edward C., 132
Stokes, William S., 72
Storer, George B., 56
Storer Broadcasting Co., 56–57
Stowers, John L., 15
Sugar industry, 129, 149
Sukarno, 162
Survey research, 79
Szulc, Tad, 76, 159, 163

Taber, Robert, 106
Tabernilla, Francisco, 100
Tamargo, Agustin, 110, 147
Tarajano, Juan Jose, 88–92
   Clavelito (Miguel Alfonso Pozo) and, 88–89
   CMQ and, 87–92
   Commission on Radio and Television Ethics, 88–92
   Manolo Fernandez and, 88
   Goar Mestre and, 88
   Gaspar Pumarejo and, 89–92
   Juan Jose Tarajano and, 88, 91
   Amado Trinidad and, 88
   Ramon Vasconcelos and, 91–92
Tax legislation, 138–139
Tele-Color, S.A., 110, 135
Telegram, 131
Telemundo, xvi, 49, 51, 78–79, 109–110, 123–124, 136, 163–164
   Amadeo Barletta and, xvi, 49, 51, 79, 163–164
   beginnings of, 49, 79
   CMQ and, xvi, 51–52, 79
   confiscated by the Castro government, 163–164
   coverage of the 1952 U.S. presidential election on, 78
   facilities of, 51
   Carlos Lechuga and, 123
   El Mundo and, 78
   network expansion of, 49, 79
   news coverage of Batista's flight from Cuba, 123
   Philco Corp. and, 49
   programming on, 51
   Gaspar Pumarejo and, 78
   ratings of, 79, 136
   "School of Television" on, 82–83
   Otto Sirgo on, 136
Telenovelas, xiv, 48, 64
   Mario Barrall and, 48
Teleproducciones Independientes, S.A. (Teleinde), 121
Teletigre (Colombian television), 117
Television, xiv, xvi, 5, 34–41, 37–41, 43–46, 50–51, 55–57, 59–64, 70, 77–92, 109, 111–112, 115–118, 120–121, 123–124, 127, 138, 143–144, 163–164, 167–168. *Also see* names of television stations and networks
   E. F. W. Alexanderson's contribution to, 35
   Manolo Alonso and, xvi, 36, 44–45, 47, 79
   Applications for stations, 50
   in Argentina, 37, 70, 117–118, 120–121
   Amado Barletta and, xvi, 47–48, 49, 52–53, 57, 59, 77–79, 82–83, 101, 163
   baseball on, 38, 40, 59–61
   beginnings of, xvi, 34–38, 168
   Paul Bethel and, 143–144
   in Brazil, 36, 70, 77–78
   in Colombia, 77–78, 115–116
   color television (in Cuba), xvii, 110–114, 124, 134–136
   color television (in the United States), 112
   confiscations of stations, 138, 163–164
   cost of operating, xvi, 36
   coverage of Batista's flight from Cuba, 123–124
   coverage of the executions of Batistianos, 127
   coverage of the 1952 U.S. presidential election, 78
   criticisms of, 37
   in the Dominican Republic, 37, 78
   English-language television, 57

escapist programming, 167
ethical issues related to. *See*
  Commission on Radio and
  Television Ethics
experimental television, 34–35, 39,
  51
high frequency and ultra high
  frequency television, 35
impact on radio, xvi, 62–64
international television, 35
Frank H. Jones' contribution to, 5,
  34–35
kinescope recordings, 59
Goar Mestre and, 55, 73–74,
  114–115, 123, 157–159
in Mexico, 36, 37, 70, 77–78
"Over-the-horizon" television, 61
in Peru, 118
post-war boom in, 34
Gaspar Pumarejo and, xvi, 36–37,
  38–41, 43–46, 48, 59, 69,
  77–86, 89–92, 109–114, 124,
  134–137, 164
in Puerto Rico, 115
race to build, 35–37
ratings methods of, 55
reception problems, 57
sets, 39, 41, 111
soap operas on, xiv, 48, 64
sports on, xiv, 56, 59–61, 164
statistics on, xiv, 41, 50, 51, 56, 70,
  77–78, 79, 109, 112
in the United States, 28, 34,
  111–112
U.S. programs in Cuba, 37, 55
in Venezuela, 37, 70, 118
World Series (baseball) on, xiv,
  59–61, 164
Television Camaguey, 109–110
Television del Caribe, 56–57, 59
Television Habanera, 58–59
Television Interamerican (TISA),
  115–116
Television Nacional, 49, 52, 55–56,
  58, 59, 63, 79, 157
  Amadeo Barletta and, 49, 79
  Angel Cambo, 49, 56
  Miguel Humara and, 49
  Julian Lastra and, 49
  Goar Mestre and, 55–56, 59
  Jose Ignacio Montaner and, 49
  ratings of, 63

sold to the Mestre brothers, 55–56
Alberto Vilar and, 157
Television Quarterly, 120–121
Television Revolucion, 163
Testar, Agusto, 15
"This Is Your Life," 83
Thomas, Hugh, 73–74, 160
El Tiempo, 104–105, 125–126, 131,
  133
  circulation of, 126, 131
  confiscation of, 126
  Rolando Masferrer and, 104–105,
    126, 133
  U.S. Embassy in Havana and,
    104–105
Time (magazine), xv, 101, 160–161
Time-Life Corp., 117
Times of Havana, xv, 95, 108, 128,
  129, 131–132, 135–136, 138,
  142, 148–149, 155, 157
  ceases publication, 149
  circulation of, 131–132
  creation of, 108
  criticizes Communists, 129
  The Havana Post and, 108
  Julio Lobo and, 129
  Carl Moore and, 95
  Clarence Moore and, 95, 108, 149
  refuses to accept press subsidies,
    128
  reports Juan Luis Martin incident,
    138
  Carlos Todd and, 129, 135–136,
    142, 155, 157
Tobacco industry, 51, 145
Todd, Carlos, 129, 135, 142, 149, 155,
  157
  Cadena Nacional and, 157
  Fidel Castro and, 149
  charges conspiracy by Castro
    government to discredit the
    press, 129
  criticizes Communist influence, 149
  describes government takeover of
    Channel 12, 135
  Clarence Moore and, 149
  opinion of bribery of journalists, 129
  opinion of Jose Pardo Llada, 155
  opinion of Gaspar Pumarejo, 135
  opinion of Otto Sirgo, 135
  Manuel Urretia and, 142
  sued for libel, 142

Tolstoy, Leo, 6
"Topper," 55
Transradio Columbia Co., 15
Trinidad Velasco, Amado, xv, 12–14, 25, 27–28, 32, 44, 63, 73, 77, 80–82, 137
  and Luis Aragon Dulzaides, 13
  background of, 12–14
  Edmund Chester and, 80–81
  Ethics Commission and, 88
  creates radio network, 13
  Ingeniero Cristobal Diaz and, 13
  financial troubles of, 80
  Miguel Gabriel and, 13, 27–28
  Goar Mestre and, xv, 25, 137
  plans for television, 77
  programming for the countryside, 13
  Gaspar Pumarejo and, 44, 80, 137
  right-to-reply law, 73
  Sabates and, 14
  sells RHC–Cadena Azul, 63, 80
  suicide of, 82, 137
  Trinidad y Hermanos (company), 12, 44
  Jose Manuel Viana and, 14
Trinidad Velasco, Diego, 12
Trinidad Velasco, Ramon, 12
Trujillo, Rafael Leonidas, 52–53
TV-Difusora (Brazil), 36
TV Guide, 127
TV Marti, 61
"Twentieth Century," 119

UNESCO (United Nations Educational, Scientific and Cultural Organization), 32, 70
Union Carbide Corp., 15
Union Radio, xvi, 35–36, 38, 40–43, 44–49, 63–64, 66, 69–70, 77, 79, 112
  Manolo Alonso and, 44–47, 69
  Amadeo Barletta and, 47, 77, 79
  beginnings of, 69
  Luis J. Botifoll and, 47, 69–70
  Angel Cambo and, 49
  CMQ and, 35–37, 48
  Confederacion de Trabajadores de Cuba (CTC), 69–70
  Miguel Humara and, 49
  Julian Lastra and, 49
  Goar Mestre and, 45
  Jose Ignacio de Montaner and, 49
  Jose Pardo Llada on, 41–42, 45–46
  Jose Pelleya, 44–45, 47, 69–70
  plans to expand into television, 35
  Carlos Prio Socarras and, 45–47
  Gaspar Pumarejo and, xvi, 31, 38–44, 48, 69, 79, 112
  ratings of, 63
  sports programming on, 38, 40, 43, 47
  stations in the radio network, 66
  Telemundo and, 49
  Alberto Vilar and, 39–40, 49, 79
United Action Party, 93
United Press (UP), 78
United States, viii, 3, 8–9, 34, 83, 104, 109, 112, 116, 143–145, 149, 155
United States Department of State, 50, 57, 143, 164, 166
United States Embassy in Havana, 43, 104–105, 143
United States Information Service (USIS), 143–144
"Universidad del Aire" ("University of the Air"), 99
University of Havana, 37, 41, 46, 76
Urretia Lleo, Manuel, 122, 141–143, 154
  Avance sued by, 142
  Fidel Castro and, 122, 140–143
  Luis Conte Aguero and, 141, 154
  Hoy denounced by, 141
  Abel Mestre and, 141–142
  regisns as president, 142–143
  sues for libel, 142
Uruguay, 70, 89, 90
Uses and gratifications theory and research, 23
USSR, vii, x, 10, 141

Vadia, Alberto, 157
Val, Luis, 66
Valdes, Pedro, 5
Valdes Gomez, F., 126
Van Doren, Mamie, 61
Vardes, Milos, 91
Variety, 58
Vasconcelos, Ramon, 90–92, 126
  Censorship of, 92
  Ethics Commission and, 90
  publishes *Alerta,* 126

Gaspar Pumarejo and, 39, 42, 45, 79, 86, 91–92
Juan Jose Tarajano and, 91–92
Velasco Alvarado, Juan, 118
Venevision, 118
Venezuela, 70, 104, 115, 118, 142
Ventura, Alberto, 65
Viana, Jose Manuel, 14, 88
"Victory at Sea," 59
Videotape, 111
Viera, Bernardo, 142
Vigil, Constancio, 89
Vilar, Alberto, 39–40, 42, 45, 49, 56, 64, 79, 86, 157–158
  advertising methods of, 64
  Manolo Alonso and, 79
  Amadeo Barletta and, 49, 79
  baseball broadcasts of, 40
  Cadena Nacional and, 157
  Angel Cambo and, 79
  flees Cuba, 79
  Goar Mestre and, 56, 79, 157
  Jose Pardo Llada and, 42
  Gaspar Pumarejo and, 39, 42, 45, 79, 86
  Television Nacional and, 49, 56, 157
  Union Radio and, 39–40, 49, 79
Villarino, Jose, 15
Voice of America (VOA), 61
"The Voice of the Air," 7
"La Voz del Aire" ("The Voice of the Air"), 7

La Voz del Camagueyano, 109

Wah Mon Son Po, 131
Wall Street Journal, 132
WAPA-TV (Puerto Rico), 115, 137
Warner Brothers, 26
War of Independence (Cuban), 3, 148, 156
Wayne, John, 158
"Welcome to Cuba," 57
WGY, 34
White, David Manning, 120
"Wide Wide World," 61
Wire services, 147, 156
WKAQ-TV (Puerto Rico), 115
World Press Congress, 33
World Series (U.S. baseball), xiv, 59–61, 164
World War II, 34, 53, 148
WQBA (Miami), 30

XEQK (Mexico), 29
XH-TV (Mexico), 36

Yiddish-language newspapers, 130

Zapata, Fernando, 67
Zayas, Jorge, 146-147
  Fidel Castro denounces, 146
Zayas Alfonso, Alfredo, 3–4
Zig Zag, 105–106, 126–127